Barrio Gangs

**Street Life and Identity
in Southern California**

Mexican American Monograph Number 12
The Center for Mexican American Studies
The University of Texas at Austin

CMAS Editors
Ricardo Romo, *Editor*
José Flores, *Associate Editor*

Barrio Gangs

Street Life and Identity in Southern California

by James Diego Vigil

Foreword by Robert Edgerton

 University of Texas Press, Austin

Fifth paperback printing, 1994

Requests for permission to reproduce material from this work
should be sent to Permissions, University of Texas Press,
Box 7819, Austin, Texas 78713-7819.

∞ The paper used in this publication meets the minimum require-
ments of American National Standard for Information Sciences—
Permanence of Paper for Printed Library Materials, ANSI
Z39.48-1984.

Library of Congress Cataloging-in-Publication Data
Vigil, James Diego, 1938–
    Barrio gangs: street life and identity in Southern California/
by James Diego Vigil: foreword by Robert Edgerton.—1st ed.
        p.   cm.—(Mexican American monographs: no. 12)
    Bibliography: p.
    Includes index.
    ISBN 0-292-77613-6 (alk. paper). — ISBN 0-292-71119-0 (pbk. :
alk. paper)
    1. Gangs—California—Los Angeles. 2. Mexican American youth—
California—Los Angeles—Ethnic identity.   I. Title.   II. Series.
HV6439.U7L78 1988
364.1′066′097949—dc19   88-23386
                                                       CIP

To my brother Richard (Dickie from Li'l 32nd),
who shared many street experiences with me.

Contents

Tables

Foreword

Gang violence has turned many parts of our nation's cities into war zones. In New York, Miami, Chicago, Detroit, Philadelphia, Los Angeles, and many other cities, youth gangs have long and sometimes violent histories. Now that gangs can make huge profits by controlling the drug trade in their territory, violence has reached unprecedented levels. Young men, often dressed in military uniforms and armed with UZi submachine guns and AK47 assault rifles, battle young men from other gangs for control of their territories and their lucrative drug trade income. Nowhere is this gang violence worse than in Los Angeles. Los Angeles District Attorney Ira Reiner said late in 1987 that "we are the gang capital of the United States in terms of numbers, in terms of violence, in terms of its overall impact on the entire criminal justice system" (*Los Angeles Times*, November 12, 1987). By the end of 1987 street gangs in Los Angeles had killed 205 people, an all-time record for the city. Los Angeles Police Chief Daryl Gates reported that 60 percent of the victims were innocent bystanders, several of whom were young children playing near their homes (*Los Angeles Herald-Examiner*, January 8, 1988).

Although there are some white street gangs in Los Angeles, as there are in other cities and as there were in our country's past, the members of most of the street gangs in Los Angeles, as elsewhere, are from ethnic or racial minorities. In Los Angeles, there are violent gangs of Vietnamese, Chinese, Filipino, Samoan, Korean, Jamaican, Guatemalan, Salvadoran, and other recent immigrant populations. But the largest number of gang members are still black Americans or Mexican Americans. Police estimate that in 1987 there were at least seventy Mexican American, or Chicano, gangs with at least three thousand members in East Los Angeles. However, while violence increased in other gangs, paradoxically it decreased among Chicano gangs. From a high of 24 gang-related killings in 1978, Chicano gang killings dropped to 4 in 1987 (*Los Angeles Times*, November 12, 1987).

The principal reaction to violent street gangs by city officials and much of the citizenry is to call for better police protection and tougher judges. City Attorney Reiner spoke for many when he said, "In a mood of frustration, you feel like the only effective way to deal with street gangs is with a flame thrower" (*Los Angeles Times*, November 12, 1987). Police budgets for special units to combat street gangs have risen, laws have been proposed to make enforcement easier, and community-based antigang programs have been instituted, all for the purpose of eliminating gangs or at least neutralizing them. Attempts to understand why gangs come into being, why they persist over the years, and why they become more or less violent have received far less attention. It is for this reason that James Diego Vigil's book takes on added importance. He is as horrified by gang killings as anyone else, but his purpose is to understand gangs and the young people who belong to them. He brings impressive credentials to his task. As a young man in East Los Angeles, he was well acquainted with street gangs. Later, as a high school teacher, he worked closely with the various Chicano youth groups, and, still later, as an anthropologist he has carried out extensive research on street gangs in the barrios of East Los Angeles.

Dr. Vigil introduces us to the history of Chicano gangs in Los Angeles, pointing out that many of these gangs have existed in the same neighborhood for three generations. Using the concept of multiple marginality, Vigil examines the underlying factors that contribute to the formation of gangs: residential segregation in low-income areas, poverty, poor school performance, little parental supervision, discrimination, and distrust of law enforcement. In these conditions, young people spent much of their lives together on the streets where a gang served them, as Vigil puts it, as surrogate family, school, and police. He describes the culture of these gangs, their distinctive *cholo* dress, *caló* speech, and "low-rider" cars. He also provides vivid accounts of the underside of gang life involving alcohol and drug use, fights, and more serious violence as young men compete for acceptance by displaying their courage and daring by, as Vigil nicely puts it, "counting coup." Sometimes, their daring leads to "drive-by" shootings and tragic deaths. We also hear from gang members in their own words about the appeal that gang membership has for them—friendship, pride, prestige, belongingness, identity, self-esteem, and a desire to emulate their uncles and older brothers who were gang members before them.

Dr. Vigil's book is welcome for several reasons. It is an intimate account based on long and close familiarity with Chicano gangs that allows us to understand how gang members feel and think. It is also a broad account that examines Chicano gangs in the perspective of Mexican culture and U.S. history. Although Vigil cannot tell us why only 4 percent to 10 percent of Chicano youth become affiliated with gangs or why only some of these young people will engage in serious criminal behavior, he has told us what sustains Chicano gangs and why young people who join them can find membership so meaningful.

Countercultural youth gangs go back at least as far as the Middle Ages in Europe, and in one form or another they are ubiquitous in American life today. Because efforts to eradicate gangs through police power have seldom been effective, the need to understand gangs should be obvious. This good book is needed. We need more like it.

Robert B. Edgerton

Preface

Individual Chicano gang members' private, personal backgrounds and motivations are the subject of this book. Neighborhood and home realities and the ineffective influences of several social institutions have made these members seek the street gang as a source of identity and support. There are multiple crises and turning points in the trajectories of their lives, which, in turn, have created voids that must be replaced by something. That something is the gang.

Analysts and practitioners familiar with delinquency have long argued that early childhood experiences predict intense gang involvement during adolescence and young adult years. The life histories of this study illuminate this process and shed some light on the background reasons for the differences among various types of gang members. In addition to this descriptive account of the commonalities of gang members' backgrounds and the dynamic conditions that facilitate gang forms and gang membership, this study also makes a preliminary examination of what interconnections there are among several factors. A historical and structural interpretation suggests that residence in isolated and physically distinct barrio enclaves and a low-income life, especially for the most impoverished underclass members, makes for particularly troublesome ecological and economic problems. Repercussions from such conditions, in turn, generate social and cultural strains and stresses that make the youth within this segment more at risk to an orientation to street life. In fact, when home life becomes overly problematic, it is the streets that become the main socialization agent in their lives.

Much of the gang patterns and behaviors can be largely attributed to the realities of the streets. Ways of acting and thinking are fashioned to aid coping with the streets. An institutionalized way of life is now firmly rooted in many Mexican American enclaves and the "*cholo* front" (e.g., dress, talk, gestures), street rituals (e.g., initiation, gang warfare), and symbols (e.g., tattoos, graffiti) comprise the primary source of identity for many youth. In short, the creation and perpetuation of a Chicano gang subculture is the end product of various inter-related influences that give rise to, and provide a means for dealing with, specific problems of identity in certain youths.

The assistance and participation of untold numbers of people made this study possible; they represent various roles and perspectives both within and outside the barrio and gang life. The strongest and most obvious contributions were from the gang members themselves and other *cholos* and street youths. They include individuals I have known on the streets from my youth and as a gang worker and watcher over several generations and, particularly, the contemporary populations that constitute the bulk of the life histories and observed street dynamics of this study. To them and all *cholos* of the barrios of Southern California, I hope I accurately and fairly depicted what this street reality is all about—warts and all.

A special expression of thanks is also extended to the many students at Chaffey College in Rancho Cucamonga, where I taught for over ten years, who were my field researchers and key informants. Denise Miller, Carole Edens, and Jessie Ortega (né Deputy) come especially to mind for their long-term participation and contributions. In addition, students in a Chicano Studies seminar at California State University, Los Angeles (1980), contributed invaluable insights on East Los Angeles gangs. My advisors in graduate school at UCLA, Tom Weisner and Pete Snyder, are greatly appreciated for their guidance in my early gang research; and Robert Edgerton for writing the foreword.

Individuals and families from Cucamonga deserve special praise in their always open and constant efforts to aid the undertaking, as they enthusiastically felt, as did residents from other barrios, that the "record on gangs should be made straight." Space does not permit me to give all their names, but some of them are Luis and Roseann Gonzales, Don Reyes, Mary Nuñez, Romelia Olivas, and Miguel and Manuel Nicasio.

The researchers and staff of the Chicano Pinto Research Project (now Community Systems Research, Inc.) were also instrumental in providing insights and data to guide the purpose of the study, especially Joan Moore, Robert García, and John Long. Their longitudinal and multidimensional look (over nearly fifteen years) at El Hoyo Maravilla and White Fence, two long-standing urban barrios, have provided in-depth historical evidence of gang dynamics. In addition to this help, Joan and Burt Moore read earlier versions of the study and offered instructive criticisms and suggestions. Particularly helpful in this regard is the critical and editorial advice that John M. Long has provided throughout all phases of the research and writing.

Finally, the opportunities to gain insight from various levels of criminal justice and educational systems were aided by a number of people, namely, David Tristan, Chuck Pineda, Fred Martinez, Al Ortiz, Steve López, and Pete de la Peña of the Gang Violence Reduction Project; Al Villanueva and Harold "Wardie" Walker from the Nelles School for Boys; Mike Duran, Aaron Rosenthal, and Ramiro Castillo from the Probation Department; Bob Eicholtz and Dick Torres from Pioneer High School in Pico-Rivera; David Brooks and Frank Garcia from Glenn High School in Norwalk; and Sergeants Wes McBride and Richard Valdemar from the Sheriff's Operation Safe Streets (OSS) program.

Partial support for this research was provided by a NIMH fellowship (F 32 HM0795-01), a sabbatical leave by Chaffey College, and an independent study grant from the Ford Foundation during overlapping periods in 1979 and 1980. Estella Tilley and Mae Horie deserve my heartfelt thanks for having contributed many hours typing various versions of the book. My wife Polly was most patient and helpful throughout all the years of my research and writing, and to her a special embrace of appreciation. Also, my son, James, and daughter, Joan, are appreciated for the general remarks they made. While all the above are credited for facilitating and informing the study, I am solely responsible for the collection and filtering of facts and analytical interpretations.

Barrio Gangs

**Street Life and Identity
in Southern California**

1. Introduction

A look behind the scenes of Chicano youth gang behavior is long over-due. It is important to know how the streets have become such a strong socializing force in the barrios of Southern California and why certain adolescents and youth there are particularly motivated to iden-tify with the street gang. Many of the street gang habits and customs make better sense when considered in the context of street pressures and group identification processes. To survive in street culture, one must have a street identity. It will be revealed in this study that there are many intricacies and complexities to this street identity.

Chicano street gangs in Los Angeles and Southern California have been around for several decades (Bogardus 1926). Over the past forty years they have been viewed as a menace to society, wreaking crime and violence on the rest of the populace, or as a serious social problem with roots in the urban experience of low-income minority groups. Several explanations of Chicano gangs (McWilliams 1968; Griffith 1948; Tuck 1956; Heller 1966; Rosenquist and Megargee 1969; Klein 1971; Snyder 1977; J. Moore 1978; Horowitz 1983) advanced our understanding of the problem. However, the complexity of the street gang requires a careful separation of the cluster of factors that con-tribute to its formation and persistence. The lives of the street youths who comprise the barrio gang reflect multiple stresses and pressures, which result in a multiple marginality. This multiple marginality derives from various interwoven situations and conditions that tend to act and react upon one another. Although interrelated, the un-folding and interpretation of these ecological, economic, social, cultural, and psychological features of the street gang suggest a developmental sequence.

All of these considerations are integral to the relationship between multiple marginality and gang patterns. In particular, it will be clear that barrio children whose lives are most intensely affected by marginality in these dimensions are more at risk to become gang members. Moreover, use of the concept will permit an examination of gang violence and related behavior within the context of a cumulative, additive experience. My self-reflexive life history involvement with various facets of street and gang life and the life histories of different types of contemporary gang members provide insights and nuances and shifting levels of insider/outsider analysis to this perspective. This combination of ways of examining and describing the street gang will promote theory building and the integration of more narrowly focused explanations for gang phenomena that have emerged over the years.

Anyone who regularly works with street gangs can learn the answers to such questions as, Where they are located? Who are the members? What do they do and how do they do it? However, even after having gained such knowledge, few observers understand what the sources of this behavior are or when in a person's life does such behavior emerge. It is these and other such questions that should guide our discussion if we are to better comprehend the gang phenomenon. Partial, incomplete, and narrow assessments do injustice to the general public as well as to the communities where gangs are common. As an example of this narrow attitude, I once inquired of a city official, the director of community programs and affairs, what recreational and social programs were offered to the local barrio youth and whether he was familiar with some of the conditions that caused the formation of the gang. He gave a testy response: "We don't want to understand the problem, we just want to stop it." While desiring to "stop it" is understandable, such lack of analysis can only impede the official's desire.

Chicano gangs are made up largely of young males, from 13 to 25 years of age. The gang subcultural style is a response to the pressures of street life and serves to give certain barrio youth a source of familial support, goals and directives, and sanctions and guides. Although gang members typically constitute a small minority of the young in a barrio, they represent a street style that both conforms and contrasts with familiar youth patterns (Klein 1969). On the one hand, most of their time is spent in the usual cohort activities found in any neighborhood where adolescents and other youth congregate. They talk, joke, plan social events, and exchange stories of adventure and love. Their alcohol consumption and drug use shows some parallels with that of other American adolescents. Yet it is their other, violent, socially disruptive activities that distinguish gang members from most adolescents.

Reflecting the tendency among adolescents to develop new modes of dress and speech, Chicano gang members have adopted a distinctive street style of dress, speech, gestures, tattoos, and graffiti. This style is called *cholo*, a centuries-old term for some Latin American Indians who are partially acculturated to Hispanic-based elite cultures (Wolck 1973). The term also reflects the cultural transitional situation of Mexican Americans in the southwestern United States; it is a process strongly affected by underclass forces and street requisites. Many of the cholo customs symbolize an attachment to and identification with the gang, although many individuals copy the style without joining the gang. As we will note, there is a wide difference among members in degree of commitment to the gang, but generally it is those members with the most problematic lives and intense street experiences who become regular members. Over the decades, the gang has developed a subculture, that is, a social structure and cultural value system with its own age-graded cohorts, initiations, norms and goals, and roles. These now function to socialize and enculturate barrio youth. Though the emergence of a gang subculture initially resulted from urban maladaption among some segments of the Mexican immigrant population, it is now a continuing factor to which new Latino immigrants must adapt. To understand developments in this area we must look to the starting point, the inception of this country's urban revolution.

Gangs in Urban Immigrant Communities

Gangs have been an urban problem in the United States since the beginning of large-scale immigration to this country before the turn of the century (Thrasher 1963 [1927]). The processes and patterns of immigrant adaption, although different in important ways, stemmed from remarkably similar sources. The early groups were European immigrants, especially from southeastern Europe, who came to this country to find work and a better life. Most of them settled in urban areas and established their own communities. The process of finding work, locating a place to live, and adjusting to urban life was repeated many times over for different ethnic groups, and the Mexican immigrant population is no different in this regard.

What characterized most of these groups was their poverty, their lack of skills. As a result, they were treated as a cheap source of labor. In addition, they came from different cultural and (by contemporary definition) racial backgrounds that contrasted sharply with the dominant Anglo-American one. Anglo native-born Americans tended to view the ethnically different newcomers' appearance, behavior patterns, and poverty as a single entity; the immigrants thus faced discrimination from the native born. Their cultural difference acted in two ways to affect them. One stemmed from the changes they had to make in their own cultural values, beliefs, and patterns to adjust and acculturate to Anglo-American lifestyles. The other was a result of how the dominant Anglo culture received and accommodated them. Their own attitudes and behaviors and those of the predominant society operated to affect where they would live, what they would do for a living, and how, when, and even whether they would become "Americanized" (Handlin 1951). Exploitation and discrimination, in particular, dominated the early period after their arrival and extended to the lives of their children. The pressures and anxieties of urban poverty, of the struggle toward a better life, and of overcoming feelings of ethnic and racial inferiority made immigrant cultural adaptation problematic. Such an experience often resulted in gangs.

Throughout most of this century, researchers and writers have compiled evidence on urban gangs. The focus of these accounts varies as to ethnic group, time, and place and the theoretical emphasis. Nonetheless, there is widespread agreement among writers that gangs are an urban phenomenon, particularly so in the cases of ethnic minorities (Clinard 1968), and they represent a pattern found among lower-class adolescents (Cloward and Ohlin 1960). In fact, there is a complex of other factors that make the urban experience so remarkably uniform: a breakdown in social institutions, especially the family and schools (which often impede rather than accommodate adjustment); a first- and second-generational conflict within each ethnic group, which creates loyalty discord and identity confusions; and a noted predisposition among youth to gravitate toward street peers for sources of social associations and personal fulfillment.

Within a generation or two, most members of each early ethnic immigrant group improved their standard of living and stabilized themselves as wage earners and homemakers. Problems associated with urban adaptation, such as youth gangs, crime, poor housing, and unemployment, were initially severe. Eventually, these problems were worked through and became less serious as each group acculturated. Hence, after two generations of severe culture clash both within the ethnic community (intergenerational) and between it and the other communities, the issues that sometimes became a source of national concern, such as culture conflict, economic exploitation, and associated social disruptions, tend to dissipate.

The Nature and Persistence of Chicano Gangs

Although Mexican Americans in urban settings largely share with earlier, mostly eastern U.S. ethnics a similarity in how adaptation proceeds, there are also distinct differences between them. For one thing,

Chicano youth gangs (unlike those of other immigrant groups) have shown a remarkable longevity. Moore, Vigil, and García (1983) suggest reasons for this difference: "the gangs are long-lasting, not transitory phenomena ... With few exceptions, the Chicano communities of Los Angeles never have been invaded by another ethnic group, nor has another ethnic group succeeded them, nor has there been total cultural disintegration. Instead, there has been more or less continuous immigration of yet more Mexicans, with a reinforcement of some of the traditional culture" (p. 183). Mexican Americans remained more visually distinct from the majority than did the third-generation descendants of European immigrants, and the continued presence of fully unacculturated Mexicans made their communities more culturally distinct.

Many familes and their children experience acute poverty and limited social mobility opportunities in these barrios, and thus, over time, there developed an underclass with its own set of problems. It is from among these children that the youth most intensely involved in the gangs tends to come. As members of a persistent underclass within the Mexican American population, these youths come from households with even lower incomes than those of other barrio families and a higher incidence of stressful family situations. (This is perhaps reflective of what Auletta [1982] refers to as the 9 million, a subgroup of the 25 million below the national poverty level, who experience a grinding cycle of poverty. Recent reports seem to support the existence of this strata in urban centers [Bearak and Meyer 1985:14; NALEO 1985].) Poor school records and limited job options have combined to make them even more street oriented. As part of their survival on the streets, especially during adolescence, they adopt cultural values and customs that help shape their personal identities.

The youth gangs of Mexican Americans have arisen in the context of the broader pattern of Mexican adaptation to urban life in the United States. Mexican immigration has been the primary factor in the growth of the Mexican American population. The first large wave (1920s) brought anywhere from 1.5 million to 2 million immigrants, doubling the native Mexican American population (Samora 1971). In subsequent waves in the periods from 1940 to 1964 (4 million) and from 1969 through the 1970s (anywhere from 6 to 12 million), the population has continued to swell (Cornelius 1978). Throughout these decades of immigration, the population increasingly settled in urban areas, and today close to 90 percent of the Mexican American (native and immigrant alike) population is in urban areas (Alvírez, Bean, and Williams 1981). A recent report (Muller 1984) on foreign immigration to California since 1970 found that, of over 2 million who have legally settled there, "at least 1.3 million of them have settled in its seven southern counties" (p. 1); and this figure excludes the uncounted and undocumented (Cornelius, Chávez, and Castro 1982). Southern California, and Los Angeles particularly, is the urban area that has received most of these immigrants. Their adjustment and its social and cultural developments have taken different forms, depending on the work opportunities, places of settlement, and, generally, the standard of living attained by immigrants. Such continuous waves of immigrants ensure that there is always a large pool of second-generation Mexican Americans.

Bogardus (1926) noted that in the early years of Mexican immigration there was a "boy" gang problem and characterized it as an incipient form that could be remedied. However, in the following decades it was clear that the gang problem was becoming a serious one, with a formal structure and emerging set of norms and rules to attract and guide members (Bogardus 1943). Cultural change over the years was affected by barrio and underclass life and was particularly acute during the Depression, when even more Mexican youths experienced the intense pressures of urban poverty, especially the second generation. It is a second-generation urban American experience that, in the Chicano case, is a continually renewed phenomenon because of continued immigration. The second generation in the 1930s-1940s originated the *pachuco* lifestyle (a label created for those who wore zoot suits and spoke a mixed English-Spanish slang language that borrowed heavily from *caló*—this in turn, was a continuation of what the Gypsies had started in Spain and later was diffused, by bullfighters it seems, to Mexico [McWilliams 1968; G. C. Barker 1950]). Pachucos were a group who strove to reconcile the conflicting values and nascent pressures that urban adaptation brought; prolonged lower-class status and immobility shaped how Mexican culture was relinquished and American culture integrated into a street style. This style served as a mechanism of adaptation for many youth who needed a source of personal identification and human support, especially during the adolescent self-identification process where ego and peer groups merge to simplify age/sex identification. Pachucos were more than a "boy" gang of loosely aligned street children who participated primarily in street mischief. They had passed the incipient phase of gang formation, as pride in barrio affiliation, barrio conflicts, and some amount of drug use and abuse became a part of their lifestyle. Because most pachucos preferred to look "cool" in their zoot suits and have a good time, these damaging group activities were not as widespread or intense as those practiced in more recent decades. As the practice of negative group activities has escalated, the early generations of gang members, even most pachucos, can be viewed as a transitional form of gang.

A gang subculture eventually formed and became a pressing force in barrio life. Earlier, youths would join the boys on the street for play or mischief. Later, pachucos began to add their distinctive elements to the emerging street gang style. With the passage of time, and the perpetuation of situations, conditions, and social practices that helped to create it, the street style now works to socialize and enculturate youth to a rooted gang subculture with its own group norms and cholo role fronts. The street violence and other debilitating activities that are common features of barrio life can only be understood in terms of this subcultural socialization and its appeal to barrio youths with particular types of personal backgrounds that give rise to particular forms of self-identification processes.

In the 1980s, Chicano gangs comprise at least one-half of the four hundred gangs that exist in Los Angeles County (Decker 1983). This number, of course, is larger when the counties adjacent to Los Angeles are included. Notwithstanding the absolute number of Chicano gangs, however, only a small percentage of Chicano youth, perhaps only 4 to 10 percent of most barrios, are affiliated with gangs (Morales 1982). Of this relatively small percentage, there are subcategories (based upon degree and level of commitment) of regular, peripheral, temporary, and situational. For the most part, gang affiliation and gang-related behavior are primarily male phenomena, although many barrios also have smaller female cliques. The great majority of youths, as in other ethnic groups (cf., e.g., Whyte 1973), find other sources of identification and emulation.

The cultural style of the gang subculture arose partly as a response to street life. However, its major cultural forms are a reforging of Mexican and American patterns. This recombination, of course, borrowed heavily from the earlier pachuco syncretic formulation of creating a culture of mixed and blended elements (e.g., language). Cholos (the present term identifying the style as well as its bearers), share a cultural orientation that makes them distinct from other barrio youth. Although cholos are Americanized, either by accident or by design, they refuse or are unable to be totally assimilated (Vigil 1979; Buriel et al. 1982). In important ways they consider themselves traditionalists and retain certain Mexican customs, however attenuated, as part of their cultural repertoire. For example, they have retained the caló idiom of expression; the strong sense of group as family; the adolescent *palomilla* cohorting tradition (Rubel 1966), which includes many daring and bravado male patterns; and an antiauthority attitude, which is, perhaps, a reaction against *gabacho* (originally a term used for foreigners, such as the French in Mexico during the 1860s intervention, but now designating Anglos) racism (Vigil 1984).

The gangs that have been addressed by researchers range from those that began in the 1940s, and that have over time established more than a dozen identifiable age-graded cohorts (Moore 1978), to those of more recent vintage. An individual gang might include as many as two hundred or more, or as few as ten or twelve, members. It is mainly in the suburbs that the newer, smaller gangs are found. Older, larger gangs, on the other hand, are usually located in long-established urban and semirural barrios. Semirural barrios, and the gangs associated with them, have often been engulfed in recent years by rapidly expanding suburban growth. The deep-rooted presence of older barrio gangs has become a model and a stimulus for gang formation in other areas, as well as a major socialization factor throughout the barrio and nearby areas.

Acculturation is a major factor in a large urban region, such as the greater Los Angeles metropolitan area. Barrio and underclass life has shaped each new immigrant population in different ways, however, creating generational contrasts. As the decades pass, each generation, depending on sociocultural environment and historical conditions, becomes part of a process of cultural change and accommodation. What once began as a Mexican subculture is now transformed into different subcultures. It is in the second generation where the children of Mexican immigrants undergo acculturation shifts resembling a transitional (cholo subculture) phase. Sometimes the phase involves culture conflict, whereby both the donor culture and the host culture become problematic. This ambivalent cultural (and personal) identity makes the gang subculture attractive for a small but significant minority of barrio youth. Their lives are often regulated by the age-graded *klikas* (cliques, or cohorts within the gang). Older gang members also lend some sense of order to their often confused interpersonal interactions by providing vertical lines of organization (Klein 1971); and the gang's involvement in some forms of criminal behavior affords avenues for prestige and income to those who have limited chances of acquiring meaningful jobs (Moore 1978; Chicano Pinto Research Project 1979, 1981). Increasingly, in recent years, both immigrant youths from Mexico and third-generation Mexican Americans have become peripherally involved with street gangs. The Chicano Pinto Research Project (1979, 1981) has found small numbers of third-generation Chicanos, who are themselves offspring of gang members, involved in the core membership of some younger age cohorts.

Multiple Marginality and Street Adaptation

The Chicano youth gang began and grew in ecologically marginal areas of the city and surrounding countryside. It was fed by pressures generated by a marginal economic role. It is peopled by youths with marginal ethnic and personal identities. Each feature of gang life merits scrutiny by itself, but once this task is completed the next step is to search for the links between these features. For example, the interrelationships between socioeconomic condition (e.g., mother-centered households) or social event (e.g., sex identity strivings) must be assessed to understand why gangs are so important during adolescence. A multiple research strategy employing the concept of multiple marginality, which is especially useful with broad and in-depth self-reflexive and life history information, will enhance this understanding. This type of information reflects various times, places, thoughts, and events that must be unpeeled layer by layer, and thus a multiple construct facilitates such a discussion. It is a construct that views reality as a constellation of forces tending to act and react upon one another.

Multiple marginality encompasses the consequences of barrio life, low socioeconomic status, street socialization and enculturation, and problematic development of a self-identity. These gang features arise in a web of ecological, socioeconomic, cultural, and psychological factors. The use of such a concept in an analysis of Chicano youth gangs will help to avoid the difficulties stemming from single-cause examinations of previous gang studies; Cartwright et al. (1975:25-45) have addressed such problems in the second chapter of their review of juvenile gangs. The use of the concept multiple marginality can lead to what Geertz (1973:3) has called a "thick description." Looking at various circumstances and forces in a combinative way increases our understanding of the similarities and variations found within and across groups. It also affords an opportunity to make use of an analyst's personal experiences when merited. Having watched gangs and gang members for many years as an insider has enabled me to chart the flow of events and decision-making processes of street gangs.

An eclectic multiple marginality analysis makes it possible to integrate key elements of the several theories that have been formulated to explain gang delinquency and that emerged in the middle 1950s to early 1960s. (This is no coincidence, as the post-World War II urban explosion led to the development of problems among new minority groups, such as Puerto Ricans, blacks, and Mexican Americans, that were perhaps even more threatening than what had transpired earlier with white ethnics. These new phenomena led, in turn, to the reformation of old theories and the development of new theories.) In summary fashion, these theories are (1) male maturation process, "becoming a man" (e.g., Bloch and Niederhoffer 1958); (2) subcultural, collective solution of lower-class boys to acquire status (e.g., Cohen 1955); (3) lower-class cultural values (e.g., W. B. Miller 1958); (4) lower-class means and upper-class goals disjunctures or simplified means-goals discrepancy (e.g., Cloward and Ohlin 1960); and (5) sociopathic personalities that make "near-group" (e.g., Yablonsky 1959). There are several ways to assess these theories: they can either be reclassified as sociogenic (e.g., 3, 4) and psychogenic (e.g., 1, 2, 5) or, examined another way, as fitting within explanations that focus on strain (2, 4), cultural deviance (1-4), and (in varying degrees, all five) social control (Edgerton 1973; Dembo et al. 1984; Cartwright et al. 1975). Although the authors argue that their particular theory is most salient to the gang phenomenon, each theory accounts for only an aspect of the gang pattern. Yet, all the authors in fact rely on a number of related factors to arrive at their theoretical formulation. For example, Bloch and Niederhoffer (1958) maintain that the gang outlet for becoming a man results because society (through such phenomena as poverty, family stress, and urban disorganization) has failed them; and Cloward and Ohlin (1960), working on a variation of Merton's (1949) means/goals disjunctures, elaborate on the nature of low-income slum life to explain gang subcultural variations. This suggests that a cluster of factors needs to be examined to understand gang delinquency; Cloward and Ohlin say as much with these words: "gangs, or subcultures . . . are typically found among adolescent males in lower-class areas of large urban centers" (p. 1; cf. Short and Strodtbeck 1965:19).

The multiple marginality framework better allows for descriptions and interpretations of particular (and perhaps peculiar) facts of people, time, and place. Such a larger framework simultaneously provides for a broader and more in-depth portrayal of the various realities that gang members experience. The intensity and duration of the individual or group experience in gangs as such are better gauged in this broadly integrative way. There are several marginal situations and conditions that are a part of the Mexicans' overall adaptation to urban life. In such circumstances of "long duration . . . the individual can be born into it and live his whole life in it," becoming a participant in "even the development of a 'marginal culture' " (Dickie-Clark 1966:24).

Some researchers have noted that the concept of marginality should be carefully applied because it tends to diminish the important role of lower-income workers in a capitalist economy (Peattie 1974). Perlman (1976), in providing a sweeping critical summation of marginality theory, nevertheless recognizes the need for a construct that looks "to some set of circumstances outside individual control," such as one that "explains these conditions as expressions of the social structure and the historical process" and that looks at "different dimensions of marginality and seeks rather to examine the specificity of their interaction in each instance" (p. 251).

Mexican and Mexican American labor has definitely been significant in the economic development of the southwestern United States, for example, in mining, farming, railroading, and so on. These contributions, however, have not assured them of commensurate political and economic power, as they are excluded by leaders from decision-making processes. This marginality, moreover, is maintained by structural features in the environment to which they must adapt (Kapferer 1978; Lomnitz 1977; Barrera 1979).

The background to the current gang situation is also important, for multiple marginality has cumulative, diachronic sources, especially in group history. A *macro* (group history), *meso* (family history), and *micro* (life history) descending order of analysis is undertaken to show through time how ecological and economic conditions create sociocultural stresses and ambiguities, which, in turn, lead to subcultural and psychological mechanisms of adjustment. Descriptions of group and family history are well documented in the archives (Bogardus 1926, 1934) and in such studies as the longitudinal investigations of Moore and her *pinto* (ex-convict) associates (Moore 1978; Chicano Pinto Research Project 1979, 1981; Moore and Mata 1981). Moreover, my personal life experiences with numerous families who exemplify the multiple processes that lead to gang patterns provide for a unique insider/outsider interpretive perspective to inform these life histories and to show how these personalized events of places and living actions are refracted through the prism of multiple marginality. For example, I have gone through many experiences similar to those of gang youths recounted in subsequent chapters, including being set upon and beaten by gang members into whose "turf" I had strayed. Such personal experiences inform my interpretation of such events.

A macroexamination of Mexican adaptation provides the backdrop for understanding Chicano youth gangs, for there are several areas that need to be traced. Clearly, a key focus is to examine how an emergent underclass life has affected many Mexicans. The underclass phenomenon entails the longitudinal effects of poverty. The youth groups that are produced in such nascent circumstances are quite different from, for example, the earlier nonviolent "street corner" groups reported by Whyte (1973). In fact, endemic racial barriers and cultural strains have combined with status to make this so (Wolfgang et al. 1972; Bogardus 1943). The historical record of cultural and social disparagement experienced by Mexicans is indicative of such developments (Moore and Pachón 1976; Acuña 1981; Vigil 1984).

Urban adaptation for immigrant Mexican families was problematic initially and continues to be so today. Low-paying jobs led to residence in older, run-down interstices of the city, such as sections of East Los Angeles (Gustafson 1940:25-40; Ginn 1947:18-19). Such circumstances created repercussions in other social, cultural, and psychological realms. Moreover, and similar to the experience of other immigrant groups (Feldstein and Costello 1974; Shaw and McKay 1942), schools and law enforcement often operated to aggravate rather than ameliorate problems in Mexican cultural adaptations (U.S. Commission on Civil Rights 1970, 1971). This segmented integration into American society and subsequent fragmenting of traditional social practices and cultural customs resulted in a new cultural orientation. In short, economic hardships undermined social control institutions: family life became stress ridden and schooling and contacts with law enforcement were problematic. The streets and older street youths became the major socialization and enculturation agents, with the gang representing a type of street social control institution by becoming in turn a partial substitute for *family* (providing emotional and social support networks), *school* (giving instructions on how to think and act), and *police* (authority and sanctions to enforce adherence to gang norms). The experience created a new social identity and thus a need for a new personal identity, and for street youth, the gang, both good and bad features, became a coping mechanism to ameliorate social pressures and develop avenues for personal fulfillment.

Collecting Data for This Study

This study has developed in several phases, both informal and formal, beginning with my youth in downtown Los Angeles in the early 1950s and continuing to my current research affiliation with the Community Systems Research, Inc. (formerly the Chicano Pinto Research Project). As a youth I was in moderately close association with street life, having more than casual acquaintanceship with the Thirty-Second and Thirty-Ninth street gangs. The former was in my own barrio, and one of the main hangouts was at the Santo Niño Community Center, a Catholic Youth Organization (CYO) agency and mission church on Sundays. Thirty-Ninth was a congeries of Chicanos just southwest of the Los Angeles Coliseum who made 39th Street and Normandie their hangout. Later, as a young adult and high school teacher, I worked with various youth groups in Carmelas (Norwalk 1964-1965), at the Barrio (Montebello 1966-1967) and Pico Viejo (1967-1968) Teen Posts, at the Norwalk Centro Aztlán (1969-1971), and at the Cucamonga Contact Station (1971-1973); and I was high school advisor to the Mexican American Club at Excelsior High School (1966-1968), which included youth mostly from the enclaves of Varrio Norwalk and One-Ways. The work in the Barrio was particularly intensive and involved daily interactions with mostly male youth in such areas as work, family, school, and social and recreational events (including problems associated with alcohol consumption and drug usage). Interestingly enough, I happened to return to the Barrio the summer of 1986 to do a qualitative ethnographic study for the U.S. Census Bureau (Vigil 1987). Several associates from the Teen Post days (now adults) remembered me. In Cucamonga the involvement was also intense, since I lived nearby and watched several generations of youth experience the "Cucamonga Kings."

When I undertook an acculturation and school performance study among Chicano adolescents in the early 1970s (Vigil 1976, 1979, 1983), the issue of marginal cultural placement and gang membership figured prominently in the findings (1979:183). Following the lead of the research, with the experiential background noted above, I undertook a formal study of the gang phenomenon in the 1976-1981 period.

The first years, 1976-1978, were spent in fieldwork with the help of my students from Chaffey College in various barrios in the area (Cucamonga, Chino, Ontario, and so on). I was introduced by students to new youth groups and gangs and some students assisted me in gathering life histories, conducting interviews, and administering survey questionnaires. When I had established rapport with some of the respective gang members, I was able to spend time with them at the hangouts, street corners, parties, car cruising sorties, and homes as a participant observer (Brandt 1972). Some of these individuals became key informants on the general nature of their barrio and gang; older adults, usually supervisors in a youth program, did likewise. In 1978, I became research associate and consultant with the Chicano Pinto Research Project (CPRP), a collaborative team of academic and community-based researchers in East Los Angeles. This experience gave me insights into the histories and dynamic qualities of two traditional urban gangs, El Hoyo Maravilla and White Fence—barrio gangs I had known about when I was a youth. Many of CPRP's data and findings (partly reported in Moore 1978; CPRP 1979, 1981) on older *tecatos* (habitual drug users) and pintos and their relatives have been made available to me.

In addition to this experience, I independently embarked on fieldwork in East Los Angeles, beginning in 1978, employing similar life histories, questionnaire interviews, key informants, and so on. Some special gang programs (the Gang Violence Reduction Project [Torres 1979] and the Probation Department Specialized Gang Unit) and detention facilities (Nelles School for Boys and Chino Youth Training Services) provided me with numerous opportunities to interview gang members from throughout Los Angeles. Later, in 1983, I was able to accompany the Los Angeles Sheriff's department's Special Gang Unit (termed OSS, Operation Safe Streets) in their patrols throughout East Los Angeles. In sum, the data that follow are composed of evidence on mostly younger gang members (and some older members who recounted early experiences) who are found in urban, suburban, and rural barrios. Sixty-seven complete life histories highlight some of the main points in the above experiences. There are twenty from the Los Angeles County areas (urban barrios like White Fence and rural ones like El Monte Flores), forty-two from San Bernardino County (urban Casa Blanca, rural Cucamonga), and five from Orange County. The ages range from 12 to 40 at the time they related their story, with more than one-half (37) under 19 years of age. In terms of the extent and intensity of their involvement, twenty-nine of these informants were regular gang members, thirteen were peripheral members, twenty were temporary members, and five were situational members.

The life histories are thus cross-ecological and reflect a variety of what Hallowell (1955) calls behavioral environments, including points of view, and "gang" self-images of the informants. Most are recorded in the informant's own words, with observed instances added where appropriate. While there is no illusion of distance in the recounting, it is apparent that remarkably similar themes emerge from all the life stories. In short, they know their own lives and know a little of the gang life, and collectively these stories provide a broad fabric. It is also important to stress that my background as an insider at various times, places, and levels of gang reality enables me to examine and pinpoint the dynamic, multidimensionality of gang behavior and plumb the deeper private motives behind the public "gang" or "cholo" image. Likewise, I claim no distance here, for a self-reflexive examination provides liberties to speak to several levels of the issue (Langness and Frank 1981:98).

In addition to the life histories, more limited observations concerning several hundred additional gang members and their contemporaries who did not join a gang comprise an important data base of this study. Most of these data were derived from participant observation or single-session survey interviews. Other information comes from youth workers, police, probation officials, teachers, and other informed adults working directly or indirectly with gang members.

In the chapters that follow, these data are organized, integrated with the findings of earlier studies, and interpreted in terms of the multiple marginality construct.

2. Ecological and Socioeconomic Background to Emergence of Street Gangs

Ecological and socioeconomic facets of the multiple marginality construct comprise a necessary phase of the discussion of Chicano gangs, especially in the context of underclass life. Urban ecology as a major focus of social science research was developed in the United States by the "Chicago School" of theorists and methodologists. Redfield (see, e.g., 1962) systematically introduced these concerns into anthropological analyses of human behavior, and Bogardus employed similar research methods and concepts in directing early studies of Mexican American communities (including the developing gangs within them). Most barrios eventually produced a gang, but the variation among different barrios—in income levels, opportunities for work, even physical appearance—helps us understand the different types of gangs. In fact, the duration and intensity of a marginal ecological and socioeconomic situation contribute to interbarrio differences, as well as to the individual differences within the gang. This ecological and socioeconomic marginality also leads to the development and continuation of other human features of marginality and, thus, for historical and analytical purposes deserves primary consideration.

Coming to America, Settling in the Barrio

Many of the problems that Mexican immigrants, and subsequent generations of their children, have had to face stem from where they settled. Low-paying jobs, of course, necessitated residence in areas where land and rent values were low. The discrimination that they encountered also often forced the immigrants to congregate in areas separate from the dominant Anglo majority. Additionally, rapid technological and economic changes often result in poor city planning—for example, inferior land sites for development, unsurveyed and unpaved streets, lack of such public utilities as lights and sewers

(Hauser 1968). The rapidity of such changes, and the degree of urbanization stemming from the influx of large numbers of new residents, resulted in haphazard conditions to which certain segments of the population, especially Mexicans, were forced to adapt (Epstein 1967; Fox 1977). Settlement patterns in Southern California attest to this fact, as numerous barrios and *colonias* (rural barrios) were founded in the most neglected interstices of the cities and outlying rural areas.

The Mexicans' initial adaptation to America in such inferior ecological situations exacerbated other social and cultural adjustments that revolved around the broader issue of American lifeways and institutions. Bernard and Pelto (1972:4) have noted that under conditions of rapid culture change, where technological and industrial advancements require large-scale human labor, "governmental or private planners who make the decisions about large-scale physical sturctures often do not make much attempt to weigh or - predict the effects of their constructions on the surrounding populations." The importation of large numbers of Mexican laborers was required for the industrial and agricultural sectors (Romo 1983:3-4), but their residence and housing needs were largely ignored.

Economic motives tend to prevail in this context. Even today, poor planning helps create slum areas. For example, Gettin and Reyes (1983) report on a 101-unit moderate-income apartment complex, built only fifteen years earlier in Southern California, in which the materials and construction were so inferior that the facilities quickly deteriorated. Not surprisingly, the units have become a mostly poor immigrant Mexican neighborhood in which crime, drugs, delinquency, and gangs have emerged as social problems. "Why did the neighborhood decline? The answers say much about Orange County's rapid, virtually unchecked growth and show how weak planning controls, real estate speculation and official neglect combined to produce one of southern California's worst slums" (Gettin and Reyes 1983:3).

Much of what has happened in the early decades of the twentieth century is reminiscent in some ways of what scholars have noted about "shantytown" migrant enclaves in various Latin American nations (Lomnitz 1977; Leeds 1974). In the Mexican American case, industrialization and urbanization brought problems involving the interplay among the industrial demand for workers during a boom period or early large-scale initial phase of construction, the poor integration of them into the urban setting, and the periodic lessening of the need of unskilled or semiskilled labor, which created high rates of unemployment among Mexicans (Romo 1983:73). Thus, immigration, settlement, urbanization, and resultant adaptation problems can be viewed as stemming from the ebb and flow of the industrial economy. As is the case with other immigrant groups, when the needs of the industrial machine are met or are no longer the same, then the newcomers are "repatriated" to their native lands (Hoffman 1974). Indeed, some have even argued that there is no need for permanent residences, since the immigrants will probably go back home anyway (Fogelson 1967).

Chicago School scholars of urban sociology have examined how urban structure and urbanization affect various groups (ethnic group, social class, or residential area, singly or in combination) in the city in such matters as crime, disorganization, and poverty (Burgess 1925; Thrasher 1963; Shaw and McKay 1942). Investigations on the first years of Mexican immigration to Southern California document how the new settlers established homes in neglected and inferior locations (Fuller 1974; Monthly Labor Review 1974; Gamio 1969a, b); and recent reports (Muller 1984; Siegel 1982) on immigration testify to the continuation of this pattern. During these early years, Emory Bogardus (a sociologist at the University of Southern California who had been trained at the University of Chicago) helped guide research that emphasizes ecological factors in the adaptation of these new residents. Such research discovered that certain locales were ignored in early phases of urban development—the "flats," or lowlands; the spaces underneath bridges; and the often flooded and steep gulches, ravines, and hollows—and when later settled were left with poor street planning and limited public services (Gustafson 1940; Ginn 1947).

Ecologically oriented researchers referred to these areas as "interstices," because they were socially marginal spaces of the city. It was here, they asserted, that patterns of social disorganization sprouted and flourished. Gustafson (1940) reported that "the ravines have been places where racial groups of low economic status could gravitate in inferior dwellings" (p. 36) and, moreover, that the "lowlands (Flats) have always been occupied by Mexican laborers and less favored classes" (p. 40). As a result, "crime had its beginnings there. When the police wanted a criminal they looked in the Hollow" (p. 110). Ginn (1947), in support of this notion, stresses that "isolated neighborhoods" do without many amenities and "the crowded conditions mitigate against the children developing wholesome reading habits or creative habits. This factor indicates one of the reasons why so many Mexican youth congregate on street corners, and subsequently become delinquents" (pp. 106–107). Such studies appear to support general sentiments of the problematic features, including incipient youth gangs, of these bypassed interstices. The interrelationship of social and ecological factors was also underscored by Bogardus in his studies of enclaves in Los Angeles and Southern California: "Sometimes fifty, a hundred, or more families are found living in a segregated section of the city or small town which lacks adequate social organization" (1934:19). Elderly residents of communities just east of those listed above, as Moore and her associates (1978) found, lived in such an interstice. El Hoyo Maravilla, in East Los Angeles, was then situated on terrain—hills and gullies—that urban growth had bypassed. "Lots in the tract were very cheap; its most conspicuous feature was its unsuitability for houses. An arroyo, or dry river bed, cut a series of low bluffs, and the depressed area became known as El Hoyo—literally, the hole. El Hoyo became a barrio inside an area of barrios. There was no water service, no sewer, no pavement, and no gas main" (p. 56).

Forced by low income to settle in affordable areas, immigrants developed a barrio niche for themselves. Although they wished to settle in such locations, their decision was also influenced by other social groups. Like so many other ethnic groups, Mexicans preferred to reside in communities that followed their own traditions, for this tended to soften the effects of culture shock and provided a sense of security (Romo 1983:9-10). However, the rejection that immigrants received from Americans contributed to this barriozation pattern (Bogardus 1934:27). Douglas (1928:xiv) noted such discrimination in reporting an interview with a resident of Santa Ana, who said:

> ... the Santa Fe Railroad Company brought the Mexicans there to work on the roads. This work, of course, only attracted a few families. The property down by the tracks is never as valuable as other property ... The Mexicans went down there to live because the rents were cheap. Then, too, there was a terrible feeling among the white people in Santa Ana at that time. They did not like to live near the Mexican people. A white man would let his house stand vacant all of the time before he would rent it to a Mexican, even if the Mexican and his family were clean and could pay the rent. So whether or not the Mexican people wanted to live in a district by themselves, they had to. There was no other place they could get a house to live in.

Barrio Characteristics

Such forces led to the spatial and physical separation of immigrant settlers from the surrounding community. It also resulted in their occupying decaying older homes and neighborhoods. The common inference of the words "across the tracks" (or irrigation canals, highways, river, or freeway) underscores this physical separation and visual difference (Bogardus 1934:70). This condition persisted in subsequent decades: "Housing has always been a problem for the Mexican-American. In the early days they spread along the river beds for the sake of water. As the population of the county (Los Angeles) grew, they were literally pushed into more concentrated groups and transferred to other areas, generally remote from Anglo housing districts" (Ranker 1958:7). Further, small homes and a larger number of household residents characterize barrios, as do inadequate public services.

Los Angeles started as a Mexican pueblo (Griswold del Castillo 1980). After the flood of Anglos in the late nineteenth century, the Mexican residents comprised a barrio, just east of the town center (Camarillo 1979). In subsequent decades they spread farther east (Romo 1983). Colonias, or pockets of Mexican American residents, were also found in outlying rural districts, even before massive immigration in the twentieth century (Simross 1984). Los Nietos and Chino are two examples that date from early Mexican rancherías. Newcomers began to settle in these urban and rural barrios in the 1920s and 1930s and even developed new barrios. Most were of the interstitial type in the urban area, such as El Hoyo Maravilla. Gustafson (1940) reports an informant's account of one such barrio: "Maravilla Park is just west of Coyote Pass. It has always been almost 100 per cent Mexican. The first houses were the worst kind of shacks, like hobo jungles, built of old oil cans, old tin, boxes, scrap lumber, etc., that could be found" (p. 43).

Proximity to work place is what led to the growth of rural colonias. Cucamonga is an example of such a place (McWilliams 1968:218). At first the Mexican settlements were scattered in small pockets throughout the area (Guasti, Ontario) when they arrived as unskilled farm laborers to work the citrus and vineyard industries. As the industries expanded and the need for seasonal workers (and additionally for year around regulars) increased, the Mexicans eventually filled one particular neighborhood—Northtown (situated across the tracks and flood canal, predictably). This enclave had once been peopled mostly by Italian semiskilled and skilled workers who eventually bought land of their own and moved out of the neighborhood. By the 1930s it was a Mexican barrio, and it has remained so to the present. In the mid-1970s, many of the streets were still unpaved, and those that were paved had no curbs or sidewalks. Most of the homes were small, graying, brownish clapboard types with only one bedroom to barely contain a family. Outhouses, some sturdy and others dilapidated, dotted backyards. This was obviously a social and physically isolated human congregation of one thousand people (Vigil and Miller 1981). As recently as 1985, there were five homes that still lacked linkage to a sewage system.

Brickmakers settled in Simon (in Montebello, but named after a brickyard), section hands in Watts, and grape pickers in Ontario (McWilliams 1968). Romo (1983) noted that "Mexican laborers recruited to Los Angeles by the Pacific Electric became the first group of immigrant residents whose residential locations were directly related to interurban transportation. At every major junction or end of the line, the company constructd labor camps for track hands" (p. 69). Whether old or new, urban or rural, all of them shared the qualities noted earlier: spatial separation and visibly inferior housing. Kienle (1912:8) early underscored this association between work and living place: "Some of the houses are like long rows of sheds. These can scarcely be called homes. They are so arranged that each family has two rooms, with partition walls that leave large cracks between the boards . . . . This makes them resemble so many stalls for cattle instead of homes for human beings . . . . Such houses are usually along the railroad track, built by the railroad company for their section hands," with rent taken out of their earnings by the company. Other contemporary reports (e.g., Culp 1921) also noted these conditions.

Ecological stressors in time began to take their toll, especially with increasing barriozation in a rapidly growing Los Angeles area. Shortly after his words on "boy gang strains," Bogardus (1943) was urging the city officials to heed the problems created by such settlement processes. The federal government by then had initiated housing projects to help stem social problems for low-income enclaves in the Los Angeles vicinity. There are five such projects in East Los Angeles, and these have become barrios in their own right (i.e., mostly low-income Mexicans and stressors that contribute to gang formation). Despite the good intentions of the government to help such communities, the projects were overwhelmed by the nearby larger barrio patterns. Gustafson (1940:112) addressed this issue, in part, at the beginning of one of these projects: "The social distance existing between such residents and the heterogenous inhabitants further north will be too great for the maximum community benefit. Furthermore, residents . . . will be renters, not homeowners. As such the community will represent a stage of community development lacking in community spirit and indicating the first stage of sociological decline." With this insight, the Methodist minister had no idea that this area would become home to one of the biggest gangs in East Los Angeles.

Ecological conditions have improved, of course, since these early barrio beginnings. There is more infrastructure since the 1940s, and some barrios have spilled over into areas where housing is better. As time has passed, even in the first barrios, dwellers have often upgraded their own housing. The introduction by city and county authorities of paved streets, utilities, and services has also brought benefits. Even with these changes, however, the older and more recent urban barrios in the vicinity stand in sharp contrast to the quality of residential conditions in most other locales within the city.

Moreover, new types of suburban barrios have formed in greater Los Angeles. They appear to have surfaced in working-class tract-home neighborhoods. In such locations Chicanos have become second and third owners of the dwelling (the Orange County housing complex previously mentioned is evidence of this). There are also changes in the former rural and semirural enclaves that are now being engulfed by suburban housing growth, a process begun after World War II. It is clear that colonias have lost their rural isolation, and in the process their gangs have begun to resemble urban ones. Suburban youth gangs resulted because of previous barrio influences and their efforts to follow tradition, especially to defend against aggressions of nearby colonias. Underdevelopment still characterizes some colonias, such as Cucamonga described above. Suburban barrios might be better, but in relation to areas nearby they are more deteriorated. For example, the Norwalk tract now known as the barrio Neighborhood (most of the suburban types have English names, reflecting their anglicization) shows this distinction.

Social networks were disrupted under such types of social strains and spatial isolations. As underdeveloped backwashes, the barrios saw dysfunctional features, including antisocial and illicit activity, arise; and crime and criminal patterns became an everyday concern for barrio residents and nonresidents alike. Residents may be lawful but they are often as much a victim of the vices and antisocial activities as would be any outsider. Locales with dense populations and in a state of decay are known to have this pattern (Clinard 1960, 1968; Shaw and McKay 1942; Shohan et al. 1966).

Barrio youth are in general agreement that their neighborhoods constitute a separate, distinct, and different environ. All of the participants interviewed for this study mentioned their barrio by name, sometimes referring to it as a special place or a sanctuary. Barrio names ranged from early California place names (Cucamonga, Chino, El Monte Flores, Santana, and so on) to those settled and named by early-twentieth-century immigrants (Maravilla, La Rana, Carmelas). Barrios sometimes have an additional name showing direction or geography, like Southside or Northtown, especially when the surrounding population desires to separate itself from the barrio.

Some names stem from an association with workplace—Varrio Sunkist (citrus), Watts (railroad), Simon (brickyard), Hick's Camp (citrus), and so on—and some from identifying visual landmarks—White Fence, One-Ways, and Keystone. Last, many of the more recent barrios are either housing or low-income apartment projects—Bungalow Projects, Ramona Gardens, Montebello Gardens, the Apartments—or modest suburban tract homes—Quiet Village, Peaceful Valley, or the Neighborhood.

Besides knowledge of barrio names as a declaration of their home base, informants were clear about the visual signs that characterize the barrio. Housing, of course, was particularly mentioned as problematic, as homes were cited as old (sometimes forty to fifty years old), small in size (both domicile and lot), constructed of wood, and having poor plumbing and sewage facilities. (Older household members—parents or an older sister caretaker—often showed facial signs of embarrassment on occasions when I visited and observed such conditions in their homes.) Streets were in disrepair and in rural areas were of dirt that became muddy during winter rains; some barrios were without curbs and sidewalks. Driving fast cars on the streets was an activity that persons noted. Most barrios had plenty of children playing out in the streets, usually right up to bedtime. Also common were the barrio "Mom-and-Pop" stores, which carried only the essential merchandise, foodstuffs and other staples, and generally tendered credit to the locals. Several individuals spoke of, and I have often observed, the "little cigar box kept below the counter for *cuentas* [record of credit transactions]" in such stores. Given these distinctive barrio qualities, one man said, "It is a city within a city."

Barrio dwellers are cognizant of the variations found among barrios and of the often more obvious difference between barrios and other neighborhoods (Achor 1978). They are equally aware of discrepancies in official and commercial attitudes that go with that difference. Typically, this awareness is expressed as discontented grumbling, but in recent years it increasingly has been articulated in organized and quasi-organized protest. On the one hand, for example, in Los Angeles are the sustained efforts by UNO (United Neighborhood Organization) to pressure insurance companies into eliminating the higher rates for automobile insurance for barrio residents; and the well-organized (but thus far only marginally effective) efforts of a now defunct parents' group, EICC (Educational Issues Coordinating Committee), to force the local school district to upgrade deteriorating barrio schools (Santana and Esparza 1974). Less mannerly, but reflecting similar awareness of the disparity in services, were the "wildcat" student protests nearly two decades ago. Even in the outlying, formerly rural barrios is this evidenced (Casteñeda et al. 1974). One young Chino resident, for example, told me of being arrested while he was still in junior high school: "I got busted because we got on top of a hood of a car . . . . We were trying to protest . . . [the street] was all muddy and we wanted sidewalks . . . . The lady [driver] got hysterical and she took off with us on the hood . . ."

In sum, the settlement of Mexicans in segregated, visually inferior locations made adaptation difficult. A life of poverty in the hollows, ravines, across the tracks, could not facilitate accommodation or aid adjustment of new groups of Mexican immigrants to American society. Discrimination in earlier decades had already made early arrivals feel unwanted, and the years of large-scale immigration to large populated areas undergoing rapid culture change in this century created the conditions for major social problems. For example, Bogardus' "boy problem" has become a "gang subculture problem" with second and third generations of Mexican youth (Vigil 1983). Their lives, in combination with other factors, are still being shaped by ecological stressors.

Nevertheless, most barrio youth shun gang activities (although they may flirt with some cholo and gang routines at some point in their lives). Moreover, most of the barrio residents are law abiders who have learned to cope with ecological conditions, even taking great pride in how they dress and upgrade and decorate their homes and gardens. Cholos and noncholos, gang members and non-gang members do share one thing in common, however. Their social and personal identities are shaped by barrio life, for they know that a spatial and social distance separates them from their more affluent neighbors and that this distinctiveness affects one's quality of life, such as in job opportunities, education, and the like. Poverty, discrimination, and group choice helped to create Mexican barrios, but urbanization and the concommitant poor city planning and neglectful and uncaring authorities make the barrios an ecologically inferior place in which to raise a family.

Underclass Life: Problems with Jobs and Work

As in all population groups, each of the various waves of Mexican immigrants brought with it variations in social status, skills, attitudes, and temperament. Moreover, some arrived during periods of an expanding economy and others during periods of stagnant or negative economic growth and, thus, job shortage. Each urban barrio thus was established with a diversity of economic well-being among the working-class families residing within it. The number of least economically stable families grew during economic downturns, of course, but such poorer households also came into existence as circumstances for individual families changed. Such changes in a family's situation and condition might result from severe injury or death of the principal jobholder; from the breakup of the marriage and/or abandonment of the family by an overstressed parent, or from the incarceration or the deportation of key members of the family. Thus, while almost all immigrant families had to cope with stresses of economic pressures and culture change, some families were strained even greater. Most families gradually acquired a stable, if not prosperous, status, but others became increasingly impoverished. Through all these changes, there thus resulted families who were unable to become socially mobile and others who suffered long-term poverty and were left behind. Today, as Moynihan (1988) has noted, this tends to be children in single parent-households.

Family stress and instability in one generation often leads to its perpetuation in the next, because youths raised in such situations tend to incorporate additional psychological strains and because they tend to incorporate the frustrated behavior patterns of adult role models into their own adult behavior. Indeed, certain problems can thus be intensified in each succeeding generation, especially if these pressures are exacerbated by external social forces, such as continuing racial discrimination and punitive governmental policies. Within a working-class barrio, thus, can emerge a smaller underclass that is characterized by chronic unemployment or underemployment of adult men whose occupational opportunities become limited to seasonal jobs and the secondary labor market—or criminal opportunism; by highly stressful family households, often with no resident adult male, dependent on relatives' assistance, charity, or (in more recent decades) welfare assistance; and by anxiety or frustration-born rage that often leads to drug and alcohol addiction, child neglect, and asocial and antisocial behavior.

Matza (1966) and Banfield (1970) have discussed, albeit with different philosophical premises, the distinction between "respectable" and "disrespectable" poor families, even among the poor themselves. Moore (1985, 1986) has examined the stigmatization of underclass segments of low-income working-class barrios and its relationship to barrio gangs. She also examines its interaction with the stigma that the larger Anglo-American society ascribes to barrio residents generally. Parents in stable family households, however much they might or might not blame underclass families themselves for their miserable conditions, generally tend to avoid such families and limit their own children's exposure to them. They are apt to say, when one of their own offspring becomes involved with a gang: "Oh, he got in with the wrong crowd." On the other hand, gang involvement of a youth from an underclass family elicits a "like father, like son" sentiment.

For most of this century, a pattern of Mexicans providing a cheap source of labor for American industries has continued. Despite continual labor struggles to upgrade the status of Mexican laborers (Gómez-Quiñones 1982; Arroyo and Nelson-Cisneros 1975; McWilliams 1968), many Mexicans have become permanent members of the American underclass. The record of Mexican immigration patterns clearly documents the difficulties of adaptation that result from placement in unskilled low-paying jobs (Gamio 1969a, b; McWilliams 1968; Galarza 1964; Moore and Pachón 1985; Reisler 1976). At present, Mexican Americans still are far behind Anglos on most socioeconomic indicators, as is made clear in the statistics reported in Table 1. Similarly, only 55 percent of the nation's adult Chicano

Table 1   Socioeconomic Indicators of Mexican American Status

	Income	Family Size	Female-Headed
California [a]			
All	$21,537	3.24	14.8%
Spanish surname	13,416	4.00	17.1%
Los Angeles County [b]			
All	$21,125	3.34	18.2%
Spanish surname	15,531	4.10	18.7%

[a] 1980 Census of the Population-General Social and Economic Characteristics, PCU-1-C6 (U.S. Department of Commerce 1983).
[b] 1980 Census of Population and Housing—Los Angeles and Long Beach, California, PHC 80-2-226 (U.S. Department of Commerce 1983).

population has finished high school, compared to 83 percent for Anglos (Chicano Survey Reports 1979). The same status disparity is apparent in the fact that two-thirds (69%) of Chicano workers are in the laboring class, with 29 percent of them in unskilled occupations (Chicano Survey Reports 1979). Moreover, these figures exclude most of the undocumented Mexican workers and families, who are even worse off (Muller 1984:7).

The small percentage of barrio youth who become affiliated with a gang are generally members of the underclass and are affected by the realities of this way of life before entering the streets. These realities include troubled families, problems with schooling, poor job opportunities, and even dress styles. Most of the regular gang members with whom I have interacted came from such troubled families—that is, from larger than average families living in smaller than average homes, usually in the poorer barrios (or sections of a barrio). Their parents often were only periodically employed, and one or both might be absent. (Many of these youth were raised by grandparents, by their mothers in their fathers' absence, or by other relatives.)

Effects of Lower-Class and Underclass Life on Families

The disruptions in family life stem from these economic considerations. The social repercussions from such economic fluctuations were noted among Mexicans quite early: "Frequently the men have lost their work, they cannot secure another job, they cannot speak English, they become discouraged and take to drinking. Fighting ensues, then perhaps stabbing. They are arrested, sent to the Police Station and then to the chain gang, nobody to know the amount of hardship the wife and mother has suffered in silence" (Kienle 1912:32).

The degree of a youth's involvement with a local gang appears to be associated with the status of his or her family. Key informants in this study who were regular gang members were found in disproportionate numbers in single-parent (usually mother-centered) households; of thirteen informants from mother-centered homes, nine were regularly involved in gang activities. In contrast, of the informants who listed parents with earned incomes (and mostly skilled occupations), twelve of sixteen were from traditional households (father wage earner, mother housewife), and most were temporary or situational gang members. Interestingly, the other four households of this group had parents who both worked and three of four informants were regular gang members, a pattern that closely resembles the welfare families.

To reiterate, these types of social disorganization problems appear to be inherent in a situation of rapid technological and social change (Bernard and Pelto 1972:321-323). Early observers noted that living and working experiences undermined social control practices, and this pattern grew in intensity with subsequent immigration to Los Angeles and its environs. Bogardus (1934) noted that social stress and crime exist "in the rank and file of the poorest paid laboring classes" (p. 54) and that "sometimes idleness and unemployment are sufficient to land a vagrancy charge on the Mexican's head. Lack of training and education and lack of constructive opportunities account for the offenses of Mexicans" (p. 55). Many families, especially those who had wage earners who were unable to secure a job, became alienated, disoriented, and problem ridden. Some parents today have problems guiding and directing their own lives, much less those of their children. As a result, children may go without adequate supervision. Life histories collected from gang members reveal frequent accounts of wandering through the neighborhood alone for hours, as early as age 9 or 10. I have often seen small groups of such children, younger siblings of gang members, in areas far from home, casually "whiling" the time away.

Although somewhat reticent in belaboring the issue, over one-half of the informants mentioned, in a matter-of-fact voice, that their lives were affected by a scarcity of resources. Food, clothing, and adequate housing needs were the predominant items raised by the informants. Many of the informants for this study were reluctant to estimate their household incomes. Those with skilled jobs were most likely to provide the figure. The average family income of all the informants who could provide this data was $11,843, compared to an average of $15,531 for Spanish surnames throughout Los Angeles County. A smaller number spoke of deeper concerns, such as a feeling of shame about being poor or embarrassment over hanging around with welfare recipients.

A 27-year-old male *veterano* (veteran gang member) from South Fontana, for example, grew up as a member of a mother-centered family of thirteen children. Most of their life was on welfare income, and as he states: "Our mother tried her best to make it with all of us, but lost the battle . . . . Gabachos used to kind of make me feel bad 'cause they came to school with nice clothes. They always had plenty to eat for lunch or they had money to buy their hot lunch. There would be times my brothers and sisters had nothing for lunch. The only time we ate hot lunches was when we worked in the school cafeteria. Boy, it was an honor to work a whole week in the cafeteria." He eventually became very active in the gang and still hangs around with the homeboys today. Similar accounts of inadequate clothing or having to work odd jobs to help the parents purchase apparel for oneself were also related.

One common problem in the home situation was crowded conditions, a not unusual circumstance when the average size of family (8.5) for all the sample is considered. A male, 20, who was a temporary gang member from Chino (cf. Henry's life history in Chapter 4), belonged to a mother-centered family with four other brothers.

Although one of the smaller families in the sample, he said that in a two-bedroom house "three of us slept in one bedroom, and sometimes I moved into the living room. We had a set of bunkbeds and sometimes one of us slept on the floor." He avoided the gang until high school, when he joined, but within a year or two he gradually phased himself out of it. "I never made it as a true member," he said.

A more extreme example of a male, 22, from Pico Viejo shows even more difficulties. Currently, he is a regular gang member, who, along with three other brothers, came from a highly disorganized family, which led to all of them being placed in different foster homes. He described his early childhood when all of them were still with their mother:

> I remember my mom. They turned off her gas and every-
> thing . . . the lights. She used to cook our dinner in the
> backyard with a little fire. She used to cook our dinner right
> there because just about everything in our house started leav-
> ing. We had a lot of good things, everything just started disap-
> pearing and it was a trip. Like my mom couldn't handle it, she
> had to sell things to support us. She was working before then,
> and when they gave us back to her they gave her welfare. But it
> still wasn't doing no good. She used to work at night, I think
> she worked in a laundromat. That was the only thing she knew
> how to do, and she used to iron clothes for the old *gente* [peo-
> ple], stuff like that. I could see that she was having a bad time,
> but still I was kinda happy. The thing is that she would never
> give up. Me and my brother C. started stealing bikes. We used
> to test ourselves to see how good we were in stealing and we
> started getting caught a few times. We stole like food and can-
> dy, but we never did nothing like really serious.

Child neglect and petty crime stemmed from shaky economic conditions. One individual, a male, 28, who was a temporary gang member from Cucamonga (although two younger brothers later became regular members), felt particularly embarrassed by his life of abject poverty. His mother struggled to raise nine children on welfare, and when the children were old enough they worked picking fruit and helped out at home. But there was never enough: "Neighbors would use us as an example of just how low a family could get. Even our own family rejected us. When there was family functions, we were rarely invited to them. The prejudism [sic] in the barrio of the Chicanos to their own is worse than the prejudice toward them from others. No one gave a damn about us." Later, he completed community college and found steady employment at a hardware store.

It was fairly common to hear stories about rural poverty from gang members in those barrios. Some even spoke of participating in the migrant stream, as this Ontario veterano, aged 40, explains: "From the time I was 12 to the time I was 18 years old the whole family [9 in all] did migrant work in Northern California. We would leave the west end in early May and not return until late in September. We went to several fruit growers, and followed the same route every year. The whole family took part in the harvesting. Our living quarters were bad, the pay was low, and all of the children were expected to put in a full day's work. It was hard work but we needed to do it to survive." The children's education suffered, of course, and he had trouble getting a job as a result. Joining the army helped him mature out of the street scene and probably kept him out of legal problems, for he had just become involved with selling drugs.

Less typical, but still a common problem, is the cycle of poverty, which affects several generations, especially in urban barrios. One female, 24, a regular gang member from East Los Angeles who is presently attempting to "kick the heroin habit" at a rehabilitation center, is one such example I observed. She was raised by a mother and a grandmother, neither of whom ever married, and she does not recall ever having a father. The mother had eight other children, all raised on welfare, and the daughter, with two children of her own, was living similarly before her arrest and placement. She, in fact, talked about getting together with "five or six other girls on Mother's Day, the 1st and 15th [i.e., the dates that the twice-monthly welfare checks arrive] to party," but in asides she always brought up these other problems: "The condition of our home isn't too good. The sanitation is really bad. The plumbing is real bad and the water comes out real slow and the toilets break down all the time. And you can take a bath, come back an hour later and half the water is still in the bath tub."

Gang members also experience problems in school, falling behind classmates at the start and then eventually dropping out when they reach high school (Haro 1976). While one can blame the negative attitudes and behaviors that such youth have toward American social institutions, it is clear that our schools have failed Mexicans (Carter and Segura 1978). Indeed, patterned discriminatory practices in the past have, in large part, shaped the youngsters' negative attitudes. Bogardus (1934) noted this disparity quite early: "Mexican parents often feel certain that their children are discriminated against by boards of education, and that their children are the last to be accorded new equipment, buildings, and the like" (p. 70). A contemporary report (Douglas 1928) went even further: "Perhaps the social system is all wrong, and the Americans are actually hindering instead of aiding the immigrant to solve his conflict problems by a superficial sort of education which tends only to increase rather than decrease the difficulties of accommodation" (p. 42). Bogardus also (1926) reported one young student's reaction to a teacher's chastisement about striving for education: "Look at Manuel, Miss M. He went to high school, and he works in the brickyard the same as Pedro, who never went to school" (p. 107). Although instructors would encourage students to do well in school, high school counselors often regularly advised Mexican American students not to consider a college education. Such educational practices were also common in rural areas (Hill 1928).

Poverty, Deviance, and the Cholo Style

The problems engendered by family and school difficulties are exacerbated by the generally poor job market for minority youth (National Commission for Employment Policy 1982). With few salable skills, few recreational opportunities, and no resources, many barrio youngsters simply "hang out" on the corner with friends who share a similar plight (Ginn 1947:106-107). Several individuals mentioned how difficult it was to find a job, and most had to rely on CETA or other government-sponsored training programs. As an example of this problem, one male, 16, a regular gang member from Cucamonga, dropped out of school and secured a job at a nearby nursery and in his spare time looked for a better job. Wherever he went he was told that he was too young or too inexperienced to hire. However, he saw Anglo boys his age in the same positions and being trained. In this case, he felt that it was because of his color, and such experiences eventually took their toll and he stopped seeking other jobs.

When these youths are not going to school, or working, much of the time spent with friends is in normal, male social discourse and interaction, such as talking about upcoming social events and discussing personal trials and tribulations. Large amounts of time, however, create opportunities for the introduction of other activities, especially if an older gang member makes suggestions and leads them into exciting alternatives to daily mundane events.

Gang members who secure a good job often refocus and redirect their lives into more conventional routes; such a change in orientation is referred to as "maturing out" (Matza 1964:22-26). Contemporary evidence on hard-core adult, former gang members indicates that they had a poor job record from the beginning of their work histories (Moore 1978; CPRP 1979). Most of their jobs were of the secondary level—noncareer, without fringe benefits, and seasonal.

Such work leaves many dissatisfied and in constant search of alternative paths—too often illegal ones. On the other hand, interviews with and observations of other former gang members (from the same age levels and areas as the hard-core adults) showed that they regarded having found a stable, primary occupation as a life-turning event. Their career involvement gradually drew them away from street life and all of the more personally dysfunctional activities. Missing that initial job opportunity, becoming more deeply involved with gang activities, and eventually spending time in jails have made the hard-core members even less prepared for good jobs. Many of them have become "revolving-door" violators, in and out of jail for one offense or another (Moore 1978).

"White collar" crime patterns show that deviance is found in all status groups (Tittle, et al. 1978). Serious crime among the early Mexican immigrants was uncommon. After decades of change under urban pressures, however, crime has become a serious problem among Mexican Americans. As Bernard and Pelto (1972) have noted in their study of technological change and migration, "some members of the population find themselves unable to obtain the desired money through legal means" (p. 323) and turn to crime and theft. A rather apt, though perhaps trite, example of this is given in one of the early studies where Douglas (1928:16) quotes a Mexican teenager:

> My brother and I looked everywhere for work. We were not afraid to work and we had to have work. Finally my brother went to the Imperial (Valley) to work in the lettuce. It was a long time, and he did not send to us any money. I was in school part of the time, because I wanted to learn the English. I had to leave school, but why? I had no work. One day I saw Mr. B. (American) and I thought of all the things he had in his house. I would work for him on his rancho. But he said that he did not need Mexican boys. I went to his house, and at night I found some things which would help my mother, so I took them for her. In the drawer there was a bag of money too. I took that because I needed it. There were mostly pennies and small moneys in the bag. (Mr. B.'s daughter was the treasurer of the Sunday School and the house was entered on Sunday night.) But what could I do? My mother was hungry. Another time I went into the house of another man. All he had there were guns. I took them. They were not what I needed most, but I thought maybe I could sell them. When I tried to sell them I got caught. The boys all laughed at me. It was not bad to take the guns, because the man had lots of them, but it was bad for me to get caught.

It is fairly clear that the characteristics and consequences of deviant behavior are relatd to status. There are predictable paths and outcomes for those lower-class individuals who follow a life of crime. They often bring more public hostility toward their infractions. Many of their activities are unsophisticated frontal assaults (robbery, burglary, shoplifting, mugging), which entail risk on their part. Because of this danger, especially since it often is a public event with increased chances for witnesses, they are often caught during or soon after the crime. Limited resources, after apprehension for such infractions, also undermine their legal defense. The probability of a conviction is often assured. I once testified in court to the good character of a young male from Jardín, who was not even at the scene of the alleged crime, yet he nevertheless went to jail for a year.

A low-income life has also influenced the dress habits of the barrio gang members (and many others who wish to emulate such standards). It is a basic style, which is fairly constant—comfortable shirt, durable trousers, standard shoes. The outfits are simple and interchangeable. Khaki pants are an example of this functionality and, in addition, are part of a tradition that became fashionable after Chicano World War II and Korean War veterans continued wearing military clothing. Likewise, later on, the "county" jeans that one wore in detention became a part of the dress habits. This dress and style became institutionalized as a part of the cholo style and public persona, for private moments at home are more casual. Most cholos are good dressers and take great pride in sporting clean white T-shirts and in keeping starched and creased khaki pants. A phrase often uttered is: "I was all choloed out," which signifies that one was dressed to the hilt. It is interesting to note that the pants, at least, are from two government sources—military and penal—that are important in the lives of low-income Mexicans. Even dress habits are influenced by the dominant society.

Conclusion

Group and family histories reveal that a sense of anxiety and confusion accompanied adaptation to America. Along with the fluctuating demands of a budding industrial economy, official neglect and social and racial discrimination combined to make the immigrant population feel that they were outsiders to mainstream events. The various barrio enclaves, including modern suburban variants, became visual and spatial reminders of the marginal entrance that Mexicans had made to the United States, even though their labor was central to the economy. A continuing placement of numbers of Mexicans in the underclass, as well as the persistence within it of large portions of subsequent generations, ensured that these living arrangements would endure. These social distancing and economic obstacles contributed to profound and complex changes in subsequent Mexican American populations, as their individual life histories attest. Thus, an appreciation of multiple marginality must of necessity include an understanding of how family patterns and group and personal cultural habits stemmed in considerable measure from living and working arrangements and, in time, how these secondary features wound their web of marginality to contribute to the formation of street gangs.

3. Sociocultural Factors in the Choloization of the Mexican American Youth Population

Under the circumstances already reviewed, a cholo subculture developed among barrio street youths. As with the Latin American subcultures previously labeled cholo, this youth subculture reflected social and cultural lives wracked by conflict and strain born of marginal situations and conditions. Cholo sociocultural dynamics, for example, involve marginal and attenuated family, school, and street patterns that create personal and group voids that must be filled by something. For a small but considerable portion of the Chicano underclass population, the gang has taken over where other influences have failed. It is the case that these marginal developments produced several subcultural strata, particularly in the gang, and that such results are rooted in the environmental and socioeconomic background of the gang members.

The experiences of Mexican Americans in the United States are unique. The annexation of the Southwest left the Mexican residents a conquered minority, and racial and class antagonisms dating from that period have profoundly colored the circumstances of Mexican American adaptation to the majority society (Acuña 1981; de la Garza et al. 1973; Vigil 1984). Subsequent generations of immigrants from Mexico encountered preexisting modes of discrimination, as well as the resident minority's developing social and cultural systems. At the same time, the continuing immigration served to reinvigorate Mexican social and cultural patterns in the barrios; and the nearness of family and friends in Mexico reinforced the continuation of some aspects of Mexican American lifeways.

Notwithstanding these distinctive features of the Mexican immigrants' experiences, the newcomers did share with other ethnic immigrants common goals: finding work, obtaining a place to live, and raising families into an often bewildering host society. Typically, as with other immigrant groups, the immigrants' children grew up to improve on their parents' status (Galarza 1971). Some became thoroughly assimilated, even to the point (in some cases) of adopting the majority Americans' discriminatory attitudes and behaviors toward Mexicans. In many more instances, as much by accident as by design, perhaps, acculturation to American lifeways was accompanied by retention of varying degrees of familiarity with Mexican cultural and linguistic patterns (Vigil and Long 1981). For significant numbers, ecological and structural obstacles hampered the adoption of either of these strategies, and such persons became alienated from both Mexican and American ways of life. The continued concentration of these very marginally adapted people in the older, ecologically and economically marginal barrios thus became a factor in the acculturation of the new immigrants streaming into the same neighborhood with each generation.

The immigrant Mexicans of the early decades were primarily of a rural, peasant background. Social boundaries separated the majority and minority groups and hindered access and exposure to, and identification with, American culture (Graves 1967). Those who settled in rural enclaves were at least familiar with their slower-paced surroundings, that is, until they too were enveloped by suburban housing and light industry growth in later decades. The urban setting, however, introduced a new set of enculturation and socialization patterns. Mexican family structure was already undergoing change (Humphrey 1944; Alvírez et al. 1981:288), and the demands and opportunities of urban life accelerated the changes.

Employment inconsistency led to residential inconsistency as many families were frequently forced to change homes, although staying within the barrio or moving to a nearby barrio where rents were low. Economic struggles taxed the parents' energies and affected the time they could spend monitoring their children's behavior, especially under crowded conditions and in large families. Disruptions in family life, moreover, often brought a high incidence of broken homes, where the mother had to take on the dual role of breadwinner and breadmaker. As a result, children spent more time outside the home, where there was more space to play and cavort. Here they began to learn the ways of the streets under the aegis of older children, with minimal adult supervision. The outcome was often early exposure to and induction into the gang.

The underclass life thus affected the home socialization of the children to the point where street socialization took over, notwithstanding parental efforts to maintain control. The loosening of family supervision networks had repercussions in two other social control institutions—the schools and law enforcement. These institutions have played a pivotal role in the life of the children of immigrants and in the conflict that has generated the marginal status of so many of them. Early researchers noted schools as a problem for the second generation of Mexican Americans: schools generally failed to accommodate the culturally different (Bogardus 1929; Sánchez 1967). Law enforcement has also had its difficulties with the Mexican population. Indeed, Mexicans have had a tradition of distrust of law enforcement in their native country. As school and street specialists overseeing youth's daytime activities, teachers and police are primary authorities of social control in our society. Yet cultural barriers in the classrooms, and the high incidence of Chicanos' "dropping out" of (and/or exclusion from) schools, have led to a situation in which significant numbers of barrio youngsters are socialized to a considerable degree in the streets; and among the things they learn in the streets is antagonism toward the police.

There is much friction between barrio residents and law enforcement, much like what is found in other low-income neighborhoods. In the Mexican case, there is a historical legacy of hostility since the nineteenth century (Acuña 1981; Vigil 1984; Mirande 1987). Because of the persistence of this antagonism between the police and the community, there are instances where even law-abiding barrio citizens are "labeled" as deviants (Gonzales 1981). Whether antisocial or not, an individual might attract more police attention just by living in the barrio (Morales 1972; U.S. Commission on Civil Rights 1970).

The activities of youth in the schools and on the streets are best understood within the context of underclass life and a broad socioeconomic backdrop. Merton (1949) has suggested that low-income populations have no or little means to attain goals established by higher-status groups and thus must resort to alternative, often deviant, paths for fulfillment. Cloward and Ohlin (1960) have elaborated on this means/goals dichotomy; Moore (1978) has framed a similar argument for Chicanos in East Los Angeles.

Moreover, youths whose schooling and career opportunities exclude them from what Cohen terms "the respectable status system" encounter serious difficulties in fashioning for themselves a social identity, especially if they are alienated. "The delinquent subculture deals with these problems by providing criteria of status which these children can meet" (Cohen 1955:121). There is an internal reasoning to the Chicano gang subculture and because of its sense of camaraderie it is able to attract and socialize many youths; and "once established, such a subcultural system may persist, [and] outlasts that of the individual who participated in its creation, but only so long as it continues to serve the needs of those who succeed its creators" (Cohen 1955:65).

The breakdown in social control and the need for social status in some social grouping must be viewed in the broader context of culture contact and culture conflict. Many individuals never completely acculturate to the dominant cultural style, yet they have already altered their Mexican self-concept, perhaps to the point where they had relinquished some important Mexican traits. In varying degrees, and in conjunction with other factors, this creates a situation of being placed between two cultural modes by default, a common occurrence in the wake of immigrant-host society contact, or deculturation. Such an intermediate cultural placement is often referred to as one of marginality (Park 1928; Stonequist 1937; Dickie-Clark 1966), for there is no denying the "betwixt and between" feeling that this situation engenders in individuals, and in group life generally (Schermerhorn 1970; Frazier 1957; Poggie 1973).

There is considerable evidence that the amount of time one's family has been in the United States, especially with later generations of native-born Mexican Americans, determines the level and rate of adoption of Anglo-American patterns (Vigil 1976; Olmedo and Padilla 1978). It is also clear that the cultural transitional process associated with years of residence can often result in ambiguous, sometimes conflict-ridden mental states. This often brings confusion over ethnic identity, especially for the second generation (Jessor et al. 1968). The experiences of Mexican Americans over several generations have given rise to various subcultural strata within that group. In some ways the subcultural strata are shaped by and are representative of each of the first-through-third-generation types of experiences, reflecting the dynamics and variations of change on a process level. Thus, the Mexican American community must be examined in terms of partially nested levels of subcultures. A subculture, as defined here, is a cohesive cultural system within a larger national culture, and a broad subcultural system may itself be divided into smaller subcultures (Gordon 1964:39). Subcultures and smaller subcultures evolve over several generations (Molohon et al. 1979).

The first generations of Mexicans shared enough in common to be considered a subculture. Many of them came from the same region in Mexico, experienced a similar immigrant life of struggle with living and working adaptations, and suffered the ill effects of inferior treatment by the dominant group. Much of this past and present background made for a certain amount of ethnic cohesion and solidarity among Mexicans, sometimes lasting well beyond the first generation to subsequent offspring; even the innocuous palomilla cohorting habits persisted into this phase.

The second generation, that is, the offspring of the immigrants, are likely to experience more intense culture conflict. Culture conflict is both a psychological (individual) and social (group) phenomenon, comprised of changes involving a number of alternatives and options, and is reflective of the development of the second subcultural strata. The alternative outcomes include, as noted above, total assimilation and identification with Anglo-American lifeways and, more commonly, a new type of ethnic identity, which incorporates elements of Mexican and Anglo-American culture, including in some cases bilingual fluency (Buriel 1984).

A considerable number of individuals, however, are unable to devise a smooth, consistent strategy of adaptation. They represent yet another subculture. For them, often, the effects of racism, the persistent cycle of underclass involvement with little chance of social mobility, and the general malaise engendered by problems with getting jobs and staying in school have dominated their lives and impeded acculturation, as well as overall cultural adaptation. Members of this second subculture of cultural transitionals are referred to as cholos. In any barrio of the southwestern United States one can find cholos, although there are of course variations from one area to another. (Some recent immigrants from low-income Mexican urban enclaves, especially from border regions, are also cholos because of similar ecological and structural conditions there [Castro 1982] or through diffusion from the United States [Cuéllar 1987; Cummings 1987]. But these are the exception. The cholo referred to here is an American product.)

An individual's status as a cholo may be of relatively short duration (usually in youth), after which another mode of cultural adaptation is adopted; or it may be lifelong in nature. One can still observe, as I did on numerous instances in different barrios, cholos in their thirties and even forties hanging around with younger comrades. Most barrios have a type of gang, and the barrio gang uniquely reflects the multiple pressures and conflicts of Mexican Americans. It is made up, typically, of individuals who have had serious trouble acculturating; and its subculture arose as a response to a type of "erring" acculturation, or deculturation (Buriel 1984), or temporary cultural ambivalence, and additionally as an adaptation to street life in urban settings. It thus has become an institutionalized entity that provides many poor, barrio youths with human support networks and a source of personal ego identity that are unavailable to them elsewhere.

The rise and formation of the gang subculture, to reiterate, revolves around the broader backdrop of culture conflict and choloization of much of the second-generation Mexican American population. It is based in the streets and keyed to cultural fluctuations. This subcultural style was generated in the 1930s and 1940s when the second generation was under intense conflict (Bogardus 1929, 1943). The pachuco was a variant of that style (borrowed from the "hip" black entertainer Cab Calloway, the first "media" zoot suiter). (It was in El Paso, Texas, that the pachuco style originated, although it might be traced to Pachuca, Mexico, where baggy pants were common among males.) The pachuco dress style was particularly unique—smartly tapered bloused pants; extra long, wide-shouldered coats that tapered at the bottom; a long chain hanging from the waist; thick-soled shoes; and a broad-rimmed hat. This style made them urban "cool" (Bogardus 1943; McWilliams 1968; Tuck 1956). An important part of the style involved a new language. Some called it "Spanglish" because it combined Spanish and English patterns. Others, however, referred to it as *caló*, a grassroots speech style or creolization of the Spanish language initiated earlier (Barker 1972; Hinojos 1975; Peñalosa 1980). Culture contact situations commonly make for similar linguistic changes (Hymes 1971).

Each new generation that followed contributed to such innovations. Eventually, the cholo style emerged, especially in the 1960s and 1970s. Cholos have carried on the pachuco tradition, not only in street language (Serrano 1979) but also in dress style, which, innovatively, has shifted to khaki pants, plaid pendleton shirt, deck shoes, and a watch cap or bandana.

Police officials have often viewed such creative cultural forms as representative of deviance. The media, especially newspapers, have followed a similar course in making such dress styles a badge of dishonor. The facts belie the image, however, as most cholos and pachucos, even though street raised and undergoing culture conflict, are nonparticipants in deviant, antisocial patterns. Because of police and media influences, the public has nevertheless tended to perceive such styles as reflective of criminal behavior (Tuck 1956; McWilliams 1968; W. B. Miller 1975; W. P. Miller 1977; Baker 1979; Johnston 1979).

An acute sense of cultural marginality stemmed from many conflict sources. Cultural marginality produces persons who have "defined a certain life situation in a manner different from that of the group judging his conduct. A normal response from the person's point of view becomes abnormal in the eyes of the latter group" (Sellin 1938:43). Contraculture is a concept that lends insight to this facet of the gang subculture; some researchers rely on other terms, such as oppositional culture, in examining similar issues (Willis 1977). "In a contraculture ... the *conflict* element is central; many of the values ... are ... contradictions of the values of the dominant culture" (Yinger 1960:629; emphasis added). Derbyshire (1968:101) has found this to be true among adolescent Mexican Americans, and the same phenomenon has been documented in working-class suburban areas (Vigil 1979; Buriel et al. 1982).

In summary, it is the group situation as shaped by all the subcultural transformations, particularly the cholo and gang ones, that accounts for individual involvement and participation in gang life. Over time, enough youths adapted to their situation of marginality, and the conditions giving rise to it, to develop identifiable (and eventually institutionalized) groups with a distinct subculture. For some, the latter in many ways is even more important than one's job, income, or religion.

Generational Change and Culture Conflict

The culture conflict experienced by Mexican immigrants has generally been even more intensively felt by the second generation. For many of those youths, language inconsistency at home and school, a perceived gap in the status of their parents and the quality of their environment and those of the larger society, and the dangers and attractions of the barrio streets combine to create an ambiguity in their ethnic identity. Parents and older siblings are often unable to effectively guide youngsters in ways to reconcile the contrasting cultural worlds, and this results in an uneven adoption of acculturative strategies. In one East Los Angeles family that I visited, for example, the eight children grew up with two working parents and their maternal grandmother; the adults were hard pressed to keep the wolf from the door and had little opportunity for providing the children with insights into the subtleties of the cultural ambiguities in their lives. As a result, each child learned his or her way individually, and the outcome is that the various siblings occupy different sectors of the cultural spectrum—from cholo to quite anglicized.

The cholo lifestyle (including, but not limited to, the barrio gang subculture) is an American experience set in the strains and stresses of prolonged immobility, which affects how Mexican culture is relinquished and American culture acquired, a cultural adjustment process that spawns a mixed culture. For example, the overwhelming majority of the individuals interviewed and observed for this study, who affected cholo speech and mannerisms, were second- or third-generation Americans. A street-based amalgam of Anglo-American and Mexican features with innovative syncretisms, the cholo subculture provides a milieu in which partially or unevenly acculturated youths can seek to define themselves and their roles. Cholo language practices, employing as they do a mixture of Spanish, English, and "Spanglish" vocabulary and phraseology, afford a more accessible mode of communication for many. Numerous informants, for example, relate initial problems in communication when they first enrolled in English-speaking schools, after a virtually exclusively Spanish-language early upbringing. Most of these tales focus on bathroom embarrassments, as in this account of elementary school experiences from a 40-year-old male from Ontario: "They sent me to a school that was 90 percent Anglo and it was weird . . . . I couldn't speak a work of English and the teacher didn't know a word of Spanish. Man, was I embarrassed when the teacher couldn't understand me when I wanted to go to the toilet. The whole mess came in my pants."

Equally common in informants' narratives, however, is embarrassment about their inability to speak Spanish. With some amount of apprehension, as if betraying his ethnic disloyalty, one male said that he was the only solely English-speaking member of a family of five siblings. Another male took pains to stress that he is a Chicano, because he is able to understand what "Mexicans are saying even though I can't talk it." Identifying with the cholo style allows such youths to assert a Chicano identity (and pride in it) and to deny being *engabacheado* (anglicized). Yet these youths also seek to avoid affiliation with a Mexican heritage and, in fact, hold somewhat disparaging attitudes toward "chúntaros" and "wetbacks," as they call Mexican nationals or immigrants. The youth groups of Carmelas (a barrio in Norwalk), I have observed, have evolved from predominantly Spanish speaking in the 1960s to mostly English speaking in the 1980s and concurrently have become increasingly antagonistic toward recent Mexican immigrants. Much of this intraethnic friction revolves around economic and cultural sources. Competition for scarce job resources, especially between members of the depressed underclass and desperate immigrants, generates a part of the animosity. However, it appears that linguistic and cultural differences play at least an equal role in pitting one group against the other. For example, ethnic slurs based on cultural loyalty and linguistic abilities (e.g., Mexicans making fun of a Chicano's inability to speak "proper" Spanish and conversely) are quite common to the youth, and even the adults.

Barrio Social Life and the Shaping of a Cultural Style

Socialization to cholo ways, especially for those who go on to become gang members, is strongly influenced by family life and peer groups in interaction with the schools and law enforcement agencies. In stress-filled families with many children, for example, there is a tendency for a loosening of primary social control networks. As a result, an unsupervised child spends more time outside the home with street peers. These street peers, some slightly older and a few in their early teens (frequently including older siblings), become major agents of socialization. Concommitantly, school behavior and performance also tend to suffer when parental guidance is lacking. School problems and the influence of street-based peer groups reinforce one another in a youth's increasingly marginal development; one can witness the same small group together in both schoolyards and the street.

Thus, a street-based subculture has evolved and looms large for all barrio youth. A set of values, beliefs, and customs helps youths cope with the realities of the street, for it is based on an aura of fear where peers and older individuals dominate affairs. Even children in stress-free, stable homes have to be aware of these values, if only to avoid them. The majority of barrio youth, of course, shun a total acceptance of this street world view. Many, however, especially among those from broken, single-parent (usually mother-centered) families, adopt it wholely. According to one probation officer's case load, 70 to 80 percent of the gang members have these family backgrounds. Most of them have no choice but to stay on the streets and are more compelled than attracted to the gang. As an experienced probation officer in East Los Angeles said in an interview: "Really, it's like a naturalization sort of process thing. Most of them use it [the gang] for socialization, or for some kind of protection. If it means to be a gang-banger to be Americanized or socialized or assimilated, then 'I'm a gang-banger,' they say."

A contributing factor, as the life histories and my observations verify, to a dependence on street peers for social support is the lack of other community outlets for recreation and social events. In fact, there was a big effort on the part of various East Los Angeles community groups to solicit Olympics funds for parks and sports programs. But even with their success in gaining funds, East Los Angeles still has a low level of parks and recreation programs. The area has one of the lowest numbers of parks compared to other city locales, and those that do exist are overcrowded. Teen-aged ennui is reflected in these accounts, as in, for example, a recurrent "there wasn't much to do" or "I was out of school and out of work."

Thus, street experiences became predominant for many informants. While such individuals had to conform to street conditions and values, however, they also resented some of the detrimental aspects: "You know, you can't even have a wedding dance without someone getting hurt or even killed," complained one young man. Another, referring to his barrio, noted, "This place is always trashy and dirty." Many echoed this older male's observation: "It's hard for a young man in the barrio—there are no jobs." The young gang members feel, however, as one individual argued, that "you have to take the good with the bad."

Family Stress

Traditionally, Mexican family and extended family ties are strong, and they foster respect for the authority of elders, especially older males. Successful Mexican Americans of working-class and middle-class status commonly ascribe much of their present well-being to the stable households in which they were raised. However, the corrosive effects of economic hardship, social discrimination, and culture conflict on many barrio immigrant families have been noted above. Moreover, many of the family households established by youths who were raised in such disrupted families are, from their beginning, fragile and readily susceptible to stress. Not surprisingly, the great majority of gang members interviewed for this study report family histories full of stress, and many of them explicitly maintain that they became involved with a gang (at least in part) to seek the kind of support they felt was lacking from family sources.

Father absence was observed in many households and is often a factor in the familial problems cited by respondents. In several instances, a broken-family household resulted from the father's death. A young male from La Verne recounts how his father's death led to a sequence of changes: "I was taken out of Catholic school . . . . my father and I were very close and when he died, he was the only one I looked up to . . . . We had to move to another place. When I went to school, some guys came up to me and asked me where I was from. I said, 'nowhere,' and they said, 'Forget about it, you're from here now." At the age of 8, he was introduced to barrio affiliation and street-based peer pressure. In another case, an 18-year-old male from South Fontana intensified his until-then-minimal delinquency upon losing his father: "Then things got different when my Dad passed away. I went to a party and got all wasted on pills, sniffing, smoking weed, and drinking. I almost passed out of an overdose."

A father's death at times simply brought to a climax a long history of problematic family affairs. A 15-year-old from Corona, for example, had an alcoholic father who eventually died from the habit. The family had problems dealing with the father's drinking before, and with his demise: "My mother could not take care of the house, her children [five of them], and her work at the same time. I began to feel lonely and started a complex that my mother didn't love me because she didn't take care of me the way she used to. I felt like a stranger in my own house as I got older because I was not able to communicate with anyone, not even the teacher or the rest of the people at school."

An older *veterano* from Pomona, whose father deserted the family when the boy was very young, similarly summarizes the feeling: "I always felt that my family didn't want me. My mother had to work and support me and my brothers [five of them]. I was always searching for something but I didn't know what. I felt bad because my mother had to be away most of the day and when she was home I had to share her with my brothers. I still felt lonely."

More commonly, father absence is initiated by a divorce, rather than the father's death. In such cases, especially, there is usually also a pattern of conflict leading up to the breakup. Generally, however, there is a radical turn for the worse thereafter. A man from South Fontana, who is now 27 but still affiliated with the local gang, reminisced about this event: "Mom and Dad fought constantly; it was like hand-to-hand combat practically every Thursday and weekends. So Mom and Dad ended their marriage of nineteen years. It was mainly due to Dad's nasty habits. He even got busted for selling marijuana and spent six years in jail. She tried her best to make it with the rest of us [eleven children], but lost the battle. The six oldest kids left home real young. I was one of them." His involvement in minor gang activities as a young teen-ager eventually advanced to more serious drug-related criminal activities, and he spent four years in jail as a young adult. Similarly, a 22-year-old from El Hoyo Maravilla, whose parents divorced when he was 6, has already spent five years in correctional facilities.

When the parents separated early in the youth's life, or perhaps never formed a household together, embarrassment and/or resentment typically was clear in the interviewee's discussion. For example, when asked about his father, a 16-year-old from Cucamonga replied, "I never knew the chump." A young man from Clanton (downtown Los Angeles), as another example, said that his father left them when he was too young to remember, and he blamed him for his mother's subsequent turn to prostitution to support her six children. He often witnessed the beatings she received at the hands of male visitors.

A father's criminal activities precipitated family crises and long-term problems in several instances. The former inmate from Fontana, cited earlier, is one example. Another case involves a male, now 28 years old, from Cucamonga: "I remember going to court with my mother and seeing the policeman bring my father in with manacled hands and feet [marijuana sales charge]. I was crushed and confused and began to cry. My mother couldn't even care for herself, not even us. We did the best we could to take care of her and us. We washed and fed ourselves. But we had to stop going to school, we had nothing to eat in the house. It was very bad for everyone." This mother-headed household consisted of six children and was supported by welfare, and two of the sons who belonged to gangs wound up as *tecatos*. The informant, who escaped relatively unscathed from this long-unsettling experience, still winces when he talks about it.

After separation by death, divorce, or desertion, mothers often sought help from others in caring for their children. New husbands (or common-law husbands) were mentioned by several participants as sources of further estrangement; this attitude was easily observed when I visited such households and noted that little communication, or mutual acknowledgment, occurred between the youth and the step-father. By far the most common example of nonparental upbringing is with a grandparent. An older veterano from Cucamonga reflects on the multiple nature of his experience: "I barely remember when my father was killed when I was three years old. My Mom was left with three kids and went on social security. She married again when I was four because she was lonely and needed help. I used to stay with my grandfather all the time. My stepfather wasn't much help when he took on drinking. We used to help buy clothes for my other brothers and sisters [six more were now added to the first three, nine in all]." His gang career led him into several years of heavy heroin usage. Today, however, he has straightened out, working hard to support a wife and two children, although he occasionally gets together with guys from the gang to drink beer and indulge in light marijuana use.

Sometimes, especially when boys reached an age and size where their mothers felt powerless to restrain them, the mother or another relative would induce the absent father himself to intervene. A 16-year-old from White Fence, unfamiliar with his father in earlier years, was reintroduced to him later when he began to get into trouble: "My Dad really didn't give a fuck. He tried to sit down with me when I got fucked up a lot on PCP. He talked to me, but it would end up him fucking [beating] me up pretty well. I used to run away a lot."

There were even instances of father-centered households, the cause of which varied from a mother separation due to death, divorce, or abandonment. A Pomona Valley man, 23, stated that their family of nine children had to more or less fend for themselves when the mother died. He even "adopted a neighbor family" when he was 13 years old, about the same time he started hanging around with the local youths in the street. In nearby Ontario, a 22-year-old male recalls when his parents divorced. As a 6-year-old, he and his older brother went with the father, and the remainder of the children with the mother. They moved several times until settling in Ontario: "My Dad worked long, hard hours as a roofer. When he came home at night, it was up to me to have the house clean and dinner ready. During the day I didn't have much supervision or companionship." A male, 17, from Fullerton had a similar experience after a divorce, although the mother left them (nine children) for good before he was 10 years old. His dad, he says, was "concerned about how we were doing, and still is today, but he had to continue working, so for a year no one watched over the kids until he remarried."

Even families that remained intact, of course, were not immune to some sometimes severe stresses. Bickering parents, an off-and-on marriage, and just a precarious father-mother relationship characterized their lives. For example, Memo, an older male from Ontario, said that hard economic times were a large contributor to family tension, as the family of nine (seven children) had to work the migrant stream every May to September. His father was no help, he says, because, "He never spoke to us except to scold us or criticize and give us orders for work." Being close to the mother, as all the children were, he often found her intervening on his behalf. Arguments and strained feelings would follow.

Generally, severe strains and stresses from altered family situations tended to characterize regular and peripheral gang members. Temporary and situational members were more likely to have relatively strong intact families who redirected their lives. For example, one male, 18, from Ontario said, "My dad was right, I got nowhere hanging around with the guys"; and another (South Fontana) male, 18, said, "My parents taught me better." Mother-centered households were the most prevalent in gang members' backgrounds, although not always the most disorganized; there were other households I visited where "mama" ran a tight ship and kept a reasonably strong tether on her children, males especially. Children commonly reacted to family tensions with feelings of rejection or inadequacy, leading them to seek support elsewhere. Furthermore, the domestic climates of instability often dissipated parental energies in ways that undermined supervision of offspring. One mother I observed over several weeks impressed me with her efforts, but she was always tired after working a ten-hour day and could barely keep in tow her always energetic and adventuresome brood. Many of the accounts depict a loosening of social control and a concomitant turn to neighborhood friends and gangs as sources of support and direction. Group associations, of course, made for different socialization regimens and further cemented the individual to the group.

Street Socialization

A consequence of the loosening of family control engendered by stress is that youths spend an inordinate amount of time outside the home. On average, street associations and interactions of the gang members interviewed started between the age of 7 to 9; some of the younger siblings were also on the streets regularly at the time of the fieldwork. In addition, more that two-thirds of them said that either a brother, uncle, or other older male model had been influential in this early learning. In most instances, this early socialization pattern comprised a modification of the Mexican palomilla tradition representing "simple, congenial, and unstable associations of friends . . . who interact with considerable frequency" (Rubel 1965:93-94), reflecting, however, the more stressful ecological and structural conditions of the barrio streets. As a general backdrop for identity formulation and personal emulation, street socialization sometimes involved participation in delinquent behavior, such as vandalism and petty shoplifting. More serious habits, such as use of weapons or drugs, were even rarer at these early ages. Much of the socialization was thus normal "kids learning from kids" during play, except that some of the mischief bordered on dangerous forays.

For many of these youths, the early associations provided a sense of friendship and mutual trust that later proved useful in gang circles, especially in backing up one another in case of trouble. One older veterano from Cucamonga remembers how much fun he and his friends used to have building go-carts and taking them to nearby hills to ride; such experiences, he felt, developed a sense of camaraderie that "lasts forever." The fact that these 8- or 9-year-olds would pull their carts miles away from home, a trek that took several hours, shows how personal abilities to fend for oneself became so important. Dependence on personal resourcefulness and that of your friends made for extremely tight social bonds. Such bonds are typically expressed in kinship terms, as will be noted in a later chapter.

Street experiences, of course, are a mixture of events, some quite playful and innocent and others clearly antisocial. For those individuals who grew up in East Los Angeles barrios, of firmly entrenched and long-standing gangs, the juxtaposition of normal and abnormal activities intermixed in daily affairs can be startling. The history of Wizard, 23, from El Hoyo Maravilla (described in Chapter 4) is a good example of this. Most of his time was spent at age 8 on the streets, getting into mischief or playing with older, 10- or 11-year-olds. He recalls how they would seek reimbursement (from proprietors) of dimes they had not in fact deposited in vending machines or pretend to be lost in a strange neighborhood to get bus fare from sympathetic adults. The idea is to act to get what you want. Football, basketball, baseball, when in season, were played on a regular basis, too, as were war, cowboy, and cops and robbers games based on television and movie portrayals. Any required equipment or props—shoulder pads, helmets, baseball, and whatnot—would typically be obtained from a friend who specialized in shoplifting and stealing to get it. At times, the group as a whole would embark on shoplifting missions, with deployment of decoys, lookouts, and deliberately tough-looking "rear guards."

Another male, 16, from the same barrio recounts similar activities, including a long period where he played Pop Warner football. Mixed with his formal, supervised activity and street mischief (staying up late and running in front of cars to make their brakes screech) were other, more deviant habits—taking whites (Benzedrine) to get fired up for football, for instance. His entrance into the gang was at a young age, 9, for he was a big kid who "hung around with older guys. These high school guys would always egg me on. Me and my friends thought we were tough. They made me drink with them and when I was all drunk, they asked me if I wanted to join the klika." He not only joined and was initiated but, as he got older and bigger, he also joined older and tougher klikas and was reinitiated. By the age of 15 he was already known as *loco* (crazy; a street desperado style). Soon after, he committed a robbery, which landed him in prison.

Geronimo, 16, from Varrio Nuevo, is (as will be noted in Chapter 4) presently serving time for an armed robbery and kidnapping of Mexican nationals. His description of early life included eventful street incidents, for example, getting hit by a car. Other incidents with friends his age, or older, revolved around the usual amount of play with toy guns and the sort, but also delinquent acts. The friendly aspects of these early experiences were illustrated with his account of his friend and him receiving $20.00 from the friend's mother (she was a tecata) and showing their generosity by buying ice cream for all their friends. He qualified this account by saying that "I'm not a Mr. Goody-two-shoes or anything, but I have a good heart." However, less-productive incidents were also related, as in his account of preparations to learn (from a friend) how to sniff paint: "I went in there [a store] and stole a can of spray paint. The man comes up to me and said, 'What do you got there?' I said, 'nothing.' And he searched me and he said, 'You've got spray paint,' and he said, 'Get out and don't ever come back or I'll call the cops on you.' "

Sometimes, associations begin at school and continue and expand on the streets. A male from the Pomona Valley, 17, tells this story about being confronted by a group in third grade: "They didn't sound like 8-year-olds, they talked older like someone about 15 or 16. Then one guy pulled out a box of cigarettes and asked me if I wanted one. I said that I didn't know how to smoke, and the guys that were there just laughed at me when I said that. They said they would show me how." He was subsequently introduced to other cholo customs, like wearing khaki pants, and he became one of the group before the group became a full-fledged klika of the gang.

Uncles, brothers, and other older relatives sometimes complement street learning. Close relations are markedly impressive telling stories that sound exciting, courageous, and attractive, especially when combined with offers of instruction in how to emulate them. Mario, an 18-year-old from South Fontana, demonstrated an early streak of malice—for example, starting a fire in a man's backyard because "I wanted to do him wrong"—and determination to eventually join a gang to be with his cousins.

Uncles served as inspirations and sometimes tutors in several cases, as in this example: "At the age of 8 I started smoking weed with my uncle . . . . He also turned me on to reds." This young man grew into a very unstable adolescent, using drugs and participating in gang raids. Enlistment and service in the National Guard has helped him toward greater stability.

Bobby, a 12-year-old from Chino, is the youngest participant interviewed for this study. A self-professed "loner" (although he at times relies on street peers for help), he has threatened other youths with harm and boasts that he once "pulled a knife on the school principal." He has learned to take care of himself, for which he partially credits his uncle: "My uncle was a member of a gang and showed me a lot of neat tricks, like how to break in and hot wire a car." Presently, he is a ward of the court, awaiting removal from his family household to a foster home.

Another case history, from San Pedro, a male, 21, contains no mention of such specific tutoring by uncles but cites the uncles' tales of exploits as models for emulation as he learned the ways of the street. His criminal record was initiated at age 10, when he walked into a liquor store and stole beer, wine, and a radio. About six months later he returned to the same store with the same radio; the store owner recognized it and called the police. He subsequently had a history of violence, heavy use of drugs, and recurrent arrests, experiences he shares in common with his uncles.

Many gang youths cite older brothers as models for early socialization. A male, 18, from Chino, "naturally followed" in his brother's footsteps, although he refrained from "becoming a tecato like him."

Another male, 17, from Fullerton, recalls desiring (as early as age 7) to be "tough, and grown up" like his brother. He duplicated his brother's experience in serious drug use and juvenile incarceration. Carlos, 19, from F-Troop in Santa Ana, explained how he feels comfortable in the streets but holds reservations about his younger brother: "I've learned to appreciate the streets. You make good friends there, people you can trust. Me and my older brother learned how to live there [family life was difficult, as the father had to support nine children]. It's not going to be the same for my younger brother. He studies a lot. It's going to last, 'cause he turned out different from me and my other brother. We started out young. I don't want to see my brother go through the shit I'm going through." (Although the younger brother is doing better in school, he still identifies with local peers, and his older brothers, and is a "Chico" member of F-Troop.)

Several brothers have often been an influence, as in the case of Victor, 19, from Venice: "I was just born in the barrio and I got like a familia there, and another, and all there in the neighborhood. I got into the ways of my *carnales* [brothers; literally, of the flesh] and as I started getting older and older, I started getting my own klika . . . . ever since then I just started fucking up and everything else and hanging around." A Varrio Norwalk 16-year-old male said, "You look up to your brothers because they give you protection." Similarly, Romero, 17, from Van Nuys, said that his cousins and older brother were always getting him out of trouble (he was frail and skinny) and backing him up in fights. Romero also had as a model the experiences of his father, a former barrio gang member, despite efforts of his parents to break the pattern of socialization by moving to another neighborhood (only a few miles away from the barrio, however, in a low-income tract-home area) and placing him in a Catholic school. The legendary stories of his father and the present activities of cousins and brother were too much to resist, and Romero is now incarcerated for a gang shooting in which the victim died.

Relatives' influence was, of course, often supplemented or supplanted by the influence of other older males. Huero, 17, from White Fence, grew up acquainted with many friends and habits from the neighborhood—for example, playing and "goofing around" in alleys and vacant lots, challenging the teachers at school, going on urban treks to the inner city in a group—but he especially remembers how he learned to sniff paint: "I was 9 years old, and I used to see my brothers do it. I used to hang around with pretty old people from there. They were about 17, 18, or 19, and I was only 11 . . . . I would be seen late at night, fucking around and stuff in parking lots, and they would be around and they would see me. They thought I was 14 or 15 and I was only 11. They started giving me drugs. I started playing the role of hard core when I was about 10 years old." Just released from a youth institution after one year, he is back in the neighborhood "partying and getting high."

A Pomona Valley story from Veto, 22, a temporary gang member, highlights street and male model influences: "All the families were similar to ours as we were separated from the rest of the community [barrio enclave]. I was in the second grade when I had my first encounter with the law for suspicion of arson . . . . I used to notice older Chicanos and observed the tough characteristics they lived by. We used to write our *placasos* [personalized graffiti] on the walls and be among our camaradas, like them." Peer and veterano models were cited on a regular basis, and always the young boy wanted to measure up to the "war" stories, real and imagined, by acting out these perceived roles.

A decision to join the gang does not invariably result from exposure to older male models whom one regards highly. This story of a male, 18, from Ontario is interesting because it explains the sources of his predicament and his personal evolution: "When I was young, about 9 to 15 years old, all I would think about was girls, parties, going out to start trouble, and staying out late and being a bad *vato* [guy, dude] in the streets. My eyes started to open when I was older, because being a bad vato wasn't me. I just felt that life is what I make it, not what someone else wants it to be. I just want to be with people to party with them, and rap with them. I guess I wanted to be a bad vato because I wanted to follow my brothers' footsteps because they were all bad vatos in the barrio and I look like one of my brothers. That made me feel like a big vato just like my older brother." Nevertheless, he now regularly attends high school, where his grades are average, and has stayed away from aggressive male posturing and gang activities. Opting to join a gang is also influenced by other, perceivedly more practical considerations, as recounted in this story by a 24-year-old downtown Los Angeles man: "I was born into my barrio. It was either get your ass kicked every day or join a gang and get your ass kicked occasionally by rival gangs."

Such exceptions notwithstanding, the lives of gang members generally show several lessons. Most of them become involved with street life early and additionally spend a great deal of time there, starting off as mischief and adventure seekers. Most of the street habits and customs are normal cohorting behavior, but other deviant activities are also learned. The experiences, good and bad, are bonding events that solidify trust and closer relations among the participants.

Learning to back your friends is an early street lesson and, later, a core requirement for gang membership.

Peer Pressure

Peer pressure, as well as emulation of older models, also plays a significant part in guiding most gang members into such roles. Many of the informants indicated that such influences began as early as elementary school and most had felt such peer pressures in junior high school. Whether occurring in elementary or junior high school, the nature of the peer influence can be categorized into three types (listed in order of importance): friendship, direct confrontation, and psychological disposition. Friendship was the most commonly cited and entailed a desire to be with associates one had made earlier, following in the footsteps of friends, or generally an explicitly felt need to be with peers that made one feel socially comfortable. Direct confrontation, the second category, involves a peer helping another to make a decision to become a part of the group, even though other conditions are also operative. Only a few cases fit into the last category, psychological disposition—that is, fear, tendency toward loco behavior, need for respect or protection—although my observations seemed to have detected a sense of apprehensiveness or fear on more occasions than gang members would admit. For fully committed, regular gang members, the pattern of peer pressure appears to follow a predictable sequence. First, there are the contacts, experiences and friendships that are made on the streets during preteen years. If the person remains, more or less, in the same barrio in later years, this early social bonding is solidified during adolescence, when the propensity toward gang involvement is strongest. Even if one changed residences quite often and the early bonding relationships were lost, they were still attuned to such peer pressure, having already learned the cues and expectations.

Peers also expect a person to share whatever they may have with others, and only subtle pressure, a look or a gesture, is ever required as a reminder. One young man, talking about passing a six-pack of beer around, said, "You get the whole case if you want it." Anticipating the needs of one's peers makes a person feel good, for it is usually implicitly understood that they are watching, gauging, and evaluating your behavior. (On more than one occasion I mistakenly misread the cues and expectations and slowed the flow of conversation and fieldwork.)

This pattern of establishing and maintaining social relations with peers was a normal, everyday activity for gang members. A male, 27 (South Fontana), disliked school because of the mistreatment he and his sisters received as the only Mexicans in elementary school. He explains the feeling he had upon going to junior high: "The first day I noticed there were more of my people there; it made me feel good. The guys made friends with me real fast." From the same barrio, Ray, 22, reminisced about following in his brother's footsteps but noted specifically that the guys gave him "a lot of respect and a feeling of brotherhood" upon joining. (He also shared pleasure in the group feeling of being feared by other people.) A male, 22, from San Bernardino, was more succinct: "I was influenced by my friends, and all of them were influenced by their friends." Larry, 20, from Chino, said that when he joined "I never thought of us as a gang, we were just friends. As I got older, I knew that doing things like stealing was what they expected me to do. I didn't want to go against my friends."

A search for a social niche made a person even more susceptible to peer pressure. A male, 22, from Ontario opines: "My first year in junior high I was an observer looking for a place." Chuy, 18, from Ontario, reported: "The vatos made me feel like they cared. They really stick with you and back you up, well at least some of them. When you were called 'Homeboy' you felt good because you were one of them."

George, 18, from the same area, explains why he joined a gang drive-by: "I didn't want them to think I was a sissy, so we did it." Backing up your friends is also a part of peer relationships, as this story of Sam, 16, from Norco shows: "It got to the point where 'you back me up and I'll back you up!' You get respect by not backing down." In his case, participation in a gang shooting dampened his enthusiasm for gang membership and hastened a disaffiliation from peers. Another case from Corona, a male, 17 (one of the life histories in Chapter 4), had a similar ending. After a close call in a drive-by shooting, in which he was wounded in the leg and for which he spent a short stint in a county juvenile camp, he decided to go straight and try another less volatile Chicano style: Hollywood Swingers.

Moving into a new neighborhood brought several youths into contact with new peers. Tato, 16, from La Verne, recalled his early gang contact: "That same day, one guy told me to get rid of those honky pants and to start acting like a Chicano. The guy showed me some khakis, and I said, 'You want me to wear these?' And he told me, 'Ya, tomorrow!' When I got home, my mom seen me walk in with the pants and told me what I was doing with those pants, those are the pants that the cholos wear! My mom said she knew that we shouldn't have never moved down here." Loco, 15, from the Pomona Valley had already been threatened several times by local gang members after he moved into the new neighborhood. Finally responding, he fought and beat the ringleader. Within a week, he had another visit from the guy he beat: "He started telling me that I was a good fighter and that he wanted me to join his gang. He told me I had passed his test. 'Test,' I said, 'what test?' He then said that the fight the other day was fixed, because he wanted to know if I could fight. I didn't want to join because they weren't my type, but I was tired of hearing my mom tell me I was a sissy because I didn't have friends. So I joined."

The case of Hugo, 24, from Chino, was similar to the one from La Verne. He had moved into the area in junior high school and had begun hanging around mostly with Anglos, who comprised a majority. In the aftermath of a school race riot, the Chicano kids pressured him to "stick with his group. I started getting hassled about the way I dressed, the way my hair was cut, who I hung around with, the whole thing, man! About five of them jumped me . . . . they wanted me in their gang, man! Anyhow, this kind of thing went on for a month. I knew I had to decide something, regardless of how good my parents had brought me up or how much they loved me. I was the one getting his head banged around school." Subjected to continual prodding, he joined the gang.

Ethnic loyalty and overt pressure were clearly factors in the rural areas (now rapidly becoming suburban) where the Chicano population was a minority of the student population. Richard, 19, from Chino, maintained: "Even if I lived with whites I would receive pressure from all the vatos and cholos and Chicanos everywhere in Chino. I wouldn't have a choice, especially where I live right now. I might not be alive right now." Carlos, 22, remembers a similar experience, except that it was a marked change from what had existed before in his life: "One day I was with my friends at school, and a Chicano who was already involved with a gang went up to me and said, 'Hey, man, you're supposed to be with us. Don't hang around with those honkies, they're your enemies!' Later, they told me if I didn't hang around with their group that they would jump me. So I gradually started hanging around with the guys who were involved with the gang." His gang activity comprised mostly normal cholo behavior—socializing, cruising, and getting high; and soon after high school, he left the area and the gang.

A few informants indicated that conforming to the peer group was, in effect, a response to their own psychological dispositions more than to peer pressures; as noted, however, there were also covert indications of this tendency. The 12-year-old whose uncle taught him to "hot wire" automobiles sought out peers principally to help him vent his own aggression. While this explanation certainly pertains to other individuals, for there were plenty of personal incidents, family and early life experiences, that would cause frustration and tension to build, only a few persons were explicit about this phenomenon. Henry, 20, from Chino, whose life history is summarized in Chapter 4, was motivated to seek peer interaction for personal aggrandizement: "I thought I was going to the joint once. I wanted to go, I wanted to make it. I thought all my friends would look up to me. They did. Pretty soon they started talking better to me." Others adopted cholo trappings, usually temporarily, to "survive," that is, overall acute personal fear.

Peer pressure, in sum, is woven into family experiences and barrio socialization situations. Usually, persons develop close peer associations in their youth. The passage of time and the accumulation of bonding events make peers even more important, reaching a high mark during adolescence. Eventually, peer expectations become internalized. Although some individuals were overtly pressured into the gang, the need and desire for friendship made the gang attractive for most.

Schooling

Problematic school experiences are woven into participants' accounts of family, street, and peer influences in their backgrounds. Indeed, the Mexican American history of prejudicial treatment, language and ethnic identity problems, and difficulties in acculturation often is focussed on educational institutions. Schools in America are next in importance to the family in providing structure and meaning to children's lives and as an agency for social control. They succeed the family in assuming responsibility for the bulk of each youth's daytime activities. For Mexican Americans, however, schools have historically often been as much a hindrance as help for youth aspiring to productive adulthood. For example, ability "tracking" and a high incidence of work permits (allowing one to leave school at age 16, way before graduation) in minority areas of Los Angeles still characterize school policy.

Bogardus documented the racial prejudice of school officials toward Mexicans early in the twentieth century (1926, 1934) and recorded Mexican perceptions of the schools in Los Angeles (cf. Chapter 2). Other studies indicate similar conditions in other towns (Alvarez 1988) and rural settlements (Hill 1928). One rural California schoolteacher was quite explicit in explaining why she conditioned her Anglo elementary schoolchildren to assume leadership roles and attitudes, while training the Mexican American children to be "followers" in performing classroom tasks: This would better prepare them for the day when they would grow up and fill their expected occupations—farm owners and farm workers, respectively (Anonymous 1966).

Such overt and blatant racism has not been typical of school personnel, of course, but institutionalized academic "tracking" (through which disproportionately high numbers of Mexican American youths were placed in "remedial" classes); selective counseling strategies (resulting in "good students" being steered toward skilled crafts rather than college); and employment of teachers unable or unwilling to constructively deal with problems arising from culture conflict all combined to produce effectively similar conditioning (Carter and Segura 1978; U.S. Commission on Civil Rights 1971). Pressures generated by community activists and federal civil rights legislation, as well as the influence of more recent generations of school officials, have resulted in improved conditions since the 1960s. Bilingual education and enrichment programs are common, for example, and many postsecondary institutions actively recruit Latino (and other minority) students. Yet the legacy of racism in the schools persists (as it does in the general society), not least in the perceptions of barrio youths and their parents. In my observations of schools throughout Southern California, I often attended meetings of parents and school officials where the issue of racism was in contention. Several parents even publicly cited their own experiences, which had occurred at the same schools when they were students.

Early Mexican immigrants, confronted with hostile or indifferent school personnel and hardpressed to provide for large families, often encouraged their adolescent children to forsake school in favor of immediate (although poor-paying) employment. Subsequent generations of poor barrio parents have done likewise; and those who, through diligence and good fortune, have attained modest prosperity without high school educations are also often inclined to disparage the need for schooling. Barrio youths' perceptions are affected by such parental attitudes, as well as the relative absence of successful role models for themselves. Bogardus (1934), as noted earlier, also underscored how discrimination shaped a sense of futility toward education among the youth.

Thus, many of the informants' school careers began with skepticism, limited parental encouragement, and early exposure to street experiences that did little to promote self-discipline. It is clear that by the third or fourth grade they had not effectively adapted to the school situation. Many at this point had become self-conscious of their special reading classes and lagging academic records. Withdrawal from the learning situation would often resolve the conflict, as one 16-year-old male from East Los Angeles said: "Let's say you sit in the back of the class. 'You don't bug me and I will pass you,' that's what the teacher would say." Cholo subcultural mores reinforce such attitudes, as reflected in the words of Henry, 20, from Chino (one of the life histories in Chapter 4): "Well, you never carry books with you. If you did, they [the gang members] would make fun of you. You'd just throw your stuff in your locker and hang around at the wall." By junior high school, if not earlier, ditching and absenteeism characterized their solution to school. School authorities who had to deal with class and campus disruptions by erstwhile dropouts resorted to expulsions and suspensions, and nonacceptance of anyone returning to school if they had been tainted by an arrest. The result, all too often, is similar to this young man's account: "My three sisters and one brother all dropped out of school before reaching the tenth grade. My younger brother is in the fourth grade, but he probably will be badly influenced, too. No one really expects me to finish school. My parents don't really care because they tell us to do this or that and they themselves do the same thing."

Prejudice

Many of the participants in this study describe their school experiences in terms of insensitive treatment at the hand of teachers and administrators and overt racial antagonism with non-Chicano peers. One result of this was to reinforce ethnic identification, often with a sense of alienation: "I did poorly in school because I couldn't speak English. We used to segregate ourselves at school, because that's what everybody did. It was expected. I never went outside the barrio except to go to school. This didn't make me conscious of the injustice, because I took it as the order of things." Informants from later generations were more apt to actively protest discrimination, as in the case of a young woman who (in junior high school) instigated and helped organize a "walkout": "We had about half the students on the front lawn with signs saying, 'Pay attention to us, we're people too!' We were asking the staff to say they were sorry for calling us names. Before long, the vice-principal . . . with tears in his eyes, apologized. We were all admitted back to classes."

A Cucamonga girl of 16 was equally forceful but less constructive. Cucamonga barrio students are bussed in to a mostly Anglo, middle-income high school located in Alta Loma. The literal translation of these locations, "Sandy Place" (the Indian name for Cucamonga) and "High Hill" (Spanish), can be taken to represent the spatial and social distance that separates them. The barrio junior high school is right in the middle of the Chicano community. In the move to high school, the students become a minority among Anglos. Race and class differences deepen the sense of anxiety among the Chicano students, and the disparaging attitude of the Anglos toward them helps foment trouble. Students report their Anglo peers calling them "beaners," "chili peppers," and similar pejorative terms. Barrio leaders and activists regard the school as one that "pushed out" Chicano students; school officials confirm a high incidence of Chicanos "dropping out." The young lady describes her experience on transferring to the high school: "Everything was going all right, but then one day I got into a fight with this Anglo girl. I got into trouble. So after that I kept getting into fights. I also started ditching school. The next year in school . . . I got into a fight with my math teacher because he took my book from me, so I got a box and threw it at him. I got kicked out of class . . ."

At times, frustrations engendered by such experiences have generated wider violence. A veterano from South Fontana describes his longstanding problems with school:

> "I think I'd rather have gotten a beating every day than to go to school. I attended elementary school. I didn't like it, 'cause there were only five or six Chicanos in the whole school, besides my sister and I. The rest were gabachos. They used to kind of make me feel bad 'cause they came to school with nice clothes. They always had plenty to eat for lunch or they had money to buy their hot lunch. I guess nothing would've changed my race. Well, I would be harassed by all the white kids. They'd call me "dirty Mexican," "greaser," "beaner," "nigger," and names like that. It was a real lowdown. At times I wished I was a white man. I thought I was being punished for being born a Mexican. Thank God, as years rolled by, I understood more and more why all the stereotype calling. One morning my sister and I were called to the nurse's office. I wondered why. Well, we both got there, and she began to bitch. She said they had a report of a couple of kids who had lice on the bus the day before. We were sent home for it. I said to myself, I would never go back to school 'cause everybody knew about what had happened.

By the time he finished junior high school, the youth had joined the local gang. His school problems had compounded, which he responded to by frequent "ditching." He reports on one of his occasional re-entries to school:

I thought I'd go back to school to see what's going on. Well, lucky me, a riot breaks out. The Chicanos and blacks group together and started kicking ass on the whites. We broke windows, lit trash cans on fire. They brought in the police. Many kids went back to class, but some played stubborn jackasses and stayed out of class. We were all gathered, suspended and taken home. They had a bus come take a whole bunch of us home. We were suspended until our parents had a conference with the principal . . . . I went back to school. Things had quieted down. But not on the bus. All the Chicanos sat toward the back of the bus. Anyways, all the white kids would try to sit back there, so we started kicking their asses. So here comes the bus driver to the rescue, so all us Chicanos began to talk Spanish . . . planning on what we were gonna do to her. Anyways, she hated us to speak Spanish, so I spoke up . . . "I was born a Mexican and I was blessed to speak two languages." She replied, "I'm sorry you were born a Mexican." When she said that, everybody with brown or black skin began to throw pencils, paper, and cussed her out. Well, I was thrown off the bus, and so were the others. My mom had another conference to attend with the principal, who also was a prejudiced son-of-a-bitch. She also had a conference with the guy who is in charge of transportation. I was thrown off for two weeks. The results were heavy for me.

Such discrimination experiences made for personal insecurity, but usually other factors were also involved, as in the case of this veterano from Pomona: "My own life was a continual feeling of insecurity, partly because of discrimination and partly because I didn't feel wanted by my family." Nevertheless, much of the resentment toward schools was rooted in such experiences as personal shame for being "labeled" in special tracking classes and other practices that segregate Chicanos from Anglos. One male, 18, angrily said: "Let me tell you, when I entered high school, things were way different. Chicanos were completely isolated from school activities, major events, and school sports." Larry, 22, from Ontario, was even more adamant about it: "The schools weren't teaching me anything. The teachers just saw me as a troublemaker, and their prejudices kept them from seeing if I had any potential at all."

Turning Off, Ditching, and Dropping Out

Most of the informants of this study left school soon after attaining the age of 16, before which attendance is mandatory under California law. Before leaving school, a "turning-off" process occurs; their behavior and performance showed clearly their disdain for school long before they "dropped out"(or were "kicked out" by administrators).

Grades for the great majority of the informants were always a problem. Academic achievement and school behavior usually began on a discordant note and steadily declined. Several mentioned problems as early as kindergarten, citing language as the source. Others spoke simply of a general malaise toward school. Discrimination against them subsequently reinforced their difficulties. It is worth noting that school problems generally predate involvement with a gang and that many nongang youths from the barrios report similar (although generally less severe) school difficulties, including early "dropouts."

The young male, 12, discussed earlier, was not only the youngest informant but also the most emotionally unstable, capable of only second-grade-level work. His teacher maintained that he was not a "behavior" problem, but she had given him special, individualized treatment. As she says: "He is a proud boy who wants to learn. So I've given him a special place in the room. He calls it his office. My main concern is that he graduate." As indicated earlier, however, he instead got in trouble and was made a ward of the court. Freddie, 17, from Fullerton, never a good student and always behind his age group academically, at age 13 was suspended when he came to school under the influence of drugs. Soon thereafter, because of gang activities in which he was involved, he was placed in juvenile hall.

An East Los Angeles veterano recalls being put in a "special school because he didn't pay attention to the teacher . . . my grades were lousy," he said. Several others said more or less the same thing. Cricket, 16, from El Hoyo Maravilla, gives an account with multifaceted reasons in an interview: "In the first grade I always had trouble reading. Everybody in my family knew Spanish but me. I could just understand it. But I spoke in English to them. They sent me to a special school. I couldn't stay still, I'd like to move around a lot, and I'd get in fights. Even in kindergarten I couldn't do this." He remained in a special school for at least five of the elementary school years and to this day still has problems with reading.

Avoidance of school was the upshot from such distasteful experiences. By the time they were in junior high school, most of the informants were regularly "ditching." Ditching occurred in various contexts, but it was generally a group affair. In some cases, it was an expected code of behavior to show that one belonged to the group; it was a way of demonstrating their allegiance to the group belief that the school "no vale" ("doesn't matter"). Roddie, 27, from South Fontana, started the habit in junior high: "We used to ditch school, and if we didn't have anybody to buy liquor, we just stole it . . . and [would] drink it in vacant fields." Sam, 21, from Colton, ditched in order to get kicked out of school and thereby acquire prestige in the eyes of the group.

One young man, 17, from Corona, had his first encounter with the police because of school truancy and later, in another incident, was suspended: "I used to ditch school and the police would stop and arrest me and see if I was causing any trouble. They always let me go, though, after they took me in. One teacher grabbed me by the hair and yelled at me when we argued. I pushed her and she fell on the floor and injured one of her fingers. I was suspended for six months for this." An East Los Angeles woman, 24, remembers a similar outcome in junior high: "I would go to school, but then I would split with my friends, toke up, sniff, or take pills. I got busted a couple of times. I never made it to high school." An older veterano from the same area explains it in this way: "I hated school. I was ditching all the time and would tell my mother I was on my way to school. I would write my own notes for school to dismiss myself from school. They found out about it . . . I ended up in Jackson High School, which was a special school in East Los Angeles for guys like me."

Ditching behavior, partying, and getting high were an expected part of group associations. In fact, part of the attraction of the streets was to join friends, ditchers-turned-dropouts; one male, 15, from Pomona Valley, recalled being pressed into the gang whose members "were all dropouts." A male, 18, from South Fontana, gives an account that hints at the group pressure and expectations that are an integral part of the process: "I was always ditching school in junior high just to be in the barrio. Later I got started on acid and sniffing. The vatos used to talk about it so I tried it for myself. After school, just for kicks, we went out and broke windows at the school. We used to write 'South Fontana RIFAMOS,' even though we didn't know what RIFAMOS [controls; we're the best] meant. We seen the older guys write it, so we did, too."

Schools, in sum, have for these youths failed their social mission. The students' generalized negative attitudes, in part, can be traced to the early school practices that discriminated against Mexican children, and, we have observed, the issue of prejudice is still considered important by them. Notwithstanding this fact, it was also shown that the students did little to help their own educational development—ditching and dropping out are hardly viable solutions to the schooling problem. The backgrounds of such youths have created a social and emotional climate that is not conducive to learning, and the schools have not successfully addressed this problem. As a result, the gang youth disaffiliation with society is reinforced and prospects for a constructive adult life are severely diminished.

Conclusion

When Mexicans adapted to America, they underwent intensified social and cultural changes in a contact situation that was colored by previous historical experiences (a war of conquest and racial discrimination). The effects of living in segregated locales and working at low-paid, unskilled jobs had repercussions in other social and cultural realms for Mexicans. Adjustment was particularly problematic in the transitional phase when the move from Mexican culture was not yet complete nor was the incorporation of Anglo culture total; thus, the dynamics of adaptation and change generate even more layers of marginal situations and conditions. We have observed the alterations in social control practices in these contexts. New working conditions, oftentimes unstable, affected family life. The transformation of the family was accompanied by another change, that is, the shift from a primary means of social control, such as the family or neighborhood, to secondary institutions, like schools and police. Schools increased their responsibility at a time when parents were having trouble maintaining their hold on the children and (especially in earlier times) regularly and consistently discriminated against Mexicans by various means—segregation, programmatic disdain for Mexican traditions, academic tracking, and so on. Despite considerable improvements in recent years, an attitudinal residue remains in the stories of prejudice recounted by several of the informants and in my observations, especially in schools where Chicanos constitute a minority.

Such beginnings made for an uneven foundation in which to acculturate. Culture conflict started at these structural levels and combined with linguistic practices, ethnic identity and other cultural patterns as problem sources. These conflicts are particularly acute with gang members, who generally lack strong attachments to the home and schools and are particularly low in academic achievement (Emprey 1978). Conventional pursuits are thus denied them, as they show more of a need to associate and identify with other marginal street youths like themselves. In large part, the gang subculture has arisen as a response to this conflict situation. The gang has constituted a secondary "fringe" organization to resocialize members of the group to internalize and adhere to alternative norms and modes of behavior. Such gang patterns play a significant role in helping mainly troubled youths acquire a sense of importance, self-esteem, and self-identity. In short, rather than feeling neglected and remaining culturally and institutionally marginal, the gang members develop their own subcultural style to participate in public life, albeit a street one. As we will note, this lifestyle is another example of the potential human ingenuity in syncretically creating something new from multiple and sometimes diverse and contradictory sources.

4. Four Life Histories—Wizard, Geronimo, Freddie, and Henry

There are multiple processes of gang involvement, commitment, and identification. A comparison of representative examples of barrio gang youths will afford us an opportunity to highlight those barrio features and processes that perpetuate Chicano gangs. Toward this end, the utilization of life histories will provide a deeper and fuller depiction of barrio reality. The histories will also show how the multiple strands of that reality are interwined. While accounting for similarities between these lives (e.g., structural, social, and cultural features), the case histories will also outline the varied differences that distinguish one gang member from another (e.g., role modeling, self-identity, and level of commitment)—in effect, how their social and personal identities mesh and diverge. It will also illuminate the choices and adjustments that a person makes, particularly during adolescence, which are crucial to understanding why some and not others join the gang. While it is relatively easy to adopt the external cholo style, especially in dress and general demeanor, it will also be made clear that there is considerable variation in the psychological and temporal commitment to the gang. I have often observed that less committed and less active gang members dressed more "cholo" than regular ones, as if the image they struck would compensate and draw them closer to the core.

Group features deserve our attention, but the study of group dynamics must be interwoven with that of individual drives and motivations. As we will see, the life histories help clarify the distinction that researchers make between "hard-core" and "fringe" gang members. Some gang members have early and longstanding gang careers, while others are only peripherally, temporarily, or situationally involved.

All of the case informants are from a predominantly Mexican American barrio and of low-income background. Thus, they share, more or less, similar ecological and structural features. They begin to vary from each other in the social, cultural, and psychological realms.

Emerging from each of their accounts are nuances and peculiarities of family life, street associations, school and law enforcement interactions, and personal motivations, with some individuals experiencing more stress and instability that others. Even though a life of poverty in the barrio is the breeding ground for gangs, it is not necessarily the sole determination of who becomes a gang member and why, for how long, with what commitment, and so on. A closer look at the socialization experiences and enculturation patterns of each individual would provide answers to these and other questions. This happens during adolescence. Self-identity concerns then become critical, and a person must reconcile and resolve early life experiences through peer networks in relation to the wider social world.

What follows are life histories of male gang members. They include the histories of two regular members and one history each of a peripheral member and a temporary member. In summary, the regulars have had a more problematic early life. They become street oriented earlier. They become gang members sooner, and they participate in the destructive patterns over a longer period of time. The peripheral member is just as intense as the regulars once he is a member of a gang, but his level of commitment is mediated less by a problematic early life and more by a life-turning event (e.g., incarceration), which causes him to contemplate pursuing another lifestyle. Finally, the temporary member is neither as intense nor as committed as the others and primarily associates with the gang during a certain phase of his development. These cases, of course, are merely illustrative and not exhaustive, for the intent here is to broaden the perception on the nature and quality of gang involvement and the variations of multiple marginality leading to it. For example, there are also situational members (who pick and choose the more social, constructive gang activities) and female gang members, but they are excluded here since they comprise such a small number. (However, vignettes concerning them will be provided, when appropriate, in discussions of the roles and functions of gang participation.) Each individual story is presented in the same sequence frame. This ordering will facilitate, in each instance, a comprehension of the cumulative nature of involvement in the gang subculture. Additionally, it will afford us a comparative basis for all cases.

The individuals whose lives are recounted in this chapter were particularly instructive in talking about themselves. They were also helpful in providing insights about fellow gang members. They and other individuals served as key informants. In most instances, the accounts were given and recorded within the home of the person or at a place close by. There were also opportunities, for example, at parties, to verify and authenticate the nature and quality of their gang behavior when I joined members and their friends for group discussions and activities.

Wizard, an Example of a Gang Regular

Wizard is a member of El Hoyo Maravilla, a barrio that goes back to the 1920s and has had a street gang since at least the 1930s. For several decades this barrio has held a reputation as very tough, with at least fourteen separate age-graded klikas in that history. El Hoyo was engulfed by urban expansion in the years after World War II and lost some of its isolated quality, gained from its mainly first-generation, Spanish-speaking Mexican immigrant population. With the proliferation of nearby neighborhoods, or barrios, rival youth gangs developed to vie with El Hoyo for street supremacy. Interestingly, these new barrios took on the Maravilla generic name, adding distinctive street or regional modifiers to distinguish themselves from El Hoyo (there are seven such barrios, such as Arizona Maravilla and so on).

Wizard was born at the county General Hospital, and at the time of our interviews was 23 years old. He is the second child of a sibling group of four (one brother, 21 years old, and two sisters, aged 26 and 12). After a long marriage, his parents eventually divorced; in any event, his father was often in and out of jail and seldom around the household during Wizard's formative years. Wizard's mother never remarried, but his father did, rearing five more children with his second wife. During his preschool years, Wizard's mother worked at small factory jobs but also collected welfare when she was unemployed. Although she did reasonably well caring for the family under the circumstances, financial problems and frequent lack of parental attention characterized Wizard's early years. By the time he was 8 years old, the family had changed residences six times, mostly within the same geographical area of East Los Angeles. During this time, he recalls, he associated mostly with older, 10- and 11-year-olds and spent most of the time in the streets, either playing or getting into mischief. At age 7, while playing in the streets, he was hit by a car, and the bump he received on the head hospitalized him for a month with temporarily impaired speech and motor abilities.

One of the family residences during this period was the Maravilla Projects. Although he had been in fights even earlier, mainly with relatives and neighbors of the same age, he remembers that his first formal fight was in the Projects. It was arranged by his cousin, who wanted to prove that Wizard, the newcomer in school, was able to take care of himself. By winning the fight, he gained the respect of the onlookers and, especially, of the loser. *"Chingazos"* (blows, fighting) was a main topic of conversation in that neighborhood: "it was a way of life," according to Wizard.

Street activities and associations continued during these preadolescent years. He engaged in petty shoplifting at the local market, taking pastries and sweets. He and his friends conned older adults by pretending to be lost and asking for bus fare. Most of the time, however, they just played sports or ran around the neighborhood playing street games, like "war."

Despite such early experiences, he was still able to proceed with a fair-to-moderate school record. He especially credits the efforts of one sixth-grade male teacher, a Chicano, who "brought out the better student in me. He said the class consisted of the cream of the crop. He always said that. Maybe he said it to psychologically make us feel good . . . I always thought I understood him, 'cause he acted like he understood me. He would talk to me after class and say,'Why do you want to act like the class clown?' He would talk to me man to man and I respected that."

Wizard's contact with law enforcement was always bad, though. He even recalled a time, as a 3-year-old, when he was riding along with his father. He had a toy gun and was "play" shooting the people in cars alongside theirs. One of the cars was manned by police officers, who, for no apparent reason, proceeded to stop their car and search it, finding "reds" (Seconal, barbituates). He remembers that his father was arrested and jailed on that occasion. Later, when Wizard was a teen-ager and young adult, his contact with law enforcement increased and sometimes involved physical altercations, especially when he was incarcerated in county institutions. While he claims that police have harassed him and his friends, as for example when they were cruising, he also cites instances where the police occasionally checked him out as a potential suspect because of his reputation.

He had by the age of 10, in the fifth grade, been initiated into a type of street gang. His elementary school cohort group was known as the Maravilla Project Boys. They would play games and marbles after school each day, and some would write their name and barrio on the walls. One of the boys, influenced by an older gang-member brother, came up with the idea of starting their own klika—the Pee Wees. Shortly after, several of them underwent the initiation ritual of fighting. Wizard explains it in this way: "Two minutes, all the time you fight back anyway you want. If you fall down, it gets longer than two minutes. So you try not to fall. What I did was I fought against the wall. I fought six guys. After it was over, we shook hands. Then, I helped get several other guys in." Thus, the first klika from the cohort began. The remainder of the Maravilla Project Boys subsequently broke up into klikas from distinct barrio gangs, even if only one street separated the barrios. Wizard intensified his involvement with the klika upon entering junior high school. More time was spent with the cohort, and the time was often oriented more toward such activities as breaking windows, smoking marijuana, taking reds, shoplifting from the local supermarket, and, of course, fighting with the local enemy of the same age. "Our rivals were X [other barrio] Pee Wees. We used to battle with them for control of the area, and we did this for about a week and won. They changed their names and we were the only Pee Wees. Killer and Lil' Man used a hatchet on some guy's head, and sometimes they would get into stabbing '*movidas*' [actions, or modus operandi]. I had a fight with a guy at Griffith Junior High." The young males in the klika had an inordinate influence on him, for he spent most of the time in the streets where their attitude and behavior dominated the scene. Fearful of being rejected by them, or of being outright abused and taunted as "a sissy," he conformed to their expectations and gained in stature. Killer, who had started the klika, was particularly influential because he had a fearless reputation and, thus, a fearful presence.

Wizard had early learned to cope with fear by just throwing himself into a volatile situation without regard for life or body. He suffered numerous bloody noses, scratches, and bruises but no knife cuts or bullet wounds despite occasional encounters with those weapons. He explains his fearless stance in terms of the respect it gained him: "Like if they would steal like sandwiches, they would turn me on to them. The respect was there. They would brag about me, like 'you know what Wizard did, man? He stole this and that . . . or kicked so and so's butt.' I got a good feeling of respect, status, and excitement out of it." He mentioned on several occasions that it was an "ego trip" for him because personal recognition would come from the guys, and he would feel like he had accomplished something. In a rather elaborate explanation of how he involved himself in the gang lifestyle, he touched on other influences and motivations. "Like, *It Takes a Thief*, you know that movie. He [the hero of the movie] takes a lot of chances. He does a lot of things but he has to be a pro at it, if he is going to get away with it. It is an image that you have to project. And it is exciting because it is like acting—no lie! Like I could make myself act and be a real *vato loco* [crazy guy], and I would change and used to wear football jerseys and things like that to look not like a cholo, but to look more respectable, dressed-up, neat. There were times I would act tough to let them know you're a violent guy. They would keep an eye on you. You'd be watched more carefully."

These and other similar antisocial activities characterized the life of Wizard through the first years of adolescence. By this time, school played a minimal part in his life, and his earlier average level of performance declined to failing levels. The drop in school performance was matched by an increase in street affairs, which brought more negative contact with law enforcement. Throughout this time, his mother and older sister, with the help of an uncle, tried to separate him from the barrio klika, even to the point of moving to a better section southeast of the barrio. But his peer attachments were already confirmed, and, along with the personal "street" qualities noted above, Wizard became one of the klika's best "Lover Boys," attracting young girls either when alone or when the group was cruising Whittier Boulevard and he was doing the talking.

A series of arrests, mostly for burglaries, eventually led him to juvenile hall and county detention camps. During one stay, he succeeded in acquiring a General Education Diploma (GED). However, he also met other young boys from Maravilla. Because his father had a highly regarded and widely known reputation in one of the first klikas back in the 1950s, Wizard joined a new klika from El Hoyo Maravilla—a different barrio gang—despite his initial affiliation with another. Continuing the gang lifestyle outside the juvenile institutions, he later was arrested for robbery and spent one year at the county prison. When he returned home at 19, a combination of factors began to make him re-examine his life. A close girlfriend (who was later to be the mother of his son) regularly admonished him for his street ways. Additionally, the continuing counsel of his uncle (himself a college graduate) now began to sink in—"get an education and get a good job." Wizard was attending a community college at the time of the interview and was always optimistic about securing a job, although setbacks were frequent. I even observed him attempt to counsel younger El Hoyo members into more productive activities, like school and sports.

Geronimo, Another Gang Regular

The second example of a regular gang member is Geronimo, a member of Varrio Nuevo Estrada. This barrio's beginnings are traced back to the 1940s Hunter Street gang in Boyle Heights (Ranker 1957:33). Some members of this barrio were relocated to the Estrada Courts Projects (government-subsidized apartments originally intended to combat urban social disorganization) when the Santa Ana Freeway was built, destroying their homes. Until that time the Projects had been inhabited mostly by lower-middle-class Anglo and working-class Mexican American families, and there were no indications of a gang. In combination with the settlement there of gang members and the changing, transient nature of the Estrada Courts, by the late 1950s there emerged a youth group that became known as Varrio Nuevo (New Barrio)—thus, VNE, Varrio Nuevo Estrada. Because the project complex was so large, and the rents lower than other nearby residences, there was an abundance of low-income families with a large number of children who would constitute a barrio of a different sort. The more than five hundred apartments provided boys in sufficient numbers to often form more than one clique of the same age grade (a not unusual habit in large barrios). Sometimes these cliques within the same barrio have had conflicts with each other. Usually, however, older members intervene to remind the factions of barrio unity. Moreover, because the barrio is so large and strong, it has expanded beyond its original boundaries (the Projects) to incorporate contested areas. Now, VNE encompasses a corridor of varying width reaching as far as three miles east of its original setting. This new area was once, like Estrada Courts, mostly Anglo, lower middle class, but in contrast to the Projects the homes were single-family dwellings. Varrio Nuevo is now one of the biggest barrios in East Los Angeles and, of course, has produced one of the biggest gangs.

Geronimo was born in the county General Hospital and was 16 at the time of our interview. His mother and father were divorced when he was 2 years old, and he never saw his father again until he was 12. His mother remarried, and, of the six children in the family, he and his older brother (18 years) and younger sister (15) are from the first father and the three younger sisters (ages 13, 11, and 10) are from the stepfather. Before the family settled down in the Eastmont neighborhood, living there for about ten years, they had changed residences six times, each time near the southern periphery of East Los Angeles. Geronimo recalls that one of the neighborhoods had a busy thoroughfare on which both he (at age 6) and his sister (at age 3) were, in separate incidents, hit by cars. Neither suffered serious injuries in these accidents. (I have observed this street on several occasions and noted how front yards and sidewalks were teeming with children of all ages until dusk or dinnertime.) The relationship between his mother and stepfather sometimes involved fights and separations. During such separations, when his mother was unable to secure gainful employment on her own, she relied on welfare for maintenance of the family and home. Throughout these years, it was his mother who supervised him, occasionally calling in his grandfather for aid.

According to Geronimo, his father and several younger relatives, including cousins a few years older than Geronimo, affiliated themselves with Varrio Nuevo. Eastmont had now become a part of that barrio, and his formative years were spent there, playing with neighbor children and relatives in the streets. He was in the third grade when he transferred to the elementary school there, and both at home and at school he exhibited a rebellious nature—running away from home or creating classroom disturbances.

His defiant attitude can be seen in his account of an incident that occurred when he was 8 years old. Most of his street playmates were older, by about three or four years, and shoplifting for toys was one of their regular activities. Geronimo himself was caught by a store employee stealing a cheap toy and was turned over to the police. Police officers took him home to inform his mother about the deed, and upon their departure she proceeded to "whip his ass." Recalling this, he says of the police: "They didn't scare me, because two weeks later I went back and did it again. This time I took marbles." "Mean ass-whippings" were very common for these and other such infractions, and he says, "I wish my mother did it more, so that maybe I could realize that she wasn't just doing it to just hit me."

During the same time period, he remembers playing with toy guns and play-acting at robbing stores, a game that preceded reality. Meanwhile, he also got involved in sniffing spray paint (usually the metallic silver or gold type) or airplane model glue with his older cohorts; since the paint inhalation often involves immersing one's head in a large brown paper bag, a telltale sign is a metallic-streaked face. Most of these inhalants were shoplifted. "I remember the guy that I was with, his mother was a tecata, she would deal and use, so she really never knew what was going on, because she was dealing and using. So when his mother used to come home she would give me some money, his little brother some money, and him some money. We would take his little brother's money and tell him that we were going to buy him a car with $20.00. That's one thing I remembered doing. Then that's when I really started sniffing the glue. We would sniff and then go swimming after that." Once his mother caught him sniffing and, realizing that the previous punishments were not helping, called in the grandfather: "She just went home and called my grandfather and the next day she didn't send me to school. I didn't know why my grandfather came and then he took me to the police station. He wanted somebody to talk to me. She [a police officer] came up to my grandfather and she tells him, 'Is this the kid you're talking about?' She said, 'how long have you been sniffing?' I say, 'I don't know.' I guess I had a chip on my shoulder and they couldn't take it off either. She told me that I had only two years to live. It's been eight years ago." During this period, Geronimo says he also would take great pride in sharing whatever resources he had with others. "I can't say that I have always been bad. I have a good heart, I consider myself as having a good heart. Some people realize that, they respect me for that."

Most of his early life revolved around activities of this sort. Street fighting was not a regular routine, for he became very skilled at bluffing his way through most potentially volatile social encounters, especially in the later years at Eastmont Intermediate School. Since the school was a bridge school, encompassing fifth to eighth graders, and he was already hanging around with older youths, he began to emulate their cholo dress and walking styles. His performance throughout school was below average, as he regularly had confrontations with teachers. He recalls one exception, a Chicano counselor who tried to help him, as well as other cholos, to join school activities. To some degree his problems in school stemmed from language sources. Although he speaks Spanish in a halting way, he has an adequate comprehension of it, for his mother and grandfather would speak to him in Spanish and he would reply in English. In the seventh grade the school authorities placed him in the remedial classes, doing what he characterizes as "3 plus 3" work; he regularly sat in the back of the room. At about this time he began cutting classes and days of school, for which he was suspended from school several times. He also became actively involved with a gang klika.

He recalls a rather prosaic event from that time (at the age of 13) as symbolically significant: "I remember my mom used to comb my hair. It ain't really nothing special. I always wish I could go back to those days, when my mom would wake up in the morning. She would play some Spanish music on radio KALI and she would get dressed and cook breakfast, comb our hair. I remember she used to comb it to the sides. So one day I took the comb from her and started combing it back. That's when I started thinking I was all *chingón* [tough guy, in control]." At approximately the same time, and with increased associations with other cholos, he was initiated into the klika—the Spantos of VNE. There were several similar-aged klikas around at that time from VNE, but the one he joined was with boys he knew from the Eastmont section. The initiation took place in the afternoon on the front yard of a neighborhood house. Three initiators surrounded him and beat him. It was to last thirty seconds, but the observers counted in a slow, deliberate way, "like this: one [5 seconds elapse], two [4 or 5 seconds elapse], and 'what comes after two,' " and so on. One's proficiency and bravery in fighting back demonstrate that he can back up the barrio, and "everyone knows, *no te rajas* [you don't chicken out]." After the initial test, he had to be prepared at all times to "claim the barrio." If anyone approached and said "*¿De dónde?* [where are you from?] You've got to say you're from VNE. If you say nowhere, they can say *órale* [hey, guy], this and that, and whatever, but the tradition about being in a barrio is that they'll jump you in. A day, a week, a month later they'll send some more vatos that you don't know and they'll ask you where're you from. If you say I don't know, if you say nowhere, they will fuck you up right there. But if you say Varrio Nuevo, they'll come on like this other barrio that they don't get along with, to see what you'll do."

Geronimo's liquor and drug habits began during this time. Beer, wine, *polvo* (angel dust), reds, and marijuana were consumed on a regular basis with the klika and other friends and cousins. While there were some minor gang fight incidents, such as at school or after school, he especially took pleasure at instilling fear in the hearts of other schoolchildren by walking around the schoolyard and having everybody move out of the way; "I guess they didn't like us, they were afraid of us." Notwithstanding these bullying activities, he clearly demonstrated his bravery to peers by conducting robberies of stores or people. His explanation clarifies the multiple dimensions to this deviant orientation:

> I never hurt nobody, I never really robbed people until I was older. The first robbery that I did was for kicks. In fact, all of the robberies I did were for kicks, not for money or to hurt anybody. One time I went into a store, me and my homeboy, and I had a paper bag over my head and I cut two eyes in it. We went up to the manager, I was about 13 then, and I socked him in the mouth and he landed in back of the market. I seen how they do the robberies on T.V. Actually, that's where I think I learned everything, on T.V., and I haven't got caught in a robbery yet. I haven't got caught for something that I thought of in my own head. Everything else that I've got caught for was nothing that I wanted to do, I just got involved with others. I thought I was slick and I didn't leave fingerprints or nothing.

Several other similar incidents took place with at least one homeboy associate. The last robbery he committed was carried out under the eyes of several homeboys, whom he wanted to impress since he was the youngest. The group was drinking beer and smoking marijuana in a front yard of one of the members. Geronimo went into the house of a friend's girlfriend and took $18.00 from her sister's purse. "I guess they [homeboys] were looking at me, and I knew it, so I wanted them to respect me. They respected me, but I wanted to be accepted, and it's the truth, too." The money he acquired bought more beer. Feeling very good after drinking it, he and his cousins, also members of the group, decided to leave, but their car wouldn't start. They saw two *braceros* (Mexican nationals) in a car nearby and asked for a ride. When refused, Geronimo went away and returned with a pipe to force them to comply. Upon coercing a ride, they first went to get a gun to ensure that the reluctant drivers would follow further instructions on where they wanted to go. After a long drive and more beer drinking, they were apprehended in Corona. Geronimo was charged with robbery and kidnapping at age 14. Tried and convicted, he is now serving time at a state youth penal institution.

Freddie, a Peripheral Member

In the immediate outskirts of Los Angeles and continuing outward to agricultural regions, there have existed for decades a number of colonias with youth gangs. Freddie is a 17-year-old who belongs to just such a barrio in Riverside County. This barrio, named Corona, was initially settled by Mexican immigrants who worked in the nearby citrus orchards and later in the Sunkist plant, which processed citrus products. As a Mexican pocket surrounded by mostly middle-income and working-class Anglos, it early and uniformly took on the appearance of a separate community—its own church, park, and older, smaller homes in an area populated by about 150 to 200 families. Youth groups have always been a part of this neighborhood, but only in the last two to three decades have street gangs become a problem. Rivalry with nearby barrios in San Bernardino and Riverside has been around just as long.

Freddie was born in Riverside and grew up in the Corona barrio with both his parents. His father worked at a furniture plant and his mother at home, together raising five children, Freddie the eldest and two other sons and two daughters. His childhood years were mostly pleasant memories as his family regularly joined with their extended family members, grandparents, uncles and aunts, and cousins for all sorts of affairs—baptisms, birthdays, and so on. He particularly recalls playing with the other children on the block, day and night it seemed to him, and credits two teen-aged paternal uncles for shepherding him. All of this changed when his parents divorced and the experience left 10-year-old Freddie and his siblings confused and disoriented. While his father soon remarried, his mother was unprepared for this break.

Without any visible means of support or occupational training, she had to go on welfare to support the children. The father, however inconsistently and infrequently, still made efforts to visit and take the children for outings. In addition to this change, other closely related families moved out of the barrio, thus disrupting the extended family network that had been in place since Freddie's youth. To compound matters, his two uncles left for the army during the height of the Vietnam conflict, thus depriving him of other male attachments.

Soon after, Freddie began to associate much more with youths like himself, who spent a lot of unsupervised time in the streets. "I started making friends with these guys who didn't want to do anything but get in trouble. We would always get in trouble at school and ditch and go party. This was in junior high. This is when I started getting into drugs and stealing from homes." Freddie learned to appreciate this street group and later joined them in reviving an old social club, which had turned into a gang, and became more deeply entrenched in street life. While cruising, partying, and social gatherings constituted the bulk of their activities, there also was an increase in delinquent activities, especially fights with rival gangs, at parties or the swap meet. The swap meets and fairgrounds in this area appear to be a regular staging ground for gang encounters, as I witnessed on at least one occasion.

Freddie particulary felt that the gang gave him a sense of belonging and a purpose in life, and as he says:

> I always felt important when I was with the guys. I liked being one of the guys they would look up to. I was big and no one would mess with me, and I enjoyed that feeling [at age 13 he was already 5' 9" and built very well]. There was nothing to do anyway, and everybody was into it, too. Anyway, you always knew you had someone to back you up and that made you feel good, too. It was fun to plan things against our enemies and the cops. Not all of it was bad, though, because we used to get together and associate with girl clubs from out of town [nearby colonias or barrios], not the guys but the girls. We had a lot of rules for how we should act toward each other. We couldn't fight with each other, and if we did all of the members had to be present. And if one of us fought an enemy, we had to back him up even if he was winning.

By the age of 15 he considered himself a full-fledged gang member. He engaged in heavy drug usage and in such activities as threatening liquor store employees for money and/or liquor. In one quick-paced cruising foray to another barrio, he and his companions started trouble by yelling out their *"placasos"* (the name of the barrio or gang) and they were shot at; Freddie received a leg wound. A successful retreat ended up at the hospital, where Freddie told police he had been wounded by some outsiders while he was just lounging with the homeboys in his barrio. This shooting appeared to fire him up even more, as he wanted to prove that he wasn't afraid of anything.

Soon after, at age 16, he had an opportunity to fulfill this prophecy:

> We went to a party out of our neighborhood and when we got there, there were some white guys who thought they were tough. I walked in and started looking around to see who I knew. There were a couple of girls I remembered from junior high school, so I started talking to them and dancing. One of them, the one I was dancing with, was pretty and all the guys liked her. When I wasn't dancing with her this one white guy, he looked like the leader of the other guys, would ask her to dance, but she wouldn't dance with him. This got him mad and he just started staring at anyone who danced with her. When I danced with her, he acted like he was walking by and bumped into us real hard and just looked at me like it was my fault. The girl got all excited and told me to forget it, but he just kept on giving me dirty looks. When it [the record] was over, I walked over to the guy and told him to watch it next time. He threw a punch at me and then pulled a knife. I took my knife out and we started fighting out in the front yard, where I stabbed him in the stomach. I didn't want him to die, I thought, because I didn't want to kill anyone. Everybody thought he was going to die. I was worried real bad.

Because the act was in self-defense and the victim survived, Freddie was only given eight months at boys' camp. This charge, despite his other undetected crimes, was his first serious one. However, he disliked camp tremendously because one had to always to be on "your toes" to survive there. He spoke about "the officers who would tell us to finger on each other, and if we didn't we would get punished. If there were gang fights the Chicanos would get together and so would the blacks and whites. No one would walk alone, we would walk two at a time because if the enemy [other gangs there] would see you walking alone, they would jump you." This unpleasant atmosphere and experience led him to run away from the facility two times, thereby adding a total of eight additional months to his detention.

Upon returning to the community, as part of a process introduced by camp counselors, he continued to re-evaluate his life and make projections about the future. This incipient life-path reorientation is symbolized by how he reacted to friends and associates, as for example: "When I went to parties I would walk in and people would look away. I could tell that they were a scared of me. So I would start talking to them and let them know I was all right." This attitude contrasts sharply with his previous habit of instilling fear, and enjoying it for its effects. However, I have noticed that among strangers he still likes to strike this pose to remind everyone that he could revert to "street," if necessary. One could offer the judgment that, now that he had gained respect for his knifing fight and incarceration, there is no need to seek fearful respect. Nevertheless, he appears to have turned over a new leaf. At present, he is working as a mechanic and helping in the support of a child from his girlfriend. He still goes out with the guys for parties and casual cruising, but now he is trying to be a Hollywood Swinger and keep away from trouble. As he says, "I don't blame anyone but myself. I love both my parents very much. If they had not put me away, I would still be out there doing who knows what and I might have been killed by now."

Henry, a Temporary Member

Another rural barrio, Chino, is the locale of the next case history, that of Henry, 20. This neighborhood is also spatially and socially segregated from the middle-income residents of the city and is situated right in the middle of a dairyland region. It is an enclave of 24 square blocks, 500 homes, and 2,500 people of mostly Mexican background. The rest of the city of 33,000 is of mixed Anglo and Mexican ethnic background, with Anglos in the majority. Chino is interesting for several reasons: It was a small ranchería during the Mexican American war of 1846 and, in fact, is the location where a noted battle took place between Anglos and Mexicans in that conflict (Acuña 1981). Economically, it has gradually shifted from an orchard and ranching environ, with mainly walnut and orange groves, horses, and cattle, to that of dairy farms. With all the changes it is still the Mexicans who provide most of the labor for these enterprises. Finally, this area has one of the oldest rural youth gangs. The latter fact is important because since the 1940s some adults from the barrio have attempted, with scattered and inconsistent success, to redirect the youth into a social/car club, but, instead, over a period of time the club has solidified into a gang: the Chino Sinners.

Henry's early life was somewhat unstable, as his father died when he was only 3 years old. His mother sought and gained work as a machinist and with her earnings, and Social Security benefits, she struggled to raise five sons. She never remarried or lived with a man, although one son was born out of wedlock. All of the family resided in a rented, clapboard two-bedroom home under cramped conditions, the older sons sleeping on the front room floor. Although on the edges of poverty, the mother was able to shield the boys from her childrearing struggles, as Henry does not recall any early deprivations. Later, though, he remembers joining a barrio protest aimed toward improving street drainage and the construction of curbs and sidewalks; as was noted earlier, rural barrios are often characterized by a lack of such amenities.

Henry's mother scrimped and saved to send all of the boys to parochial school up to the sixth grade, for she felt that they would receive a better education there and, especially, avoid the bad street elements in the barrio. Unfortunately, this did not materialize in Henry's case as he struggled to maintain a "C" average. Further, although he lived in the barrio, his close peer friends were in Pomona, the location of the parochial school. When he left the sixth grade for a public junior high school near the barrio, he had to establish new associates. At first he was able to "do his own thing" and remain a "square," but in high school he began to associate with some of the gang members at school. His reasons for associating with them are varied, however:

> And then ninth grade comes along and that's when everybody changes, no matter what. All the Chicanos hang around the benches and when other guys came around, we would start making fun of them—that's the way fights started. You make fun of someone and they don't like it. Usually the group would stand behind you, this is where it's at. And you felt pretty good, you know, as you hung around with them more and more. Then you'd go home, and it's all over, you know. You listen to your mom yell and your brothers are fighting you. "Man," you say, "this is getting me mad, I got to do something." Some guys would ask you, "Hey, why don't you come over to the Projects." So I would go over.

Getting away from home and feeling good with the gang resulted in learning a number of other gang customs, without Henry undergoing an initiation. Of course, many of the customs were quite positive, such as fixing cars: "Yeah, to have a good time, the guys would have a couple of beers and a whole bunch would get under the engine." However, there were also habits that contributed to Henry's poor educational record. For example, in school: "Well, you never carry books with you. If you did, they [the gang members] would make fun of you. You'd just throw your stuff in your locker and hang around at the wall." But the bad was accepted because of the good: "I felt good. At home you just got yelled at. With my friends, you could relax, have a few joints, and drink beer." His mother regularly and consistently admonished him about going and staying out late with "those guys," but "by then I didn't care what my mom thought."

For several years, Henry learned what the gang experience was all about—cruising and raiding, the vato loco style, and the interbarrio gang conflicts—but he was more an observer than a participant. He even carried a switchblade around to "act bad" and wanted to "do time": "I used to think school was stupid. I thought I was going to end up going into the service, or maybe end up going to the joint. I thought I was going to the joint once. I wanted to go, I wanted to make it. Yeah, I thought all my friends were going to look up to me. They did, pretty soon they started talking better to me." The warmer cohort reception he's referring to was gained by his spending a night in jail, after being charged with resisting arrest. The charge stemmed, he says, from an altercation deliberately provoked by the police officer, who had detained him for "cruising." On another occasion an older veterano asked him for a ride. He obliged, but the person put his "stuff" (heroin) under the seat to be "clean" in case they were stopped by the police. This subsequently happened several times with that person, and others, and it made him feel uncomfortable, because "I could get busted for that."

Such incidents, in part, led to his gradual disaffiliation with the gang. He was able to remain on the fringes of the gang, however, moving in and out of selected situations most of the time, such as only committing petty shoplifting for items from the auto supply stores. Because of this manuevering he was able to avoid an initiation, although the veteranos, from time to time, would say things like "we're going to take you to Pomona and leave you off there." The crucial turning point for him stemmed from his clear distaste for violence of any sort, "that's why I never made it as a true member. No, I told myself if I fought with my hands, it would be okay. But I never wanted to kill anyone. All my friends had guns like it was nothing, but guns kill people, and I didn't want to do that. Yeah, at the *'remate'* [swap meet] in Chino, I was with the group when they started stabbing a guy. They even kept chasing him after they stabbed him. It turned me off. I wanted to fight only with my hands. No, I never wanted to do nothing that would hurt anyone but me."

One day, two years ago, he and a close friend got drunk, "toked up," and he recalls thinking of the "Projects" as "all concrete and like a prison cell." This led both of them to reflect on and discuss ways of getting out of the gang. Henry's solution was simple, but as he states, "other guys really got hassled if they wanted to get out, they would be beat up like my friend." He merely avoided them to make his exit:

> When they invited me to go with them, I made excuses. I guess they got the hint. After a long time they stopped asking me. I didn't know where to hang out. I would be watching out for different cars. I was wondering where can I hang out, when I don't want to hang out here anymore. Then I started working full time. I would work at anything to stay off the streets. I didn't go through what some guys I know went through. They started treating me like I was invisible. Now [age 20], when I see some of the guys sometimes, they ask me, "Hey, how you doing?" But we never get together.

Since leaving them he has continued to work as a mechanic's helper and is presently attending college to improve his work skills. Clearly, he now belongs to the larger group of youth who live in the barrio but do not belong to the gang.

Analysis of Life Histories

These cases are rather representative examples that highlight the dynamics of barrio life and the resultant personal adjustments that have to be made during adolescence, especially with the formation of an age and sex identity. Both Wizard's and Geronimo's routes to gang involvement and group identity reflect common experiences for regular gang members. On the one hand, it was clear that they had undergone similar experiences: a low-income background, family disruptions, mother-centered household, street socialization (with its petty mischief and food and toy theft), conflict with social control institutions, street role models, and generally an adjustment to the multiple realities and pressures of barrio life. Although coincidental, the fact that both were hit by cars testifies to their early and continuing involvement in street life. Despite their mothers' efforts to supervise them, the lack of consistent male adult guidance in Wizard's and Geronimo's household situations made the streets even more attractive as a place for companionship and a play arena as an outlet for physical energy. Involvement in street life was part of the reason for gang membership, but it was during adolescence when equally, perhaps more, important factors began to operate in their lives. Here too, however, the two cases resemble each other. Lacking an appropriate male household role model, both emulated young associates and refined and buttressed this adolescent identity source with television role imagery. At approximately the same age, in junior high, they became closely associated with a clique of their barrio, although the initiation took place earlier in Wizard's case, perhaps because he lived in an older barrio. The gang initiation itself was an obvious rite of passage, as the group witnessed the initiates withstand the psychological and physical shock. This event allowed them to demonstrate that they did have the mental and physical mettle to contribute to the gang, by adding either fighting power (Wizard) or daring ability (Geronimo). A number of cholo characteristics were adopted to assuage the personal fear and apprehension that accompanies joining a gang. Many of these personal qualities had begun earlier, such as sharing resources and backing one's friends, and were intensified under the group's supervision. They had to now show that they were responsible, loyal, and dedicated to group goals. A style of dress, speech, and personal demeanor was incorporated into their persona and was affected when they were with other members of the gang. In addition, the group network provided values and norms for personal affection (within) and aggression (without), and the attainment of status, prestige, and respect through various ways—fighting, leadership, drugs, car cruising, and so on.

These broad strokes give an indication of the similarity of the many themes that reflect the cumulative, combinative nature of gang life. Within that way of life there are nuances and differences in how these two individuals' lives unfold. Geronimo had an ineffectual stepfather but apparently a grandfather who gave occasional chastisement. His mother punished him severely but failed, as did other authority figures; and, as noted, his mother's "ass-whippings" clearly left him confused. Taking the comb from his mother indicates that he wanted to show that he was grown, a man, especially in conjunction with his later attempts to gain older male recognition for his daring. He resolved his concern for acquiring group acceptance by conducting robberies. Wizard, in contrast, had an older uncle who, with his mother's prompting, represented an alternative model to those available on the streets. To a degree, he also modeled himself after his father, especially mythologizing this attachment of following in his father's footsteps when he joined another Maravilla barrio, El Hoyo (his father's). This worked to solidify his fearless reputation, for there was a longstanding tradition and series of personal networks (his father and his) behind it. Fighting and unpredictability (loco behavior) were his means to acquire gang approval and respect; he also played this role to manage fear and be "watched more carefully."

Comparing the peripheral and temporary types of gang members is a more difficult task. Nevertheless, there are similarities between them, such as the following: they were barrio raised yet able to avoid very early street socialization, they had stress-ridden homes, they received necessary acceptance and identity through gang membership, and they had negative contacts with gang habits, which caused them to re-evaluate their involvement. The differences between them are more striking than are any similarities. Freddie, the peripheral member, was apparently stable until a divorce and residential and social separation from his extended family traumatized his life. Thereafter, he spent more time with street peers and particularly enjoyed instilling fear in others. In his case, the gang provided an outlet for his aggressive "needs." This aggression, coupled with his body size and toughness, made him somewhat of a leader and induced him to participate in fights and other hostile acts. After spending some time in camp for a stabbing at a party, he decided to alter his lifestyle somewhat by identifying with the Hollywood Swingers style, a much more socially oriented subgroup. Yet he continued to cruise and party with the homeboys. In contrast, Henry, the temporary member, was only a casual participant, more oriented toward cruising and socializing, successful at coping with the gang peers and lifestyles but never entirely associating with them until high school. His mother tried to get him educated and conforming (Catholic school) and regularly admonished him about hanging out with the wrong crowd. Her efforts apparently affected his decision to leave the gang, though it must be noted that one of the reasons he cited for joining the homeboys was to get away from home. Group support and security and "kicking" back with his friends was what made him feel good. In time, a number of unsettling brushes with detrimental gang activities made him reject gang associations, and thereafter he sought steady employment to avoid contact with them. He appreciated the sense of camaraderie in the group but disliked losing control of his own person and being "used."

Life Histories, the Gang Subculture, and Self-Identity

What all four cases tell us is that the words of many law enforcement officers must be read with caution: "If he looks like a duck, walks like a duck, then he must be a duck." Such words are often used to describe someone who adopts the cholo front, and inferred gang membership, but it is clear that the phenomenon is not so easily categorized. A tremendous range of variation exists among these youths. True, all of them share a number of barrio and structural situations and conditions that triggered other events. For example, they sought the gang for a source of peer identity and a setting for social friendship and recreation during adolescence; they experienced some type of social control breakdown (e.g., attenuated family situation, poor-to-mediocre school performance, and contacts with law enforcement); and, of course, they incorporated the "cholo front" and other group symbols—the dress, demeanor, talk, graffiti, and so on—as part of their identity. Notwithstanding these broad similarities, what distinguishes the regular, peripheral, and temporary gang members from each other are the types and degrees of experiences and involvements of each of these, as well as other, dimensions. It is especially important to know how these experiences and involvements combined and accumulated in each person to determine his level of gang membership. For instance, the cholo front is external and easily acquired with a minimal amount of practice; thus regular, peripheral, and temporary gang members can play the part with (relatively speaking) equal ease. For a consideration of deeper gang involvement, one must examine early social experiences and chart how cultural values and psychological drives and motivations arise. The poorest, most stress-ridden members of the underclass are more at risk to become and to remain gang members. In short, problematic marginality in the aforementioned multiple areas is probably suggestive of serious gang membership.

While peer associations serve multiple purposes for all types of gang members, it is the regular gang members who have had the earliest and most intense street experiences. This, in turn, tends to make their peer relationships stronger and more enduring. Peripheral and temporary members are less compelled to maintain this close a tie and thus reflect a commitment that they can change if they desire. Peer respect and support, especially if there is an absence of other male models and associations, is a cultural complex known as *carnalismo* among gang members and is sometimes the only human support system they have. To reject or avoid peers (and the gang) is out of the question for them or, at the minimum, is a difficult task. That is why some have trouble leaving the gang.

Regular gang members generally have more disruptive social control problems, but, as noted, such conditions are not necessarily a prelude to a deeper gang involvement (e.g., temporary Henry's case). One gang pattern that differentiates types of members is the debilitating activities—the alcohol and drug use and abuse, the fighting and violence, and the extended contacts with the criminal justice system (e.g., police detention, incarceration). The evidence clearly suggests that some individuals are more prone to join, find fulfillment, and continue in these activities, as, for instance, the more extended patterns reflected in the lives of Wizard and Geronimo. Some decide to remain members, sometimes consciously but just as often out of social compulsion, even after the most harrowing gang experiences (Klein 1971). Regular members, under the aegis of peers, were found to begin experimentation with chemical substances and street fighting at an earlier age. Freddie, the peripheral member, was just as committed to these activities as were the regular members but, in contrast, participated in them later in life and was eventually able to change his habits. In his case, the breakdown in social control and subsequent attachment to street youths were formalized under more loosely defined circumstances (e.g., no gang initiation). Henry, the temporary, mostly socializer member, was sheltered from street associations, and, additionally, he largely avoided the more damaging habits. In fact, his distaste for these activities (e.g., the gang stabbing that "turned him off") is the major reason he withdrew from the gang.

What has to be considered in detailing the differences among gang members is the deeper psychological propensities that stem from and are based on early life experiences—the anxieties, frustrations, and aggressions (e.g., Geronimo's "ass-whippings"). It is these motivations that later find group-sanctioned avenues for expression. Because of these experiences, we observe that more-loco regular gang members are likely to initiate, and encourage others to follow, serious deviant activities that allow them to act out their needs. This behavior is reinforced if it fulfills their needs. Of course, peer pressure, or peer expectations of this type of role enactment, is a mediating influence. In most instances this behavior required an audience to provide feedback to the actor (e.g., Geronimo receiving respect and Wizard being watched more carefully). But, as we have seen, some individuals can more easily avoid peer pressure if they are not personally driven to perform deviant acts (e.g., Henry turning off to the stabbings). In other words, the gang helps facilitate what an individual person wants to do (i.e., deviant acts); and conversely, an individual (deviant actor) can also help determine what the gang will do.

Conclusion

The life histories draw a clearer, and fuller picture of the nature and quality of the gang subculture, as will be noted in depth shortly, and of the varied social and cultural experiences that account for individual differences in gang involvement and commitment. The life histories show that other social, cultural, and psychological features and characteristics are important and indicate that living in a barrio and being poor are not the only conditions that warrant our attention. The task is to examine how all these interwoven situations, conditions, and psychosociocultural experiences affect an individual during adolescence, when a personal identity is forged with the aid of peer group members. Individuals who have had a relatively harsh and problematic early life are more likely to have personal identity confusions and ambivalences, especially of an age and sex nature, when they reach adolescence (e.g., Geronimo taking the comb from his mother). This often makes the street peer group, the gang, the only useful source in which to experiment and acquire a personal identity. This pattern has emerged over a prolonged period of marginality, involving various areas and degrees of intensity that are reflected in the group, family, and individual histories. Thus, historical and social forces continue to shape contemporary individuals who must, then, also adapt to the street life shaped by previous generations. It is this street subculture that requires our closest inspection, for it has developed a life and a force of its own.

5. The Gang Subculture as a Lifeway: Structure, Process, and Form

How environmental, structural, and sociocultural features mesh with and generate the peculiar characteristics of the gang lifestyle is also better understood within a multiple marginality perspective. An informal and formal observational and life and group historical analysis is particularly useful in clarifying why certain stylistic and behavioral traits arose over several decades and became institutionalized among street youth. The effects of multiple marginality are seen in the adoption of role models and coping strategies to adapt to street life, and in the way that group traits and processes represent a collective resolution to problems associated with, for example, territory, age-grading, and gender socialization. For example, cohorting behavior and klika formation combine aspects of the Mexican palomilla tradition with the behavior patterns developed in American streets. Moreover, the sense of personal efficacy that for many youths is lost in the margins of several arenas is reconstituted and regained, especially for males, in the postures and demeanor that control the streets.

There are clear demographic and structural properties to the Chicano youth gang that help facilitate one's involvement and encourage a deeper commitment. For instance, the age-graded nature of the gang ensures that there is a place for everyone, even the youngest member; it allows for gang regeneration with the inclusion of each new generation; and it additionally provides the social arena for youngsters to learn and demonstrate important gang customs among themselves. As with so many other adolescent innovations, there is also an initiation procedure that gangs resort to in order to test and screen available and potential members. To leave the gang, as we will see, can be a much more complicated matter.

All of these processes set the tone for gang lifestyles, but early life experiences are what mediate an individual's induction and inclusion in the gang. Gang members generally share a background of family stress, lack of success in and subsequent alienation from school, and a disinclination toward many conventional pursuits of childhood and adolescence.

Several attitudinal and behavioral customs which have been adopted to help level the personal and sociocultural differences among gang members help make for group conformity. Such traits reflect the cholo image, the dress and demeanor of which are particularly distinct. Dress, gestures, mannerisms, language, walking style, nicknames, graffiti, and, of course, car and music preferences are a part of this "front." Although mostly external and easily mimicked, this image is an important source of identification. However, this stylistic symbolism is only the form and not the substance of the gang. Taken together, the structure, process, and formal features of the gang serve to recruit, organize, and provide a source of social identity to members.

Role Models: Family and Peers

In the life histories of gang members collected for this study, peer associations and pressures of childhood street experiences were commonly noted as background influences toward joining the gang. Despite such peer pressures, however, peers were less likely to be explicitly cited as models than were male family members. The influence of male relatives who were (or had been) gang members provided an image to live up to, and encouragement (sometimes inadvertant) to join, for about half of the gang members I interviewed and observed. Most often they wanted to follow in an older brother's footsteps. The family reputation (where several different members once belonged to a gang), uncles, father or stepfather, older extended family members, and cousins were also named as family models. About half of this group also spoke of the combined effect of peer pressure and family models; the other half, only of the family.

The distinction between peer pressure and family models is important. Peers dominate the steets and schools and provide the roles for novitiates to observe and internalize. Family members in contrast, are provided ampler opportunity as role models because their living arena reinforces what takes place in the privacy of the home as well as what occurs in the more public street sector; and a family member is generally subjected to more detailed feedback information by virtue of living in the home and listening to all the stories, gossip and otherwise, of a confidential nature.

In the instance of brothers' influencing youths toward gang membership, it was mostly a case of their living through similar conditions that made gang involvement predictable. Given the similarity of background, and the brothers' behavioral examples, it appeared that very little else was available to them except to follow suit. One young man, 17, from Fontana explained it this way: "I liked to listen to my brother's stories, they sounded like fun. He said you get more respect . . . He was right because they used to be afraid of me and I liked that feeling." (Interestingly, he had to conceal his gang involvement from his traditional Mexican parents, who were totally against gangs.) Listening to such stories made such youths admire their older siblings. The brothers helped pave the way, especially in older, established barrios, making it easier for one to belong. A 16-year-old male from Corona who eventually left the gang said: "My two older brothers were into it, so it's nothing new for our family. You have to learn to back up your friends and brothers." One young man from White Fence even talked about his older brothers' becoming gang members in different barrios, thus underscoring the importance of conditions and situations that create the tendency toward gang membership.

There were a few cases where the general family outlook or gang tradition was given as a reason to belong. A gang member from Chino, 19, for example, said: "I made my decision a long time ago about being a Chino Sinner. You see my father was a Chino Sinner, it's been in the culture of my family for years. It's kind of like when white boys are brought up to play football or something else. You have to stick with it. It gives me something to do." Tico, male, 22, from Pico Viejo was even more expansive about it: "My father was from Varrio Nuevo and my mother and all her family from Geraghty. When my father got busted, my mother moved away from East L.A. We grew up in different barrios and my carnales are from different barrios."

Although uneven and inconsistent, there were instances where brothers and parents attempted to break the cycle. One interviewee, a male, 19, from F-Troop (Santa Ana) reported: "It's not going to be the same for my younger brother . . . . I don't want to see my brother go through the shit I'm going through." Such good words and intentions, however, were betrayed by his living example, especially when he told his brother "to learn to fight and not let anyone push you around"; and the brother, as I observed in one incident, acted out this advice by resisting an arrest by police officers. In another instance, a male, 17, from Van Nuys said that his parents moved away from the barrio "because they didn't want us to go through what they went through." The attempt to break the pattern failed because they moved just a few minutes away to a nearby working-class tract-home neighborhood; friends and habits were relatively easy to maintain.

The point here, of course, is not that a family member was the main socializing agent in encouraging gang membership. In fact, there was usually very little verbal encouragement on their part to join. Younger siblings were rather impelled to follow in their footsteps because they looked up to them; and of course early street associations with peers would complement the tendency. The combinative effects of early and continuing peer influences coupled with a family model illustrate the multiple sources of the gang situation. In this instance, family models, when present, act as reinforcement, especially if other factors are present, and this despite the fact that several family models tried, at least verbally, to steer younger relatives away from gangs.

The Group as Family: Is the Gang a Surrogate Family?

It is important to note the overall pattern of early street socialization, peer interactions, and the effects of family gang models in shaping a gang member. However, it must be underscored that the gang is a force of attraction that provides many family-type functions. Although this pattern is a common adolescent group phenomenon, it is significant that a more formalized version of it is found in the gang. The gang has become a "spontaneous" street social unit that fills a void left by families under stress. Parents and other family members are preoccupied with their own problems, and thus the street group has arisen as a source of familial compensation. As a sort of tradition, it is also, perhaps, the gang members' way of continuing Mexican familial and palomilla customs under conditions of uneven culture change and the press of street life, in other words, to attach them to "something" when everything else is not working or has failed.

Almost one-half of the individuals interviewed mentioned why the group became important in their lives, and their reasons can be translated into what we would call familial supportive behavior. Implicit throughout all the life histories, in the remarks about social interactions and the learning of cultural values, is the sentiment that the gang is needed and gives something in return. This is demonstrated by the constant reminders in interviews and incidents that "the group is important to me"; "I get help when I need it"; "there was a lot of good things to do, like parties, car washes, and bake sales"; "I hung around with them all the time"; "it made me feel like I belonged"; and so on. Watching the way some of these individuals cling to and put demands on each other is often a remarkably touching experience.

Getting together with friends, especially childhood ones, was a common enough occurrence for almost everyone. Many of these personally charged ties affect other gang norms and identity symbols. Feeling like a homeboy, backing someone up, and gaining acceptance are all personal motivations, but they are interwoven with the sense of familism. Several individuals, however, were very explicit about the group as family, even though strict group qualities were also mentioned. Sometimes there was a close association between the disorganized family syndrome and a personal tendency to seek in or make of the group a family. Clearly, the group represents a ready source of nurture and acceptance. Those who rely on it probably need it the most. A male, 18, from Ontario had been having family problems (he was one of twelve children) and said: "I think my mother and father were at fault . . . I felt that I was not wanted, so I wanted to be with someone who cares." Another youth from Santa Ana recalled his interaction with fellow gang members at a youth authority camp, saying: "Sometimes I think the reason we share things is because Chicano families are like that. Other groups here are more for themselves."

The same feeling pertained in car washes, socials, and dances that I attended, as well as in gang-banging (i.e., fighting) activities. Other studies have noted this familism custom among Chicano gang members and prison inmates (P. E. Rodríguez 1980:12). One male, 16, from Cucamonga encompassed the whole barrio in his familism: "Most of the people in the barrio are related, that's what makes the barrio. Like you go around and talk to somebody and he knows mostly everybody in the barrio. Most of them are like his cousins or relatives or something like that. Even close friends become like a part of the familia." Thus, some peers are more than friends, and gang members especially are quite verbal and emotional about this fact.

Gang Structure: Cliques, Locales, Level of Involvement, and Gender Roles

Collective human behavior requires some ordering of thinking and behaving, especially when the conditions that produce a collective response reflect what members of groups do (activities), whom they do it with (interaction), and why they do it (sentiment) (Homans 1950). Hirschi (1969), furthermore, has emphasized other group features in explaining delinquent patterns—attachment, commitment, involvement, and belief—that provide a psychosocial overlay to the nature and quality of gang life. Bion's statement on group dynamics summarizes the importance of collective human patterns, much as one would find in a gang: "Every group, however casual, meets to 'do' something; in this activity, according to the capacities of the individuals, they cooperate. This cooperation is voluntary and depends on some degree of sophisticated skill in the individual . . . . Since this activity is geared to a task, it is related to reality, its methods are rational, and, therefore, in however embryonic a form, scientific" (1975:12).

The gang subculture is just such a group effort, particularly during adolescence. What initially began as a group of boys gathering on a corner, normal enough on its own terms, has evolved into a street gang with a structure to recruit and direct new members. Most of the gang members grow up in the barrio (or a barrio) and undergo more or less similar life experiences. Individual barrios, gang structures, and gang members vary, of course, but there is uniformity in the structural properties of a barrio gang. For youngsters who become gang members, barrio life has determined their early associations and bonding experiences; learning the boundary and "turf" lines of the barrio is a part of that background. On my cruising forays with gang members, I was always intrigued by their interest and familiarity with barrio (and gang) territorial considerations.

Historically, the barrio youth groups of mostly first generations followed the Mexican palomilla custom of banding together, as will shortly be noted. This age-grading custom provided adolescents and youth with approved channels for social growth and maturity. The palomillas, in contrast to later gangs, were "particularistic, personal, voluntary, non-instrumental . . . [and lacked] such corporate attributes as group name, identification with a particular territory, ingroup sentiments, or even persistence over time" (Rubel 1965:93). With the proliferation and expansion of barrios, and the coming of age of subsequent generations, there were many more children and thus more separate age groups—for example, White Fence now has twelve such clique generations. Urban conditions and social control alterations made something different out of street life. It was under these conditions that the gang was forged.

Cliques and Locales

An important heritage from the palomilla is the age-graded clique, which is the nexus of the gang structure. Most barrio gangs are made up of age cohorts, or klikas, separated in age by two to three years; although, in some of the oldest urban barrios, there may be more than one clique of the same age and some cliques might have a wider age spread. The oldest urban barrios have had a succession of cliques, beginning in the 1930s and 1940s, each with its own name. In one study (CPRP 1979), for example, twelve successive cliques were listed for one well-known urban barrio and fourteen were named for another nearby neighborhood.

Occasionally, multiple cliques have developed in the largest barrios, but they are more the exception than the rule. When this happens, it sometimes is difficult to maintain barrio unity, since there are cliques who claim the same barrio but are unacquainted and unfamiliar with each other. There are instances where a numerically large and territorially diffuse but contiguous barrio has had conflict between separate cliques. For example, one young woman from an overextended urban barrio reported witnessing a large brawl. She initially took it to be a fight with outsiders but soon recognized local barrio youth participating on both sides of the fighting. In addition to this type of barrio and clique expansion, a recent "hiving-off" phenomenon has occurred among some of the oldest and prestigious (by street standards) barrios (e.g., White Fence). Cliques are started in areas miles away by members who have moved from the barrio locale. Thus, they claim an allegiance to the barrio and share similar clique problems of unfamiliarity with the home base, in a socially constructed way (Moore et al. 1983). According to some sources, there are even such East Los Angeles barrio-named cliques in Tucson, Arizona.

The Chicano Pinto Research Project (1979, 1981), in tracing the evolution of gangs through compiling clique histories, has found that the earliest cliques (especially El Hoyo Maravilla) were not unlike the palomilla. Within a few years, however, especially after World War II, the cliques began to change under street conditions. Although encounters with strangers from other barrios were common at school and parties, where fist fights and confrontations ensued, initially these were usually personal affairs that might or might not involve others. With more barrios and larger groups of youth in the streets, it became more difficult for parents and other adults to supervise their activities. Personal fights might be contained, but conflicts among groups of youths tended to escalate. The gangs, in response, became more structured and their territorial affiliations became formalized.

White Fence, as an example of how a "fighting" clique begins, started with eleven boys who joined together to offer mutual protection. A veterano explains why in an interview: "The guys from White Fence were seeing me get into fights and getting jumped all the time. They took me to White Fence. They used to come and pick up the guys from the junior high school. They knew that there were only five or six of us in school. There would be big trouble from the guys from Flats and the guys from other neighborhoods and they used to come down to protect us" (CPRP 1979:32). In later years, interbarrio conflict became a pattern in White Fence, as well as other barrios. Contemporary gang members often follow a tradition of animosity toward certain enemy barrios on the basis of incidents from the past. Additional rationales for providing protection and security to barrio associates, especially clique members, stem from other sources as well. A male, 16, from Corona stated in an interview: "We had to defend our territory" and "make sure no one else from different barrios or towns would get near our *jainillas* [girls]." This defensive posture also implied that normal social life would go on uninterrupted, as these words from a male, 18, from Chino suggest in an interview: "We usually would party, get loaded, cruise around. We would chase outsiders out when they came around. Everyone would always back up each other." With some long-established barrios this stance required strict rules for clique membership. A male, 16, from Cucamonga said in an interview: "They aren't going to pick somebody who just came into the barrio and just got into it, because we don't usually let anybody into the barrio, not unless they grew up here."

As subsequent cliques formed and followed similar patterns, there was soon a succession of cliques, making a larger barrio unit of both older and younger members. A hierarchical gang structure based on seniority and experience evolved, with younger members generally looking up to older ones. Although most of the earlier clique members, now mostly in their early to late twenties, had left the gang, those who remained active were recognized as the veteranos and were accorded a considerable amount of prestige. Vetaranos would sometimes act as counselors, but more often they served as an image for the younger members to emulate. Klein (1971:66) has referred to this cluster of cliques graphically as resembling a skinny turnip, with fewer members in both the younger and older cliques and the larger numbers in the middle cliques.

The size and the age spread of the gang are difficult to determine because some members might provide figures for their clique while others enumerate the cluster of barrio cliques. Respondents in this study were from barrios varying in population, location, history, and length of gang tradition, so the parameters of the gangs they represent should be seen as a rough estimation. The average size of all the gangs was around thirty-six members, with the lowest being ten or fifteen (suburban) and the highest one hundred (urban). The latter, of course, is representative of a cluster of cliques and the former number is for just one clique. Ages of the respondents ranged from 12 to 30 years old, with the average being 16.8. The older, established barrios usually had members who joined at younger ages and stayed active longer, while the suburban gangs were mostly clustered around the middle teen years. On the average, males outnumbered females almost ten to one, although some (especially established urban and rural) barrios had larger proportions of female members.

The rural, long-established barrio of Cucamonga provides an example of clique memberships over time, although it is not a typical gang. Cucamonga (population, about one thousand) had a clique of about thirty from the ages of 14 to 20 in 1978. This barrio is a classic enclave with ecologically defined boundaries—a main highway on the west, an open field of vineyards on the north and east, with a wash in the east to punctuate the separation, and railroad tracks on the south. As a result, there is a strong sense of community and territoriality that affects adults and youth, particularly the local street group. During the late 1970s, there were a large number of children in the barrio; the cohort would sometimes swell to sixty or seventy members when important events occurred (e.g., parties and, especially, defensive preparations for a rumored raid by a rival barrio when everybody, including a large number of adults, was "from Cuca" and joined to protect the community). Ordinarily, however, the street group of thirty were the active and consistent participants in street life (mostly regular and peripheral members). While these individuals represented the underclass (and regularly stigmatized element) of the barrio, it is clear they enjoyed a special camaraderie.

Growing up together in the barrio had made them particularly tightly bonded. Most of their time was spent at the local hangouts. The Contact Center was used for recreation and socializing. Sometimes a backyard or a parked car or an empty field served as the place where they drank wine or beer, smoked marijuana or angel dust, and dropped reds or whites (Benzedrine). Seldom were all thirty together at any one time or place, as they preferred to spend idle moments with their closest friends. Dyadic and small group activities and interactions characterize their social life. At least a half dozen of the group were actively interested in and successful at initiating and maintaining contacts with females of their own age. When available, they joined a friend with a car (quite often a non-gang member) for cruising to effect those (and new) liaisons. I once attended a party just outside their barrio with about eight of them. Some had a good time partying, including two who slipped away to have serial intercourse with a willing female who was "throwing" the party. However, the remainder (four exactly) were having neither a good time nor part of the sexual encounters and thus decided to egg each other on by breaking up the party. They picked several fights and started throwing household items around. Fortunately, one of the older members (he was having a good time) sensibly intervened and returned the early morning to order, although most of the guests, hoping to avoid trouble, had left by then.

One 19-year-old sometimes served as the unspoken leader because he initiated or redirected activities in ways that suited his purposes. He was the local loco who had a life of extreme poverty and deprivation. He also learned to box while in prison. He often decided to raid and shoot-up another barrio, roll a drunk (usually a Mexican national), or get *locote* (crazy, drunk, high). Most of the younger, more impressionable youths followed his lead in this behavior to gain his approval. Some of the members close to his age often succeeded at going their own way if they did not feel like acting loco. It was during this time that a rash of crimes (including seven homicides, mostly of Mexican nationals, in a fourteen-month period) eventually brought a "sweep" by law enforcement (over one hundred police in a door-to-door round-up) (Ziegler 1978). At least half of the thirty were incarcerated within a year. This group of youths was not generally typical of barrio gangs. Indeed, it was an unusual period of rampant violence (e.g., more individuals with serious problems and thus more loco prone). For the remainder of the decade, until the early 1980s, activities were relatively quiet in Cucamonga—until, at least, the next cohort came along.

Cucamonga is known as a particularly impoverished body, and its street gang still has a reputation as especially violent. Since 1978, cliques of active members have averaged between twenty and forty members. In 1984, I attended a gathering of the current clique and counted fourteen members, who averaged about 15 years old. A veterano at the gathering reported to me that seven or eight members were absent, indicating a total current membership of twenty-one or twenty-two. In this instance, clique size and ages remained relatively the same. Such factors as loss of interest and variations in arrests and incarcerations account for the clique expansions or contractions in this barrio. The CPRP (1979) has documented similar fluctuations for two long-established urban gangs.

On a daily basis, for most barrios, one can seldom observe more than five to ten members at the local hangout, although others, in groups of two or three, might be somewhere else in or out of the neighborhood. Weekends and special occasions generally bring most clique members together. This is particularly the case at baptisms, weddings, *quinceañeras* (15-year-old female's coming-out celebrations), or other social affairs when married former gang members show up. Together they make up one big barrio group. A male, 17, from a once-rural (now suburban) barrio, El Monte Flores, explained in an interview the pecking order of his barrio in a way that roughly approximates other established barrios: "My klika is known as the

Enanos, they are guys that are usually 18 years and under. And then there is the Costros, or gangsters, who are the gang-busters, the shock troops of the gang or troublemakers; they are over 18. Veteranos are the older, married guys, some of them are working and others are still active. I guess you would call them the night priests of the gang. They get a lot of respect."

Generally, the oldest, most entrenched barrios have the largest number of total gang members, when active members in all cliques are added up. Clique dimunition and the eventual phasing out of a gang have occurred in some barrios, especially in East Los Angeles. El Hoyo Soto, for example, had so few youths to recruit at one time (they lasted about fifteen years) that their territory was absorbed by White Fence; a similar outcome came to the short-lived barrio Tortilla Flats. Urban renewal and the replacement of homes with freeways split Varrio Nuevo off from the old Hunter Street neighborhood. Arizona Maravilla, a contemporary barrio at least thirty years old, is undergoing a similar experience with its residents being dispersed to other areas. This phenomenon occurs most often in the very complex, greater urban East Los Angeles multiple barrio area.

Rural barrios, in contrast, have generally persisted through the decades, though practicing a different clique formation pattern. Because of rural isolation (mostly agricultural) and a small population, they usually had a smaller number of youths who could belong to a gang; in fact, some have only recently evolved from less formal youth groups into structured gangs. Youth workers, some of whom were from the barrio, found it easier to start social clubs and work to expend youthful energies in constructive ways. The distance separating rural barrios, some of whom were real or potential rivals, was enough to provide youth workers the space and time to periodically redirect the lives of certain cohorts. Small cohort populations often either were too ineffectual to constitute a problem or were less inclined toward gang activities. In any event, this tended to interrupt the build-up of successive numbers of cliques, thus dissipating the force of clique clusters that are found in urban barrios and made for a looser, less militant gang structure. Nevertheless, even with these qualifications, the rural barrio has persisted because conditions that generate gang behavior remain. In recent years, increases in automobile ownership and the construction of nearby freeways have tended to lessen their isolation. With the build-up of a gang tradition, they have become more like the urban barrios.

The urban and rural gangs are considered more traditional because of their longevity and socially rooted nature (Klein 1971). Occasionally, spontaneous gangs arise in the territorial interstices between barrios, especially when there are enough young males in a heretofore unclaimed area to start a new gang. Sometimes it just lasts the life of that cohort, or perhaps for several years if their strength and reputation are enough to keep attracting new members. Usually the group dies out. Suburban gangs are more likely to fit this mold. Situated in areas near established gangs, they emerged in the early 1970s, especially in inexpensive, cheaply constructed tract-home developments. The Chicano homeowners in such locations are second or third purchasers of the property who have recently migrated from other barrios, in which their children were previously exposed to gangs. Established rural barrios (which now are surrounded by suburban tracts) have become a threat to the newer suburban residents who, in reaction, have banded together to defend themselves. Thus, the suburban gangs are a spontaneous response to threatening encroachments on the part of other, rooted gangs.

Level of Involvement and Gender Roles

Individual members differ in the level and length of their involvement in the gang. Klein (1971), for example, treats these differences in level of involvement by distinguishing "hard core" and "fringe" membership. At any given time, however, the majority of the gang would be core members, although key differences among them are subsumed in such a categorization. A more discriminating taxonomy would distinguish at least four levels of involvement, which can be categorized as regular, peripheral, temporary, and situational membership.

Regular members typically join at an early age, consistently participate in gang activities, and remain active members into their twenties (sometimes later), stretching upward the age level of the barrio gang as veterano role models. Peripheral members may have the same background as the regulars or may have a moderately stable background. In any case, their participation in gang activities is inconsistent and tempered by interests in other areas. Peripheral members typically mature out of the gang by their twenties. The temporary members have reasonably stable childhoods, usually becoming involved with the gang during adolescence, and their commitment is often tenuous and subject to ready dissolution. Finally, the situational member may have either a stressful or a fairly stable background, with episodic gang behavior. These persons gravitate to the more recreational and social habits, like cruising, partying, and drinking and talking at hangouts. Situational members generally avoid gang practices of a destructive (to self or others) nature, although occasions sometimes

Table 2   Categories of Gang Member

Typical Characteristic	Regular	Peripheral	Temporary	Situational
Age at which joins gang	10-14	14-18	14-18	14-18
Age at which leaves gang	22+	20+	18-20	16-20
Involved in violence	All	All	Some	Almost none
Criminal behavior in youth*	Most	Many	Some	Almost none
Indentification with gang	Profound	Strong	Marginal	Marginal

*Except for status offenses—e.g., minor drinking alcohol, etc.

arise in which they must honor commitments to peers. Regular gang members are most committed to the gang and most prone to illegal and destructive (to self or others) behavior, but "a brush with the law" and even incarceration are common among all categories of gang members. In fact, such experiences in some cases form the impetus to avoid further gang affiliations. One 17-year-old male from Canta Ranas whom I had observed over a three-year period transformed himself from a regular to a nonmember because his older brother was involved in a shooting incident where the victim died. To unequivocally signal this shift he even changed his school and dress behavior to conventional patterns.

Within the oldest and most active barrios, smaller social clubs, sports teams, or car clubs may co-exist with the gangs, often with partly overlapping membership. Most members of such groups have largely avoided the street gang network, and gang members sometimes frown on them. Female auxiliaries exist in the gangs and other groups. One very specialized type of clique in many barrios, which Moore (1978) and the CPRP (1979, 1981) investigations have documented, consists of drug (especially heroin) users. These are comprised of remnants of cliques who have passed their prime and now associate and interact with each other to "score" drugs and/or maintain ties to a "crime partner." Members of active, younger cliques from the same barrio harbor mixed thoughts and feelings about these drug cliques. In rural barrios, historically, whole generations of youth have shifted from their predecessors' orientation to a social focus, and vice versa. In any event, most barrio gangs who are territorial and conflict oriented also value social activities, such as parties, cruising, and so on.

Barrio youth recognize the stylistic and behavioral differences among cliques. A male, 17, from Los Olivos explains why in an interview: "And we all had respect for each other. But then some got into drugs, not just pot, pills, or acid, but heroin. We had to watch and make sure they would not O.D. [overdose] or try and rip us off just to get a fix. Later we started to getting to trust each other 'cause the heroin users slowed their habits at a pace where they didn't have to steal from their own homeboys." Another male, 20, from Chino, an established, traditional barrio of multiple cliques, explains it in this way: "In the barrio, there are different types of gangs. Each one of them [cliques] have their own activities. When the barrio is calm, two different groups will get together and have a party."

The mix of behavior orientations in one clique alluded to earlier posed a different problem for those youths who had grown up in two different neighborhoods. Their loyalties were divided. As an example of this problem, an account of a male, now 27 years old, gives some insight into how to either go straight or remain true to the "*plebe*" ("plebians," i.e., the local youths in a poor neighborhood); he did both. Growing up in the eastside projects in Colton made for a lot of childhood friendships with the plebe. He and three brothers and six sisters lost their mother when he was 9 years old, and he was raised in a fairly stable home by an older married sister. He nevertheless had some adjustment problems during adolescence, especially struggling with a poor school record. His family's efforts directed him away from his boyhood chums from the eastside and toward a westside social club. He learned to identify, relate, and get along with the lower-middle- and working-class youths in the westside, but he still remained friends with the guys from the eastside. This dual association was successful because "I tried never to fight against my friends from the Projects. In order to survive, everybody had to be in a gang. If not in one, then in the other. I liked the social club we had because we raised money and did a lot of good things. I still had a good time partying, though, and getting high at the park with the plebe."

Female cliques are interesting for a number of reasons. There had always been young girls who hung around with street boys, going back to the earliest cliques. Some even joined in the drinking, getting high, and gang fighting. Even more common then (and now) were the females who belonged to and associated with social or car clubs. Recently, however, there appear to be more barrios with girls who are cholas and who regularly affiliate themselves with the street gangs (Quicker 1983; Murphy 1978).

Initially, it was considered quite improper and un-Mexican for females to publicly join—and especially avow affiliation with—a street gang. Pachucas were part of the zoot-suit experience and had their own style to complement that of the pachucos. In that respect, they, too, were rebels, but a pattern of street gang involvement had not yet developed. Uneven culture change, underclass patterns, and intergenerational street socialization, in time, all operated as new situations and conditions to affect the female role in gangs. Thus, the dialectics of multiple marginality applies to why females now are more active in street gangs. In addition to more serious problems with alcohol and drug abuse and interactions with criminal justice institutions, there is even an increase of incidents where females conduct their own gang-banging actions against rival barrio female members. To put it another way, the female gang-affiliated member of today would be considered comparable to one of the active male members of the past (e.g., 1940s); just as contemporary male gang members contrast sharply with those of the past, so too do females. Because of this deeper involvement today and as relative newcomers, they speak more freely about their lives and provide poignant accounts of barrio street dynamics. For example, a 20-year-old from East Los Angeles told me during an interview about her clique:

When I first joined there were thirty-one members. After a couple of months there were close to seventy. Our leader was this vata by the name of Mary, better known as *Payasa* [female clown]. She was a very heavyset girl who always wore straight-legged Levi's and a lot of make-up on her eyes. She was mostly all talk. She had us do all the fighting. But she was taken out of the club because she backstabbed one of the homegirls. Then we had another leader by the placaso of Huerita. She was very light complected and she wore no make-up at all. She was very tomboyish and a good leader. When she said things she would always do them. Now there is a bunch of punks in our barrio. I guess I was a punk at the time, too. They just drive around in the neighborhood and cruising in cars, and make out with any guy who wants them to. The girls I knew well are now mostly a bunch of tecatas. If they don't have a fix, they're out in the streets stealing from others to get one.

Clearly, this style parallels the male version, even approximating the hierarchical arrangement, as this 24-year-old female from a different barrio in East Los Angeles said: "It was the older veteranas who told us what to do when we were young."

The role of females in gangs is not always appreciated by the males, however. Girls may plan and cater parties, serve as sources of social and other important information, and when needed generally back up the guys. But the males always remain in command, even if force or the threat of force must be invoked. Roscoe, 19, from Santa Ana, explains: "If they don't like us messing around with chicks from another barrio, we try to keep them away before they get jumped. But if they are with other guys from another barrio, we might jump them if we don't like them. And if they like the guys, she ain't got nothing to say, man. She's just a homegirl, ya know. We're the ones who take care of the 'hood; we protect them. They ain't got nothing to say."

Another fellow, 16, from Cucamonga makes a clear distinction between the different types of cholas in uncomplimentary words:

> The girls wear a lot of make-up, and they look good, too! Most of the girls would stay home asleep, but there would be some girls that will be out all night. And those girls who are out all night, they are just like some dudes. The guys don't really trip out on them because they are a bunch of scraps. They call themselves the Queens, but we call them the vultures. There are a lot of nice girls around here, but the ones that I'm talking about now, they're all fat and ugly. A lot of the girls have cars, but those are like the girls that go to school and who have graduated, stuff like that. Girls who could keep their act straight.

In sum, contemporary street gangs are far more formalized and autonomous today. Although some palomilla characteristics have remained (especially age-grading), new and different traits mark the barrio youth groups, such as alcohol and drug use, violence, and various symbolic events and behavioral codes. Most of these developments emerged as a result of adjusting to urban street life, as more and more children sought a source of stability and identity in the gang. In time, routines and procedures for attracting and retaining recruits took over as a clique tradition unfolded. Urban, rural, and suburban differences account, in part, for variances in clique traditions, especially the presence of social and car club habits and customs. In addition to interbarrio contrasts, it was also noted that barrios had different types of gang members. The urban barrios have experienced the greatest amount of population density and pressure, and thus over the decades a rooted gang subculture emerged. The rural enclaves, now often enveloped in suburban housing, also are homes to traditional gangs. Occasionally less formal, spontaneous gangs emerge in both urban and rural areas, but generally these gangs can be found in the suburban neighborhoods in close proximity to older, rural barrios.

Gang Entrance and Exit: Initiation and Maturing-Out

Getting in and out of the gang is sometimes a very elaborate and complicated affair. For most gang members it is a process that begins early, and later ceremonies for the most part simply formalize membership; some are even able to avoid these trials. Specific rites of entrance and exit do exist, however, and, while adherence to them varies with particular gangs and individuals, these rites indicate the public nature of both membership in the gang and its dissolution and provide insights into the processes of gang identification. An initiation ceremony to induct exists in most Chicano youth gangs. The initiation is commonly perceived as an ordeal that entails a physical beating by several other gang members. In contrast, the process of maturing-out is much more complicated and involves personal, family, and institutional considerations. Gang entrance and exit ceremonies are most commonly prescribed for peripheral and temporary members, less often for regular gang members whose early experiences lock them into the gang subculture.

More than two dozen full accounts of gang initiations were collected in the course of the life history interviews conducted for this study. In the overwhelming majority of these cases, the initiation occurred when the individual was in junior high school, at the age of 12 or 13. A much smaller number were initiated in grammar school. Each of the latter came from long-established barrios and had older relatives who were already gang members. Typically, both grammar school and junior high initiates cited desire for group acceptance or to "prove oneself," that is, to demonstrate manliness, as motivation for undergoing the ritual. Only three of these initiations, each involving a temporary or situational member, occurred when the individual was in high school. Although the three lived in established barrios, they had refrained from joining until peer pressure overwhelmed them; before high school was over they had quit the group.

Most of the initiations took place somewhere in the barrio, usually near the hangout or at the home of one of the initiators. Geronimo, from Varrio Nuevo Estrada, described his initiation (which occurred when he was in junior high school):

> If you wanted to get in, one, two, three guys, you go against them, so I went up against them. It was in the front yard of one of the guys' homes. It was during the afternoon. They surrounded me. If you just stood there and let them hit you and they whip your ass and you don't do nothing, you're going to get an ass whipping for nothing. I guess I took an ass whipping to be able to back up the barrio. They would go about thirty seconds. They would count like this: one [5 seconds elapse], two [4 or 5 seconds elapse], and "what comes after two," and so on.

It was usually a spontaneous affair. A few were initiated at a party when most of the initiators were under the influence of alcohol or other substances. One 18-year-old from White Fence, who had grown up in the barrio, recalled his initiation at age 14:

> They came up to me at a party, all at one time. It was a big party . . . They told me if I want to get into the barrio. I said I don't know, *ese* [guy], I want to get in, but I want to think about it. They said, when you get into the barrio you have to be *trucha* [alert, prepared] for you're taking a big risk and you can get killed by anyone just by being from White Fence. I thought about it, and said: "Órale [O.K.], I'll get in." . . . It was about 2:00 in the morning. I was loaded but I knew what I was doing. I went out into the alley and eight homeboys followed me. Like, there was a big crowd, you know, a lot ran out after them, but eight of them did the thing. "Órale," one of the homeboys said, take a *trago* [a drink], ese, before you do it. I drank the rest of the bottle, about half of it. Then one of the homeboys hit me in the mouth. I kept on going for about twenty seconds, I was going head-on, throwing with one of them. Throwing mine in and they would get theirs in. All the eight guys were coming at me at the same time. I never got a second of a break for every moment was a serious hit. They downed me about four times, and I kept getting up . . . I was all fucked up, I had a broken nose and everything.

When the onlookers, especially the homegirls who by now pitied him, thought he had enough, they said, "He's a homeboy now." He shook hands with everybody to confirm the fact.

Some described the initiation as a gauntlet trial of running through two lines of gang members. For others, however, especially among members of younger contemporary cliques, it was a timed affair, from thirty seconds to two minutes, with two to eight gang members doing the pummeling. Whether a small or large group and timed or untimed, the severity of the beating was dependent on a number of other factors. If members were high at the time and decided to initiate someone, which often happened spontaneously and typically was aimed at a younger, weaker youngster, the beating could be intense and open-ended, as in the example cited above. There are even instances where a nonresident of the barrio has had to undergo a stabbing to show his mettle, as this account from the CPRP (1979) shows: "They stabbed him and they threw him into the bushes. The dudes that got him in were loaded and they were muy locos, and he kept getting up and he kept saying he was from the neighborhood. They kept getting him in and getting him out and finally they just stabbed him."

More commonly, however, the beating was merely a formality, especially for a long-term barrio resident. "When they would jump us in, they would start a fight. Some other guy jumps in, then another. They would get me down, then start hitting and kicking me, to see if I had *huevos* [balls; tough]. They're not out to really hurt you, you know, they just want to see if you can take the punches." Individuals already known as "able to take it" were accordingly subjected to briefer pro forma attacks.

Whatever the circumstance, the initiate must accept the group's determination of where and how the ordeal takes place. The beating must also be endured without complaint (although this does not preclude fighting back); the slightest whimper or other expressed sign of pain could result in rejection of membership. The initiation thus acts as a prerequisite to weed out the weak and uncommitted. Successful endurance of the ordeal also reinforces the attraction of gang membership. Even those informants who admitted to substantial trepidation prior to initiation asserted that it enhanced their desire to belong to the gang. In fact, the desire to belong, prove oneself, gain respect, and show loyalty were all intertwined with the appropriate (by gang standards) role behaviors expected of the initiate. Bloch and Niederhoffer more than two decades ago likened gang initiations generally with "puberty rites in primitive societies" and added that "we may conceive of much of gang practice and the spontaneous, informal rituals of gang behavior as arising because our culture has been unable, or has refused, to meet the adolescent's needs during a critical juncture in his life" (1958:30). In the same work they noted that, for the new member of a gang, "once having succeeded in passing through the ceremony with honor, the psychological aftermath of the experience contributes towards creating bonds of solidarity with those other initiates who have shared this vital experience with him" (p. 123).

Structurally, the barrio gang (like the gangs that Bloch and Niederhoffer discussed) exists to provide psychological support for youths who have not received adequate reinforcement from family and other social caretaker institutions. Initiation can additionally be viewed as affirming one's ethnic orientation. Some of the street solidarity and ethnic loyalty is based on defiance of school and law enforcement authorities, which many adult residents and nearly all the resident disaffected youth consider unsympathetic to low-income Mexican barrios. Thus, the ritual also tends to affirm one's ethnic identification as well—as in showing they are "Chicano." (On a psychological level, of course, it may also satisfy sadomasochistic urges, opportunities to intimidate and coerce, and even simply a sense of excitement in aggressive, socially sanctioned combat.)

An exit rite also exists, and gang youths typically maintain that, just as one must be "jumped in" to gain membership, he must be "jumped out" to leave. A Latino from Echo Park reported what happened after one bad experience after another—fights, numerous confrontations, harmful drugs, family rancor over his activities—led to a day when he decided to exit: "When I told my friends about it, three of them beat me up. There are two ways to get out of the gang: by fighting, or chickening out. I decided to fight and not get hassled later on. If you run out, then you could be hassled anytime, anywhere, by anyone, even other gangs' members." Immediately after this "jumping-out" ceremony his mother sent him to live with an older brother in the suburban community of Claremont, to get him away from the barrio.

In fact, however, such exit rites appear to be limited to situational and temporary members who have expectations of continued contacts with gang members. Such members who do not expect continued contact may simply quit, for example, upon leaving school. A male, 19, from Pomona put it rather succinctly: "You have to grow out of it. When you leave high school, you don't see the same people unless you want to." He had an easier time of it than other barrio-raised members, for he was a situational member whose level of low commitment provided him with enough space to withdraw unceremoniously.

Most members of the gang simply mature-out. Maturing-out is simply explained as a process of gradual disaffiliation and breaking away from the gang (Cartwright et al. 1975; Matza 1964). Matza (pp. 28-29), in addressing the broader notion of "delinquent drift," notes how maturing-out operates in the process. Individuals who drift from conventional to delinquent behavior are common in society. However, those who become locked into a delinquent pattern become recognized as deviants. Regular gang members (and some peripherals) would fall into this category (as deviant actors) but the temporary and situational ones would not. Although the latter might on occasion commit a deviant act, they usually experience a life-turning event, mature-out, and pursue a conventional life. Matza also takes great care to distinguish between the two: "The delinquent as drifter more closely approximates the substantial majority of juvenile delinquents who do not become adult criminals than the minority who do. Some delinquents are neurotically compulsive and some in the course of their enterprise develop commitment. These flank the more ordinary delinquent on either side, and during situations of crisis perhaps play crucial leadership roles ... The delinquent drifter is less likely to command our attention and we have partially ignored him" (pp. 29-30).

Most of those who join the gang fall into the drifter category. Maturing-out for many of them is more like "wising-up" real fast to avoid problems. Temporary and situational members leave the gang early but during their tenure are able to mediate between the pro- and antisocial gang activities. The peripheral members, and some regular ones, generally take longer to mature out. Moore (1978) and her CPRP (1979, 1981) collaborators have stressed what effect a good job or a good girlfriend (or wife) can have in stabilizing a gang person's life (1979:95); such "life-turning events" often provide an impetus for maturing-out. They also noted that the older gang members were more likely to rethink their lives after extended periods of incarceration. One male, 40, from Carmelas, whom I have known for twenty years, was able to do just that for over ten years, but somehow underclass pressures (e.g., unstable job history and social instability) took their toll and led him to revert to previous street behavior—he now is in San Quentin.

Violent incidents turn numerous youths against further participation. Two male members of Ontario, one 18 and the other 19, carefully selected gang activities for participation, but regular members sometimes pressed them into fights with other barrios. These and other experiences were enough to speed their departure right after high school—one got a job and the other started college. A female, 17, from the same barrio, reported her experience: "A fight broke out and one guy pulled out a gun. Ralph, the guy that we gave a ride to, was shot and he died. I remember once sitting at the corner with some friends and a white chick was walking by. It was at the time of the riot at school so naturally we jumped her. I felt sorry for her because we left her all bloody. I began to think about what I was doing with my life."

One male, 30, from a spontaneous gang in Buena Park, spoke about how the group broke up, or "matured-out" together. After a big gang fight with a rival barrio in Anaheim, the members began to lose interest in joining together. "The last gang fight," a bloody affair according to the story, became a turning point to hasten their maturation; jobs, marriage, and the armed services, of course, preceded and followed this event. (After a few years to formalize their new adult status, they regrouped to "throw block parties.")

If gang involvement continues after high school, prison is a common experience and, for some, a catalyst to disinvolvement. For example, a male, 21, from San Pedro had experienced numerous fights and had used heroin but did not leave the gang. However, after doing three and one-half years in prison for a second-degree murder offense, he became convinced that the gang life was "dead." Upon his release from the prison, where he had learned to be a baker, he returned to the barrio, got a good job with the bakery, and married his sweetheart. Together, they are now raising their 4-year-old son (born earlier before the prison phase) in the barrio, and he avoids the gang.

In many accounts, the influence of a mate was clear. June Bug, a male, 18, from Ontario, was quite adamant about his girlfriend's role, although her influence is combined with his own personal reservations: "She really kept me from going sour and hanging out with all of the vatos . . . She really made me what I am right now . . . She made me do my homework, she would go and help me read."

Next in importance to a mate is family influence, and sometimes these factors are combined. A couple of females, 17 and 19, respectively, are interesting in this regard. Throughout their gang involvement (both in Ontario high school), they regularly were admonished by family members. In the instance of the 17-year-old, it was her mother who eventually prevailed upon her but not until after she had been in several fights and group attacks on rival girls. One day her mother mentioned that one of the victims was a sister of a boy the daughter admired; and as the retelling goes: " 'Remember the first girl you beat up, as if you and those cheap tramps were her parents—well, that is Ronnie's stepsister, you fool.' 'No sir;' I yelled, 'or he would've told me that day.' 'Maybe you didn't give him a chance,' she said. All I could think about is when we jumped her, and how she must've hurted. I cried with my mom and begged her for forgiveness. I quit the gang right after."

The other young lady, 19, had a somewhat problematic life—both parents died in an auto accident—and eventually wound up with an aunt and four cousins, a household with a strong family base. During late adolescence, she began to associate with gang friends and spent a lot of time with them, during and after school. While the usual social activities and partying occupied most of her time, she also participated in delinquent acts. Once she was caught shoplifting and had to be picked up by her aunt, returning home to a stormy family session. She said: "This time my cousins Frankie and Gilbert got a hold of me. They never let go until they knew I would straighten up. Man, they gave me a real good one. Since then I only take things like make-up and nail polishes from the market." Although not exactly an abrupt turnabout in behavior, she gradually left the gang associates that were making it easy to get into trouble.

The larger portion of gang exit stories reflect a combination of reasons or series of events. Some of the most noteworthy have a succession quality to them, where one event after another adds to a growing awareness of the problems associated with their gang membership. This was reflected in the life history of Henry (as fully noted in Chapter 4), a temporary member, when he "started thinking about how bad things were," and "would work at anything to stay off the streets." Exiting in this phased-out manner was particularly the case with individuals who still lived in the barrio.

Gang Styles: Cholo Dress and Body Adornment, Speech, Demeanor, Partying, and Car Culture

Group affiliation often entails embracing the external signs that characterize the group. Gangs, like many youth groups, are notorious for encouraging their members to dress, talk, and act in a certain way to show that they belong and identify with peers. Such behavior serves a number of purposes. Aside from the obvious show of group conformity, gang members also have practical reasons for adopting this image. Clothing is usually the first signal that novitiates send out to advertise their new social and personal identity.

George Barker (1950, 1972) has long reminded us that the cultural and linguistic differences among Mexican Americans stemmed in large measure from the effects of Anglo-American culture contact. Particularly noteworthy was the tendency among the American-born youth to establish their own group cultural style (at first known as pachuco) and to "correspondingly reject the conventional social standards of the Anglo and Mexican communities" (p. 46).

Cholo Dress. It is fairly certain that the cholo subcultural experiences helped produce the clothing styles. As with other low-income people who try to stretch their dollars, the cholos have sought to find dependable, comfortable, durable, and reasonably priced clothing; even the expensive shirts and shoes are recognized as long-wearing and lasting. Cost considerations have also influenced the cholos to limit the wardrobe to simple and interchangeable items. One good shirt and several T-shirts and pants of the same make and color are usually almost all that are needed for a wardrobe. Borrowing and exchanging clothes among friends, especially of shirts that have a different plaid design and color, is a way to expand one's wardrobe and is a fairly common intragroup habit.

The cholo style began about the same time that the group was recognized as an urban problem source. The perpetuation of the style stems in part from present youngsters' desiring to maintain the traditions of the past; in fact, the recent hit play (1978) and movie (1981) *Zoot Suit* and popular barrio-oriented magazines like *Low Rider* and *Q.V.* have generated renewed interest in these styles, with some shops, like El Pachuco in Fullerton, specializing in such wear. Thus, along with the functionality of the clothing style, barrio tradition plays a significant role. It is a way to identify with the past, one's roots so to speak, by dressing like someone from the past.

Although the style has undergone slight variations and additions, it nevertheless has remained relatively unchanged through the decades. Khaki pants, for example, became fashionable after World War II and the Korean War. It was the youngsters' way to identify with older brothers and relatives who had been in the armed services, especially those serving in such elite bodies as the paratroopers and marines. Although other pant styles (e.g., "counties" or "Frisco" bluejeans, a carry-over from county detention facilities) have also been used, it is the khakis that have persisted. Today, the pants are "stylish" if they are large and baggy (some even call them "baggies"), heavily starched with a crease that wearers try not to bend, and worn with a long and unrolled hem hiding the heels of the shoes. Ironically, and perhaps predictably, the pants style stemmed from public sources—military and penal; there is even a cut-off, below-the-knees jeans style and, lately, other multicolored styles that have been introduced by youth just out of a penal institution.

Shirt and shoe styles have remained remarkably stable over time. Creatively combining two types of shirts from the 1940-1950 period (e.g., long sleeve nonvariated gabardine and short-sleeved plaid "Sir Guys"), the present-day cholo relies on the long-sleeved plain shirt, known generically as "pendletons." Worn with all buttons fastened shirt tails outside, often in an oversized fit, the pendletons usually are darker hued and complement the lighter tan khakis. If the weather is warm, a person might methodically drape the shirt over a forearm and instead sport a bright white crew-neck T-shirt or tank top undershirt. Shoes are usually of two kinds: the long, tapered toe Imperials, similar to the Florsheim french-toes of earlier decades (but less expensive), and either Hush Puppies or deck shoes, known as "winos." Imperials are kept highly polished, and with the starched khakis and clean T-shirt or pendleton, a cholo shows a great deal of pride in dress appearance. Trench coats are not as common as before, but one still observes cholos who wear them.

Hair styles and head adornments have also contributed to the distinctiveness of the cholo. Similar to other prison-life influences, the current hair style is shortly cropped, about one-half to an inch of hair, combed straight back, and neatly trimmed around the ears and neck to affect a rather conservative appearance reflective of youth camp and prison requirements; sometimes a hair net is worn to train unruly hair to stay down. Earlier styles were longer, especially during the pachuco "greasy-kid-stuff" era and to a lesser degree the 1960s "hippie" period. Head adornments, beginning with broad-brimmed fedoras of the 1940s, have always been a major feature of dress. While some individuals might occasionally sport such hats, the present custom is to wear a stingy-brim version or a watchcap beanie and baseball cap, depending on personal resources and tastes. Since the 1960s Chicano movement emphasized indigenous customs, it has become fashionable to wear bandanas around the head, much like a "Barrio Warrior" (Frias 1982); lately, earrings also have become commonplace.

Young females in every barrio have also taken up this style and with slight variations have fashioned a chola appearance, especially for those who identify with the gang. Obviously, some dress items differ; blouses and female T-shirts and polo shirts replaced the male types, and cords and regular jeans joined the "baggies" and khaki pants wear. The manner of arranging the hair has remained rather traditional, in that Mexican women appear, beginning in the 1940s at least, to prefer long, natural hair. Cholas favor this natural look, as their tresses flow in long strands down their back and the sides of their head. Facial make-up, especially around the eyes, is quite a different story, as a lot of mascara and white shadow base paint are the custom. Long, fake eyelashes and overly plucked eyebrows with new thin eyebrows drawn in higher on the forehead stand out in the white eye shadow background that covers all of the area around the eyes—from the bottom of the eyes to the eyebrows, and from the corner of each eye to the temple region. This "peacock-hued eye shadow beneath thin, high eyebrows," as one observer said (Morrison 1983), is an integral part of the chola front. Dark, heavily applied lipstick complements the eye make-up.

The style has become pervasive throughout Southern California, for it is the easiest cholo facet to adopt. Without thinking, talking, feeling, or acting, one can just dress up and appear to be a cholo in the eyes of observers. Some adopt the style because it is both fashionable and adaptive. In effect, it conjures up the image of a group behind you, even if you are not what you represent. There is a certain amount of security created in that pause when an observer has to think about your social ties. It often works as a deterrent. However, it can also operate as a challenge, especially to a rival barrio observer.

Adoption of the dress style marks one's closer associations to the barrio gang. Of the over one-half of the youngsters who spoke of the style, most mentioned it as a source of group affiliation. Joining the gang often meant dressing like the others. There is even a change in behavior when the dress style is adopted, like when someone dons a uniform or fancy clothes, as I observed on numerous occasions with Want-to-Be's (someone who desires to be like a cholo and so dresses and acts the part). Descriptions of group thinking, behavior, and events are often punctuated by mentioning how they were dressed. A 20-year-old female from East Los Angeles said during an interview: "When we wanted revenge [for a gang retaliation] we would go to their part of town in our Levi's and khakis really creased and a boyfriend's pendleton. We thought we were fancy. But nobody could whip our ass." For most, then, dress style aids group identification. However, some individuals were very flexible about shifting to other dress styles when a new image was required. This was a way of managing their social front when they had another purpose in mind. An El Hoyo 16-year-old male made this point quite clear in an interview, even though he was a regular gang member: "But this girlfriend I have isn't a chola. When I go over to my girlfriend's house, I dress regular, with slacks and a dress shirt, and walk regular, without trying to be a chingón."

Wizard, a regular gang member (whose life history case was noted earlier), exhibited the same flexibility: "I used to wear football jerseys and things like that to look not like a cholo, but to look more respectable . . ."

Having undergone the choloization process early in life, there was no question that these males were recognized and accepted as cholos. Changing their dress, for them, meant changing social roles, especially to confuse observers. Changing dress styles can also be understood as a matter of survival: one can remain incognito when visiting a girlfriend or committing a crime or, as in the cases of Latinos and some Chicanos on the periphery of cholo life, avoid trouble by giving the appearance that one is "trouble." One 18-year-old male from Ontario, however, describes how an otherwise normal youth social activity can be tainted by appearance: "Dressing like a bad vato doesn't pay off because to every party and dance you go it seems that someone always has to hit you up . . . . they treat you like you are from a different world."

Clothes help create this different world. However, other gestural and demeanor patterns also reflect the cholo style. Though cholo attire is important and comprises a large proportion of the total social image, it must be examined in the context of other image characteristics.

Nicknames, Tattoos, and Placas. Body adornments in the form of tattoos are a worldwide practice and in recent decades have become a common enough occurrence for street youth in American cities. Explanations for this phenomenon are varied—adolescent body concerns, peer conformity, and hidden sadomasochistic desires—but in the Chicano case it appears to largely revolve around personal and social issues. The personal nickname and barrio name that make up the tattoo reflect this reality. Nicknames are created and assigned by fellow gang members to signify acceptance, and a person who places a tattoo on his or her body (nickname and barrio) confirms the alliance. Often there are public "tattoos" in the form of *placas* (literally, plaques, but used to indicate graffiti) on walls and fences to publicize a person's affiliation and commitment (Poirier 1982). The use of tattoos and placas to demonstrate personal identity in the gang is, thus, a gesture of multiple origins.

Nicknames, or stylized regular names, are often the centerpiece of personal tattoos and public graffiti, a habit often associated with gangs (Bloch and Niederhoffer 1958:99). In part, it is the adolescent's way to capture and caricature peer quirks and by the naming make them accepted and normal; it's as if poking fun publicly works to destigmatize a funny or odd personal quality. Although a nickname may be acquired earlier, it usually comes in junior high when gang affiliations materialize. While it affirms group membership, it also grants personal anonymity. According to some gang researchers, self-image problems are at the root: ". . . influences convey to the adolescent that he is a person of very little worth. It is hardly surprising that he then seeks a more favorable definition of himself" (Cartwright et al. 1975:66). In some ways, a nickname allows a person to lay aside a fragmented ego and take on an ego created in the barrio.

As in other barrios, members in one early klika of an East Los Angeles gang also used and are referred to by their regular names; some have a diminutive form, like Juanito and Tu-Tu. The sources of nicknames can be separated into two basic categories: personal appearances and quirks.

Personal appearance nicknames (with explanations) include:
  Chaparro (Shorty)
  Trokitas (Truck, shaped like one)
  Freddie Narizón (Freddie Big Nose)
  Gorilla (pronounced the Spanish way)
  Huero (light or white skin, spelled the cholo way)
  Midnite (either because of dark skin, or stays up late)
  Chuco (dresses and acts cool, like a pachuco)
  Orejón (big ears, or eavesdropper)
  Tony Fatbox (fat and boxlike body)
  Fish (face resembles fish)
  Bobby Gordo (Bobby Fatso)

Some with an ethnic twist:
  Philip Flip (Filipino)
  Black Phillip
  Chilino (Chilean)

Personal quirk nicknames include:
  Rudy Bubble Gum
  Lefty
  Chesshound (likes to play chess)
  Tony Spring (good at geting bail, springing guys)
  Deep Purple (likes song of the same name, also dark skin)

Some nicknames have multiple meanings, such as, Hando (from cholo word *jando*, meaning money, but also someone who always has funds); Sapito (from Sapo, lucky or chance, or Frog, but also diminutive, meaning little one); Ruco (old man, but also wise counselor); and Black Bart (bearded, but also good robber like historical character). Youths aspiring to the esteem of former renowned gang members may adopt that individual's nickname, prefixing it with "Li'l" (i.e., Little), as in Li'l Crow or Li'l Wino.

Nicknaming provides avenues for proving commitment and unwavering group loyalty. An indelible imprint, like a tattoo, is like a barrio imprimateur, locking a person in for what the group seemingly considers life. Members wear their tattoos with pride and gain a certain amount of status and adulation from barrio onlookers, especially siblings and younger individuals who look up to them. Often one's level of gang identity can be gauged by the amount and type of tattoo. Some might only place a small dot (•) or cross (†) on their hand, between the thumb and forefinger, while others, especially the committed veteranos, might cover large parts of the body with a very elaborate art form. (Many of the latter have a practical reason for this, as tattoos help hide injection "marks" when they are "using.")

The symbolism of the tattoo is also expressed in the graffiti on public walls and buildings, that is, the placaso (graffiti) is a nickname, barrio, and klika signature. Usually stylized, the tattoos vary from professional to homemade. Similarly, the quality of graffiti differs as to number of items, size, degree of artistic ingenuity, and type of painting/drawing material used. Although the public views graffiti as an example of antisocial, delinquent defacement of public and private property, the activity is perceived somewhat differently by gang members themselves. Sometimes romantic liaisons still appear (Freddie y Stella) and recently sociopolitical slogans and causes were common, but most graffiti is gang related.

At one level, it is a way to declare territorial dominance. Gang members proudly put their placas in their barrio, in areas that are being contested with neighboring rival barrios, or in the enemy barrio itself, as a form of boasting much like Plains Indians' "counting coup." At another level, as many interviewed members have verified and I have confirmed in cruising with them, the placas are a way to gain attention and recognition from the general public—"I always wonder what people think of when they ride by and see the name 'Puppet' there. Do they think of me?" And there are the barrio youth interested in personal matters—"I know the guys from that barrio know who I am. They've seen my placas in their neighborhood." For all these reasons, placas are usually quite accessible to the public view as the writers place them near major roads and street frontage structures. (This fact contrasts with Robert George Reisner's [1968] explanation in his book *Graffiti*, where he maintains that writers put messages in undetected places that only reach a limited number of viewers.) The prideful boasting of the placas also accounts for the frequency with which rival gang members cover them over or, more frequently, append written insults to them.

The placas vary in stylistic devices (especially over time) and are encoded in current barrio idioms. In general, however, the message in the graffiti is direct and pointed toward other gang members, who will be well acquainted with the conventions employed. The following personal example is one type of message, with the definition added for clarification:

EL = The (*El* is masculine, *La* is feminine; in cholo speech, the article is often used with first names, as it is with personal titles)

PEGLEG = PEGLEG (nickname)

DE = From

32nd = Gang name (32nd Street)

-R- = We're the best (*rifamos*)

C/S = Jointly means: There is nothing you can do about it; don't touch; or anything you do to this, twice to you (*con safos*).

One other barrio example would be:

Los NEiGBoRHooD = Gang (*los neighborhood*)

To-TAL = United (*total*)

ControZZA = Controls (*controlla*)

Such messages, obviously, constitute an extension of face-to-face challenges and often serve to aggravate tensions among rival gangs.

Although much of the gang graffiti is crudely put together (especially insults written over the original claims), not infrequently the placas display linguistic invention and aesthetic creativity. They are likely to be found on shop and business walls, fences, bridges, apartment houses, and private garages. Although sacred objects are generally considered unmarkable, the prohibition is not fully honored, as is clear from the placas covering many local churches in Los Angeles. Generally, barrio and nonbarrio residents frown on the graffiti. Some barrios have had programs to eliminate or curb the proliferation of "eyesores." One way was to paint historical or cultural murals, popular since the 1960s Chicano movement (Zucker 1978), on surfaces the gang members would then refrain from *plaqueando*. Many of these murals, however, have by now been altered substantially by graffiti.

Cholo Kinesics. As Haviland (1980:102) has noted, "kinesics is a system of postures, facial expressions, and bodily notions which convey messages." Like other subcultures, the cholo subculture has a distinctive body language. The messages that are conveyed are direct and simple and usually emanate from the facial and bodily demeanor of the individual; the eyes, mouth, and hands are particularly demonstrative. The sometimes stoic, even sullen, cholo kinesics usually portray a posture of being in control of the situation. Such an attitude probably evolved to assuage and manage the traumatic and stressful life experiences, especially the endemic fears engendered by street pressures. This attempt to gain a sense of personal efficacy becomes a particularly important task during the adolescent's age/sex role clarification phase.

Movement is generally methodical, deliberate, and smooth, whether walking out of the front door, pulling a pack of cigarettes out of a front shirt pocket and getting the cigarette out to meet the match, passing out beer to comrades, or sizing up a new group of people with a steady gaze. A walk to the corner, for example, especially when one is alone, will typically be at a leisurely gait, with stiffly postured shoulders and head leaning very slightly back, and eyes fixed forward.

Proxemic behavior is also stylized. Interpersonal encounters are typically characterized by participants stopping short of arm's length from each other and staring directly toward one another, to signify readiness to meet a potential challenge. Shortly, one participant will speak or simply step away calmly, with a last sideward glance to indicate disinterest but continued readiness. Stepping directly toward the other, however, is to issue the awaited challenge.

Gesturing is also common. Head movements often serve to punctuate other facial expressions: the mouth's corners downturned and the head slightly jerked back to indicate, "What's going on?"; the eyes motioning in the direction of a person or object and the head nodding in the same direction to show concern or interest, like "Who or what is that?"; or the hands with the index finger and thumb, like a gun, pointed and directed to a person or object that is negatively sanctioned or has a *leva* (social avoidance) thrown on it, with the head held down, eyes avoiding object, to complement the message.

Sometimes a hand, eye, or mouth movement, or a combination thereof, is the sole gesture, but more generally verbal messages accompany it. As an illustration, a gesture relaying one's fearlessness or fearfulness can be conducted with one hand and fingers that approximate human physiology. For indicating courage, the hand and fingers are cupped as if holding a heavy ball and sagged slightly downward, accompanied by the phrase "*¡Tiene huevos!*" (He has balls). For showing anxiety or apprehension, the hand and fingers, with the thumb meeting the fingers, are formed as a cone with the fingers and thumb simulating a moving body aperture (a twitching rectum) and the phrase uttered is, "*¡Está escamado!*" (He's afraid).

Much of the cholo physical presence revolves around managing inner psychic tension. Although early childhood was a tearful, painful experience for many, it must be forgotten and replaced by a more forebearing adolescent and young adult demeanor. The stoic attitude is especially useful in assuaging feelings of fear. Regular gang members, as creators and carriers of the subculture, are much more proficient at this, with peripheral and other fringe members following in that order. The projection of this image is sometimes undertaken with the expectation of an audience, as if in guarded preparation for any mistakes that would indicate a weak link to observers. For many peripheral members, as noted, it is a way of disguising personal apprehension and trepidation by taking on group-sanctioned mannerisms.

Cholo Speech. Among the most remarkable aspects of the cholo subculture is the development of its unique forms of speech. This linguistic phenomenon is widely characterized as a result of strains and stresses in the acculturation process: "Pidgins arise as makeshift adaptations, reduced in structure and use, no one's first language; creoles are pidgins become primary languages. Both are marginal, in the circumstances of their origin, and in the attitudes towards them on the part of those who speak one of the languages from which they derive" (Hymes 1971:3). Carey McWilliams (1968) noted the southwestern United States cultural milieu in which this creativity blossomed: "It is in the speech of the city gangs, 'the pachuco patois,' that the attempt to fuse the two languages is most clearly apparent. . . . Anglicizing Spanish and Hispanicizing English as it suits their purpose and often coining an expression of their own."

Contemporary cholos reflect somewhat similar historical conditions and experiences, which create this type of language style (R. Sánchez 1983). In large part, this speech style is merely a carry-over from the early pachuco days when the words were first concocted. In fact, much of the word tradition has been lost through the generations, for it was much richer and varied in its earlier form, much as the pachuco lifestyle has also changed. Language usage back then was much more bilingual (or trilingual, if one includes the patois) (Griffith 1948), thus creating a more productive cultural crucible for word invention. Today barrio gang talk is mostly English, and the degree of Spanish and cholo terms that are spoken is dependent on the tradition and generational history of the barrio; in a fashion, it is one way to show loyalty and allegiance to remnants of Mexican culture or, more basically, "us" against "them."

The association between talking like a cholo and group identity and membership is clear. Many individuals indicated in interviews that they actually shifted their speech pattern to conform to group expectations when the situation warranted; and I observed this phenomenon on several occasions. Especially noteworthy is how communication in this manner occurred when outsiders—for example, various law enforcement and criminal justice authorities—were around, much as if the group required a secret code to shield its members from the intrusions of untrustworthy strangers. Many words, of course, refer to group-related features. In addition to the constant use of exclamatory phrases like ¡Órale! (Hey! Hello!), ese or esa (say, you, he, or she), and vato or vata (guy or chick), there was regular mention of barrio (their neighborhood) networks or allegiances. Friends and associates are called by their first name or nickname, but the use of other socially bonding utterances, like camarada, carnal, vato, or homeboy, is also quite common. An age cohort in the gang is designated a klika, as noted. Both major ethnic groups from whom the cholo style derived are now considered outsiders and are given racial epithets rather than ethnic names: Anglos are called gabachos (with sometimes a long emphasis on the middle syllable of the word for special opprobrium), while Mexican nationals are referred to as chuntaros or "chunts." This attitude toward Anglos and Mexicans tends to confirm their own in-group solidarity as cholos. Other terms often allude to group activities, such as getting locote (being drunk, high, and crazy or acting that way), becoming trucha (alert), throwing chingazos (fighting, throwing blows), showing cora (heart, compassion), and declaring rifamos (we rule). Much of the usage of phrases like vato loco (crazy dude) and placaso (graffiti writing of ego and barrio name on buildings and walls) also is group centered. Other words for objects, such as lisa (shirt), vaisa (hands), calcos (shoes), pisto (liquor), cantón (house), and so on, are regularly used, but the words that hint at group associations and the strengthening of social ties provide particular insight to the functions of cholo speech.

Dictionaries of barrio (Fuentes and López 1974) and pachuco (Serrano 1979) words have been compiled, so there is no need to elaborate here on the working, contemporary terminologies in usage. The words and their usage stemmed from the choloization process initially and in subsequent decades have become another facet of the cholo "image." For individuals and barrios that are presently still in the midst of choloization, such as Tercera Flats (Third Street Flats) in East

Los Angeles, the image is shaped by living conditions. But adoption of cholo talk, similar to adopting the dress style, is also a general requisite for group membership, especially aiding the identity-conscious fringe gang members. The use of the patois helps reify gang solidarity, even if only a few choice words are known.

Cholo "Partying." "Partying," to a cholo, means a number of things—although its varied meanings almost always imply that, first, homies (homeboys from the barrio) are involved and that, second, some form of intoxicants are available. The number of participants (ranging from two or three to dozens) and the types of inebriants (from beer and/or wine to hard drugs) may vary, but the essence of partying remains the same. The context of partying can be very casual—a few guys sitting around, talking, and getting high—or more formally structured. The more common casual variety may involve gatherings on a front porch or lawn, in a car (moving or parked), at a local hangout, or at a park. The outdoor casual gatherings often include one or more individuals playing a *lira* (guitar) and the others joining in singing old Mexican *canciones* (rancheras, boleros, corridos, and other rural, folksy tunes).

While these casual get-togethers sometimes include females, they are more often all male. (Gang girls similarly gather with one another, although substance use tends to be slightly less intense, musical instruments are rare, and the songs they sing are more apt to be "Oldies-but-Goodies," that is, music derived from the black "rhythm and blues" tradition and Chicano creations based on it.) Partying between the sexes usually involves slightly more structured settings, such as house parties or neighborhood dances. Neighborhood baptisms, birthdays, weddings, and anniversaries also occasion parties to celebrate the events, and gang members often mix with neighbors and relatives from the barrio at these events. At the predominantly cholo house parties and dances, dancing is typically a slow, rhythmic rocking from side to side by couples closely embraced; music with a quicker tempo generally thins out the dancers on the floor. In some of the more isolated and Mexican-oriented barrios, canciones, rather than "Oldies-but-Goodies," will be played; both types of music evoke sentimental moods and romantic ideas. At the more generalized family-and-friends gatherings in which cholos mix, elders' choice of music is apt to prevail—"Tex-Mex" or swing music is commonly heard.

Parties—in part because of the heavy drug and alcohol consumption—often are marred by fights. Since gang members often carry knives or even handguns to such events—especially outside their own barrio—the violence can frequently occasion serious injury or even death. This is especially the case when members of different barrio gangs are invited to the same celebrations or when gang members "crash" an affair to which they were not invited.

Car Culture: The Cholo Style. The automobile is a focal concern of youth culture. Chicano "low-riding" evolved in the context of American adaptation to youth patterns (Twillen and Koren 1978; West 1976). The cholo image of a controlled, calm, and cool demeanor has affected this style, and I particularly enjoyed excursions on the streets observing it. The car style is distinctive, too, with lowered rear ends (or all around), either permanent or temporary (with hydraulic lifts of the type that raise or lower truck tailgates). This lowered vehicle can be an older 1940s or more recent 1970s model (usually a General Motors vehicle, especially a Chevrolet); it may be regular in appearance or highly decorated (multicolored paint jobs, sparkling wheels, rich leather or velvet upholstery, and so on). The image of the driver is a slumped-back low silhouette and the drive is smooth and slow. There is both form and function to low-riding, for it is a look and an operation. It has been suggested that Chicanos fashioned this style to demonstrate their difference from Anglos and "Anglicized" ways (West 1976:76). Although unintentional, there are ethnic contrasts, even though in recent years Anglos have borrowed from the Chicano variant. Most of the cholos interviewed and observed for this study considered low-riding in a positive light, as a way to socialize and court, usually when "high"; but there is also an occasional chase scene or confrontation stemming from the activity.

The first generations to participate in this car pattern were pachucos, although it was then referred to as cruising. Community and social workers attempted to redirect street youth by establishing car/social clubs in the 1950s, a practice still common in some gang worker programs (Sample 1984). These programs provided alternatives, and, with some inroads, these car/social clubs helped guide the pachuco tradition and formulate highly elaborate low-riding style. Great amounts of time and money are today expended on cars by such groups and a quintessentially institutionalized pattern has resulted. *Low-rider* magazine was very popular in the 1970s-1980s. To complement (or generate) such media hype, car shows and the weekend car cruising in different barrios (most clearly East Los Angeles' Whittier Boulevard, the "granddaddy" of them all, where sheriffs now block the route) add to the tradition.

Street youth find it difficult to join such costly and organized activities, even though some crossover cholos can mix with the car/social club types. Cholo low-riding, in fact, is different from the flashy "clubber" style. Cholos have a taste for a more or less informal, casual run of stock cars, due to limited resources. To them, to customize a car means renovating an older 1940-1950s model. Of course, this is in line with their penchant for tradition, such as in language and dress.

Youth car cultural patterns often entail matters of masculinity and maturation. Bloch and Niederhoffer (1958:131) have suggested the idea of the car as a *churinga*, an object or place in which an Australian aborigine's soul resides: ". . . can it be denied that the youthful owner of an automobile does not likewise put his 'heart and soul' into his car? He adjusts it, tunes it, cleans it, polishes it, communes with it, cherishes it." Cholos have infused their cars with their style, if not their hearts; and the nicknames for cars reflect this casual habit—"Earth Angel," "96 Tears," and so on.

The car has become a social instrument to aid the youths' sexual and maturity goals. Social encounters and interactions are generated in a new cultural way. The smooth, methodical walk that carries the cholo forward is repeated in the car movement. Slumping back, peering over the steering wheel and sill are all ways of turning an attitude into a practice. The vehicle's sounds must also measure up. An almost inaudible slow-moving engine is sometimes "revved up" to release a lowered-tone rumble from the dual exhaust system. The driver's cool image is thus complemented by cool sounds. With this look and sound, the car is easily managed. Street and male considerations have shaped this style. Slow driving helps human eye contact and creates opportunities for favorable responses from onlookers (eye movements, smiles, words, gestures). Social interaction becomes the raison d'être for driving, and why move quickly when it is social contacts one desires? Use of the car in this fashion increases territorial coverage and thus opportunities to meet more people, particularly members of the opposite sex. (However, regular peer interactions of both sexes are also common.) The low silhouette contributes to the male image of being deliberate in talk and gestures. Such posturing requires time, which cruising allows, and it produces expediencies for males and females to court each other.

Social interaction cruising is clearly the most important use of the car among cholos. It is also used as a private sanctuary when it is parked. Like so many other hangouts, someone's car is a regular meeting spot to talk, get high, drink, and just conduct normal social intercourse; sometimes it's stationed in the same spot almost every day.

There is a great amount of pride in owning a cruiser car. A 17-year-old male from San Gabriel, in an interview, said that his " '62 Chevy was something I was proud of. But I needed money one time and I had to sell it for $200.00. The one thing I was proud of." Putting a great amount of time and energy into cars is also a way of demonstrating pride. Several individuals whom I have observed boasted about working on engines. One 20-year-old male from Chino gave this answer to a query on why Chevrolets were so common among Chicanos: ". . . they know the engine well. Your father had a Chevy and showed you how to change the oil and how to switch engines . . . Yeah, to have a good time the guys would have a couple of beers and a whole bunch would get under the engine. They don't even have to say the make of the car, you know it's a Chevy when someone says, 'Hey, I just bought a '56 with skirts.' "

Although cruising and social interaction in one's barrio are appreciated, it is much more exciting to cruise another barrio. Doing so generates opportunities for liaisons, specifically meeting members of the opposite sex. Many a courting relationship has been initiated in this way, some even ending up as permanent dating arrangements. There are pitfalls to this courting method, however, for barrio youth groups are often extremely hostile toward any outsiders who appear to be "messing around" with one of their own (often a relative). As an example of such attitudes, a young girl, 16, from Cucamonga explained in an interview how she and her friends react to intruders: ". . . three carloads of girls from Ontario were here and gunning their motors at some of the guys at the corner. When they got to where we were at, we started stoning them 'cause they were yelling Ontario *rifamos* [we-from-Ontario-rule], so we started calling them putas and Ontario putos. Then this guy went by and we stopped him [car] and asked him to take us and chase those girls out, so we chased them out." A male, 25, from the same barrio, said: "We would go to Upland or Ontario and pick up girls and bring them to Cuca to cruise. The guys from there would chase us out, throwing bottles and rocks. But we used to do the same thing to them when they used to come to Cuca."

Interestingly, although many illegal chases, bumping incidents, and fights spin off from cruising forays, only a few of our informants reported incidents that involved other criminal activity. In one interview, a male, 19, from Chino gave this account of cruising and dealing: "We were cruising one night in my Monte Carlo looking for people to buy dope. It was a slow night, so my friend dropped me off at my girlfriend's. I let him drive the car. About a half an hour later the police pulled him over. They searched the car and found the drugs [reds and cocaine]." Generally, such stories are rare and occur more often with barrio members who have become crime oriented. Cruising, as we have seen, is definitely a social affair, even though some individuals instigate and create other goals.

Conclusion

This admixture in the car culture of stylistic elements, social activities, and, less frequent but more widely noticed, violence and criminal actions holds true in general for the subculture of the gang. Through the decades the gang subculture has established itself as an alternative coping strategy with socialization and enculturation processes of its own. Only a small percentage of the barrio youth population is attracted to it, and of that number an even smaller portion become thoroughly immersed in it, usually members of the underclass or the most marginal ones. The external reasons for the variance in involvement and participation are multiple—type and degree of family stress, amount of street socialization, peer and model influences, barrio traditions and sense of territoriality, and so on. However, there are also reasons intrinsic to the gang subculture. The fact that the gang mixes functional (i.e., palomilla) and problematic (i.e., street survival) activities informs us about the personal choices that operate in gang life. Some youngsters can largely ignore or avoid those customs that are detrimental or damaging yet still be considered (by themselves and others) a part of the gang, "someone from the barrio." Most members of a gang know, understand, and accept the personal differences within the group and thus maintain various expectations for each individual.

Usually it is outsiders, including especially law enforcement and the media, who tend to lump all members together regardless of their personal degree of gang involvement and commitment. In large part, these observers have based their assessment on the visual characteristics of the gang, particularly the dress, demeanor, and other easily practiced signs. As we have seen, there are other social and cultural dynamics that need to be considered in understanding the gang subculture. What needs to be clarified is the distinction between the cholo experience, for example, the transitional phase of being in the middle of two cultural traditions, and the varied group customs and habits that arise as a result of that experience. As noted, some patterns are quite normal and functional while others are definitely problematic, and both are found in the gang.

6. The Notorious Side of the Gang Subculture

Adolescence in America is generally a period in which individuals greatly increase their efforts toward independence from parental authority (and by extension from adult authority) and, at the same time, intensify bonds with their peers. It is characterized by a considerable level of confusion concerning the worthiness of competing norms and values and is typically accompanied by increased experimentation with previously proscribed behavior. Teenagers are thus apt to spend less time with their parents and more in the company of their peers, often engaged in adventuresome behavior, such as, drinking and drug use and excursions to locales conducive to flaunting social norms. Not infrequently, they may encounter a "brush with the law" or conflict with other youths in such settings. For the most part, such behavioral rebellion is resolved in young adulthood by acceptance of career and family responsibilities, and the norms and values that reinforce them.

In the context of barrio marginality, Chicano youngsters are apt to initiate such adventures at an earlier age, engage in them with greater intensity, and—in many instances—continue some of the behavioral patterns for a longer time. For those with the most multiply marginal backgrounds, that is, those most likely to become regular members of the barrio gang, these tendencies are often extreme. They tend to wholeheartedly embrace such deviant behavior as heavy drinking and drug abuse, fighting, and committing other crimes that bring them into recurrent and prolonged contact with the criminal justice system (Jackson and McBride 1985); and, for many of them, young adulthood is a period in which they intensify and habituate such behavior, rather than decrease it in favor of accepting normal adult responsibilities.

Drinking and Drugs

Drinking alcoholic beverages and using various drugs and chemical substances have become taken for granted as aspects of gang life. Individual members vary in their preference of substances and level of consumption, but drinking and drugs act as a "social lubricant" to facilitate the broadening, deepening, and solidifying of group affiliations and cohesiveness. Partying, cruising, and park and barrio hangout gatherings usually involve such liquid refreshments and substances to "kick-back," relax, talk, and laugh. It is generally a group setting that marks one's first extended contact with liquor or drugs. Drug and alcohol usage often facilitates gang youths' release from their felt obligations to social mores and thus increases their willingness to participate in other criminal acts, especially if such behavior seems to help them prove their loyalty and commitment to the group. Most drinking and drug usage, however, is undertaken simply as part of a desire to party, let one's hair down, and enjoy more relaxed social intercourse with friends.

Among those gang youths whose life histories I collected, the average age of first continuing use of intoxicants is about 12.7 years, with the youngest being 8 and the oldest 16. Generally, the regular gang members began while still in elementary school, and the peripheral and temporary members started in junior high school. In most cases it was difficult to determine the sequence of particular substances' usage, because alcohol and other substance usage was initiated at about the same time. With different generations, there were different drugs, mostly of the cheap variety. However, for those who started earliest, glue and/or paint sniffing, and sometimes the use of pills, clearly preceded the initiation of alcohol and/or marijuana consumption. Drinking beer or wine begins in earnest in at least the first year of junior high school. Liquor consumption is a decidedly group affair, and large bottles of wine (quarts, half gallons, or gallons, usually of cheaper brands) and quarts of beer are sometimes passed around in almost ritualistic fashion.

By the age of 15 or 16, extensive polydrug use is common. Regular gang members generally move from one set of substances to another in their teens and often begin to subsequently specialize in heroin. Peripheral and temporary members, on the other hand, are more likely to be marijuana users with occasional resort to other substances— seldom heroin, however. Most do not engage extensively in drug sales; of the few whom I interviewed who had become drug "dealers" at one time or another, regular and peripheral members are equally represented. However, the regulars tended to "deal" heroin; the peripherals, marijuana.

For some of the regular gang members who went on to a pattern of prolonged and expanded use, drug usage started with chemicals bought at (or stolen from) public stores. Geronimo, 16, from Varrio Nuevo, talked about sniffing substances at age 10: "It was gold or silver spray can paint. I remember one guy, he turned me on to it, and ever since then I started sniffing. We used to get it at Pep Boys, right near Beverly and Atlantic. We'd put it in a plastic bag. You'd get the bag, spraying it all over with paint so that it's all drippy, cold, and wet. You just get it and start breathing. It lasts about 30 seconds; when you're coming down you just get more and more." Another male interviewee, 19, from Varrio Norwalk started sniffing substances early but later turned to *yesca* (marijuana). However, "it wasn't a constant habit, but as I got older, 17 or 18, there was nothing else around, no pay or nada, so I just wanted to get locote quick. I did it about 7 or 8 times within a time period. It gets you all *tonto* [dumb] and shit. Smoking yesca, you end up, it gets you in a good mood so you can be *firme* [together, bonded] with your own boys. But sometimes when we sniff, too, something funny happens, or like when I sniff, I hear funny noises. You hear that same sound even after it stops. You know, zzzzzzz."

Marijuana is perhaps the most common drug used by gang members, and the habit usually begins in junior high (although some start earlier). Often marijuana use among regular gang members comes after experimentation with glue and spray paint, although there is some use of pills (both uppers and downers), too, in this phase. An increasingly common drug, in some ways a substitute for "downers" (reds), is PCP, or angel dust (polvo, in the cholo parlance). One of the popular ways to get "dusted" is to dip cigarettes, specifically the Sherman brand, into a liquid form of PCP, allowing it to dry before smoking it. It is known as a "SuperCool" or "Sherm." The traditional urban gangs are generally much more indulgent in the use of PCP, although outlying areas like Cucamonga use it, too. By middle or late junior high, at least some of the individuals have tried heroin. (With the regular use of heroin, the individual is probably headed for a different role in the barrio; he becomes a tecato, who is less frequently involved in gang activities, particularly the more social ones. However, this develops later. Some individuals at this time begin to turn more toward criminal activities for money to support this habit.)

Several accounts of polydrug users who started in elementary school and went on to try heroin were collected. An 18-year-old from South Fontana gave this representative explanation.

At the age of eight, I started smoking weed with my uncle. I liked the feeling of being loaded. It was a different feeling than everyday life. From that time, I started smoking two or three times a week with my uncle, or whenever I could get away from the house. Then one day my uncle turned me on to some whites. I liked them, so I took them every time I could get my hands on them. He also turned me on to reds, but I didn't dig on them too much. Later I got started on acid and sniffing. The vatos used to talk about it, so I tried it for myself. In the ninth grade I went to a party and got all wasted on pills, sniffing, smoking weed, and drinking. I almost passed out of an overdose, so I said no more for me. I stopped getting wasted. In the tenth grade, I was about 15, when I shot up [i.e., with heroin], after telling myself that I wasn't going to get wasted again. That really messed me all up.

Of the youths that I interviewed, most who used heroin were simply "chipping"—incipient users, who hadn't as yet developed a strong need for the drug. The 18-year-old above, for example, reported that he had not tried heroin again since age 15. Those who go on to become tecatos, do so at an older age (Moore 1978); and many polydrug users never even try heroin. This account by a veterano, 27, from South Fontana is more representative of such youths:

We used to ditch school and if we didn't have anyone to buy our liquor, we just stole it. We used to take gallons of Red Mountain [a low-priced brand of wine] and drink it in vacant fields. I used to hang out on the corner with the older guys. We'd shoot pool, sniff glue, smoke pot. The most experienced shot up with hard stuff. I just watched them shooting up at the time. I thought this was more my bag . . . [When he was older and married] . . . before work, I would drop seven or eight whites, so when I'd get to work, I'd be feeling a buzz. . . . Then at lunch time my buddies and I would recharge ourselves again. We'd drop more whites, drinking beer and wine to get the pills working. . . . Whites had gotten to the point where they didn't move me, I needed something stronger. I got some shit better and stronger than whites, it was called "crank" [uppers]. It came in a little sticklike package. You had to process it yourself . . . You'd take a pinch and snort it into each nostril. It would hit you in minutes. It makes you real tingly, light on your feet. Real neat was the feeling.

Peripheral and temporary gang members were generally less abusive in both the types of drugs used and the amount taken of each. Their accounts generally reflect a clear-cut rejection of what they call "bad drugs" (usually meaning heroin), as this experience of a female, 17, from Ontario confirms:

All the girls back at school would always go into the guys' head. There we would drink, smoke pot, or just make plans for next week's ditching party. One day things were different. The guys were all freaked out, they had shot up. A couple of the girls were going to shoot up, too, but I didn't want to go that far, so I left and I never went into the guys' head again. I was called chicken a few times, but I just threw blows with them and told them I wasn't going to waste myself like they wasted themselves . . . I was different now, and they felt it and I didn't hold it back. I let them know I was me and nothing was going to stop that.

(Female members usually start drug and alcohol usage later than males, but the same range of abuse—and its corollaries—is characteristic of them. Cf. Moore and Mata 1981.)

Gang Conflict and Violence

Conflict is a distinguishing trait of barrio street gangs and is found in many contexts. The desire to enhance one's sense of (and recognition as) being tough, as well as a desire for a measure of protection from others, is part of most members' motivation for joining the gang. One often must fight other gang members to be initiated into the gang—not always completely voluntarily, as this 31-year-old former member recalls: "My first encounter with any gang was when I decided to walk around the neighborhood to see what was going on. Well, when I got near the circle, I came upon four boys who were there [from the Varrio Nuevo gang, ages 13 to 15 years old] . . . It was then I was told by them that joining their gang was the only way of walking around the Projects without getting jumped. When I told them I didn't want to join, they didn't care. They began to form a circle around me to jump me." Fear of more severe violence deters some who grow tired of the gang from an early exit, for some cliques interpret such an action as betrayal and may inflict very serious injuries on the offender. Generally, however, fighting among members of the same clique is strongly discouraged. When tempers flare in the course of roughhouse play, other members intercede to allow the disputants to cool off. If a deep-seated dispute between two clique members cannot be resolved nonviolently, others will ensure a "fair fight," one-on-one without weapons, and will stop the violence once a clear-cut victor has emerged. One who too often picks fights with his clique peers will be forcibly expelled from the group.

Violence against others not from one's own barrio is more readily countenanced, and one's homeboys will back up a peer who fights an outsider. (Even in such situations, however, hotheads may be curtailed if the fighting interrupts other members' enjoyment of an affair, as in the case of the house party disruption discussed in the previous chapter.) Indeed, gang members feel obliged to respond with violence in defense of their barrio. This often involves repelling intruders—especially those from rival barrios—from the territory claimed by the gang. Some individuals articulate such territorial considerations in terms of fear that the invaders may be carrying out an attack or that they may be visiting some of the local females (who are often relatives to be protected or girlfriends to be possessed exclusively). As one male, 16, from Corona said in an interview: "We had to defend our territory, but what we really had to do was make sure no one else from different barrios or towns would get near our jainillas." More often, however, territorial defense is justified in terms of a perceived threat of having outsiders "show them up" by coming and going and treating them with disdain, as if they could not control their own backyard. Members often claim a sure (if sometimes intuitive or even instinctive) awareness of boundary demarcations as the 19-year-old from Santa Ana who said in reply to the question of how one knows when one neighborhood starts and ends: "Well, everybody just knows. It's like in a jungle, the animals know!" A male, 18, from South Fontana pointed out that the "public is not involved in this. It is the gang members who watch for anyone crossing their boundaries." Major barrio entryways are sometimes marked by graffiti warnings, such as "Death to Outsiders" or "Nuevo-y-Qué" (We're Nuevo. So what's it to you?) to ward off would-be intruders. Nevertheless, boundary specifications given by different members from a barrio often contrast considerably; and overlapping territorial claims by different barrio gangs are not uncommon.

Fighting between barrio gangs is at the root of most gang violence. Indeed, members of the earliest cliques of two East Los Angeles barrios have explained the origin of their gangs as an effort to protect themselves from boys in other neighborhoods (Moore 1978). In those formative years, and for the next generation or two, interbarrio violence was usually a matter of fist fighting, augmented by pick-up weapons, such as stones, sticks, and bottles. (Even then, however, prearranged gang battles would involve knives, brass knuckles, and, on rare occasions, homemade "zip guns.") Violence was normally directed only at other teenagers and young men, there being an implicit understanding that women, children, and elders were not to be targeted in interbarrio fighting.

Most youths enter the gang at the time they are in junior high school; not surprisingly, confrontations with members of other gangs are often first experienced at the school. A 17-year-old male from White Fence was once transferred to a rival barrio's junior high school and gave this story about how he was challenged: "They came up to me, so we started talking about territory and shit, that they should have this territory and we should have another territory. That way everyone would have their place and no *pedo* [fights] would start." This habit of establishing boundaries at schoolyards is particularly pronounced in the urban locales, for many barrios are in close proximity and competition. As Moore (1978) and her associates (CPRP 1979, 1981) have found for some members, this interbarrio conflict at school continues until the first years of high school.

While gang violence sometimes breaks out in schools, there is a remarkable amount of peace maintained by the fear of suspension or expulsion. However, on the streets conflicts increase, for this is where gangs face few restrictions. Occasionally, it is a premeditated affair, but more commonly it is a more or less spontaneous engagement arising from a chance meeting at a dance or a party, at a recreational area, or while out walking or riding through the streets.

Quite often there is a long tradition of rivalry and animosity between particular barrios. A male, 16, from Cucamonga recounts his understanding of one such tradition: "We've been fighting that barrio and they have been trying to get some guys for a long, long time, since 1930s-1940s, the Zoot-Suit days, and a lot of killings have been happening and stuff like that . . . Before it was mostly chains and knives. Now it's not like that no more, it's just killings." The escalation of fatalities has come about in the past two and a half decades with an increased availability of cars, drugs, and, especially, guns. Many barrio rivalries and conflicts have resulted in a long string of killings and maimings without anyone knowing the origins of the violence. What matters is that the barrio's honor (in the view of gang members) is upheld at whatever cost.

One male, 19, from Ontario waxed philosophical about the meaning of this barrio combativeness: "The only thing we can do is build our own little nation. We know that we have complete control in our community. It's like we're making our stand and we're able to express ourselves this way. We're all brothers and nobody fucks with us . . . We take pride in our little nation and if any intruders enter, we get panicked because we feel our community is being threatened. The only way is with violence."

Occasionally, personal vendettas can result in gang involvement. A male, 20, from Venice gives his explanation of how trouble begins in many instances. "A lot of people never look at the beginning of an incident. . . . they just look at it as if there were two different gangs.

What it is, you just run into another neighborhood that you don't have hassles with, and one of your homeboys might lie about what went down. Like some guy may get into a fight, it was really a personal thing, but the rest of the homeboys get involved, too. That's all it is." The personal incident may be serious enough, however, to call for stronger forces, as this male, 22, from Pico Viejo attests: "We went over and this guy pulls out these *chuckle sticks* [*nunchaku*, two wooden batons joined with a chain] like he was going to do us in. He was right there at this house and we just went over to get him. We were going to get him anyway, he needed to get his ass kicked. There were a lot of us, about twelve of us. We used a crowbar and kicked the shit out of him." For some of the *locos* (crazies) a resort to weapons is also common, as this account of Wizard shows: "He could handle himself good, too, in fighting, but as soon as he would be beating him up, he'd stab him. His brothers had been stabbed before by older guys from Mariana and the brothers taught him: 'Hey, I was down and they stabbed me, so you do the same thing.' "

Some individuals expressed the feeling that much of the conflict was something of an endless game of revenge, in retaliation for previous encounters. "We don't start the shooting, but we have to go back and do the same or else we lose," said one male, 19, from Chino. Some barrio hostilities have persisted for a long time, with alternate periods of relative peace and quiet being replaced by more volatile and active phases; for example, some rural areas (Pomona vs. Chino, Ontario vs. Cucamonga) have had a rivalry for at least thirty years. Members of each new klika remember and focus on those incidents they feel are significant and thus develop a distorted view of events that led to the rivalry, and they embrace the gang's established attitude toward the rivals.

In furtherance of these rivalries, many gang members undertake cruising excursions into "enemy territory," much like Plains Indians' "counting coup," in that the prestige gained is proportional to the type and degree of daring. For some individuals, it is enough to ride through hostile territory and come out unscathed. Many more cruise through, yelling their barrio slogans and/or stopping to write their placa, and beat a hasty (albeit cool if possible) retreat. A smaller number might plan to shoot up a house with the hope of injuring or killing someone, as this story of a convicted murderer, 17, affirms: "My friend and I went riding to shoot anyone from ———. We saw this guy and asked him to come up to the car and asked him where he was from [¿De dónde?]. He put his hands on top of the car and said ——— [the name of the barrio they were in], so I shot him in the chest. He screamed and fell. I just laughed 'cause I was loaded and I could barely see his face. We drove off and my homeboy shot his gun in the air." When I asked him how he felt now about the guy he shot, he replied: "I have dreams of the guy's face, I see him as a little boy, I imagine him as a baby playing. The police couldn't contact his mother, he was living with his aunt. His parents are dead or something."

The automobile facilitates interbarrio "warfare." A thin line sometimes divides the cruising actions that bring spontaneous conflicts and those that are premeditated "raids" or "drive-bys." A male, 16, from Cucamonga explains how his gang's intentions were interrupted: "Yeah, one day I went down there [Ontario]. We were riding around, and we stopped by this house. We were going to snuff out this dude and this dude just came up to us and asked where we were from and we said Cucamonga. He just pulled out a gun and started shooting. He shot up my tire, the side of my car, with a .38. We got lucky, we got out of there in time. We changed the tire and split, or else if they had had cars, they would have caught us." In another account, a friend of his wasn't so lucky: "One time one of my homeboys, he was driving in Ontario, a place called Ghosttown. He ran out of gas and some guys went up to him and started beating him up. Some other dude, he ran, and they started getting crowbars, and they just beat him to death. He was only 16 years old and they killed him."

Drive-bys, a more widespread gang habit in recent years, have become a common occurrence. Drive-bys usually are premeditated, although the culprits appear to be cruising, and entail traveling to a rival barrio for the express purpose of shooting somebody, and in recent years anybody. This extended interview account of a male, 18, from Ontario gives some background to the subject:

We got together to talk about how we were going to plan it. It wasn't too hard. We had a .22 automatic rifle with 18 shots and one 4-10 shotgun with only two shots. We got together in a pickup truck. I was the driver or elected driver, but I didn't mind. There were two guys in the back, one was Paulie and the other Bobby. I can still recall exactly what happened that night. As we got closer, my heart started thumping faster. As soon as we made a left . . . a white '64 Chevy started chasing us. I still don't know who exactly fired the gun from the truck, I just kept going faster. I think about eleven or twelve shots were fired at the '64 Chevy. I was going about 70 miles per trying to make it for the country . . . The '64 caught us and started ramming us. There was still five or six shots left, but it wouldn't shoot anymore. I couldn't make the truck go any faster, but the '64 kept pushing, trying to make us wreck, which is exactly what happened. We wrecked into somebody's front yard. Nobody got hurt. But after wrecking, everybody jumped out and started fighting. It took about four minutes or longer before the cops came. Even the cops were scared to break it up. They had their guns drawn. Finally they broke it up and hauled us away . . .

Like so many other conflicts, the planning for drive-by raids occurs in an otherwise normal social setting. A veterano, 40, from Ontario recalls the early days:

It was the booze and pot parties we had that made us grow wilder and go on raids against other barrios. It was a spur of the moment thing. During a party, someone, after clearing their mind with a lot of liquor and pot, would come up with a bright idea, such as "Let's go shoot up ———." We would carry our guns outside and pile up in our cars and go to another's territory. One time we cruised their main street of town, spraying bullets here and there but nothing happened. We were leaving back down the same street and suddenly we saw five cars coming around a corner in our direction. We took off spraying bullets behind us and got out. Nobody ever found out if anyone got hurt.

In another incident a male, 18, from South Fontana elaborates on the somewhat complicated repercussions in the aftermath of a raid:

Me and some homeboys were cruising around the barrio. We parked in front of this vato's pad and were just getting loaded in the car, when some other vatos . . . came by. They made a U-turn at the dead end and came back. They stopped by the car and one of the guys gets off and said, "———Rifa!! We're it." Next thing we know he is shooting at us. We all yell to run, duck! . . . Later, I found out that my two best homeboys had passed away. I felt so much hatred in me that I wanted to get revenge at the vatos . . . The court says it was a gang-related incident and that those guys shot at us in self-defense. We were unarmed. One of the guys has been convicted. One of the guy's dad put a contract out on me, so I wouldn't make it to court. A few times I have been cruising around the barrio and I get shot at. Since the shooting I make it a habit to carry a gun at all times. I'm just afraid that one of these days I wouldn't make it home.

Shootings were often a part of a wider generalized barrio warfare drama, sometimes lasting weeks or months and involving a series of events. This story of one veterano covers several weeks of an escapade that began in a pool hall:

... so this dude pulled a sawed-off shotgun out and blows Paulie away. From that day on ———— and ———— have been at each other's throats. One Thursday afternoon on ———— Avenue, some vatos from ———— ambushed a carload of us from ————. The vatos outnumbered us, they were all prepared. We got the shit splattered all over. Our car was all messed up, the windows were broken and the car was dented up bad. One of the guys was paralyzed from the waist down. They had worked him over with tire irons. Lucky me, I made it out O.K. with only a broken arm, and a mild concussion and darkened eyes. That weekend the rest of the dudes from ———— went on a rampage in ————. They blasted ———— up. They wounded one of the ———— brothers, they were the leaders for ————. A couple of weeks passed by since the battle had happened. We decided to have a dance at the contact station one Saturday night. Everything was riding smoothly until a lot of gun blasting was being fired at the station. One of the blasts hit Tony ———— in the head. He was alive for a while, 'til the ambulance arrived. He finally died. They kept on blasting our hangout. They blew my mom's store windows out frequently. One night my sister Mary was ready to close up and a car passed by, blasting up the store. Mary jumped quickly on the floor; luckily she wasn't hurt that bad, just cuts caused by the glass.

Not all gang violence is oriented toward other barrios, however. It has also included, for instance, ambushing and stoning cars (sometimes police) in the barrio; beating up a doctor who refused to provide unreported medical attention to a gun-injured comrade; jumping "chúntaros," or "wetbacks" (Mexican nationals), or Anglos; and jumping a "traitor" in their own group. Violence and aggression in schools sometimes is turned toward school authorities. Tico, 22, from Pico Viejo attended a junior high in La Puente where the P.E. instructor had a reputation of always pushing the guys around. He recalls: "And when we were together, nobody could tell us what to do. Yeah, teachers or anybody. They jumped the gym teacher once, kicked that boy's ass. He tried to play rough, real rough and tough. They jumped him right there in front of the class, around seven or eight dudes. ... This guy used to go around trying to prove that he was tough, tougher than them."

Fights sometimes involved strangers, and the provocation will often be as much imagined as real. A male, 17, from Norwalk describes one with Mexican nationals, while he and his friends were walking past a local bar:

> I had a feeling that they were talking about us, because they were pointing at us and laughing . . . I said, "What are they saying, do they want to get down or what?" Then he [friend] said, "Yeah." Then I said, "Well, let's get down with them." I thought we were just going to throw blows, but these guys had big belt buckles, so I said fuck it. There were more of them than there were of us, so they pulled it on my homeboy and my homeboy grabbed it. So we just jumped on that one dude and these other guys were surprised that we didn't run. We got a rock and hit him in the head and he dropped, and his friends, they just tripped out on it, they got real surprised. We took off running after that . . .

The situations discussed thus far pertain principally to violence initiated and carried out by male gang members and for the most part directed at rival males or their families. The overwhelming majority of gang violence is of this nature. However, many barrios have female cliques also (although continuity from generation to generation is less common than it is with males); and the female cliques can also be oriented toward fighting, as a female, 19, from Cucamonga affirms: "We have to back each other up in case of *pleito* [trouble]. We cruise around and go to different towns and get in fights. We drink to feel good. Some of the guys will come along with us to see how we do to get other gangs from out of town. They'll give us some points on how to get away from the *placas* [police]." As with the male cliques, individuals in female cliques differ in their propensity toward violence. A female, 19, from Ontario illustrates this point in this example: "We saw these girls walking on the sidewalk in Pomona's Sharkey Park. We all got out of the car and started throwing 'chingazos.' Happy, the girl who drove, had a wrench on the back seat. Mary took it out and hit one of the girls with it behind the head, very hard. The girl fell, but Mary had no sympathy for her and began hitting her more on the face with the wrench and knocking her head so hard against the cement, it cracked. It all happened so fast. We didn't know the girls' names."

In sum, conflict generally involved rival barrio gang members. Regular members usually take the lead in such affairs, but it is also clear that peripheral/temporary members show their commitment to "backing the barrio," in many instances in response to peer pressure and expectations. But gang violence can occur under various other

conditions and circumstances and sometimes end up in violent killings, not infrequently of innocent bystanders. Most of the violence,
by far, is committed by males and is targeted primarily at other males,
but female cliques also often include one or several young women
who are prone to violence.

Property-Related Crime

While the criminality attached to liquor consumption, drug use, and
fighting is strongly embedded in gang patterns requiring group efforts
and support, it appears that property-related crime is more of an individual nature. Moore and Vigil (1988) note that "comparatively few
gang members actually adopt a lifetime deviant or criminal lifestyle"
(p. 1), and "the gang may reinforce the deviant acts of individuals by
tolerating or even encouraging them" (p. 2).

Mischief and minor offenses, such as stealing bicycles, shoplifting,
and vandalism, are strewn throughout the life histories. Wizard and
Geronimo, the two regular gang members whose lives were summarized in Chapter 4, reflect this early age behavior. Later in life, they
escalated into serious offenses that led to detention and incarceration.
The life histories of the temporary and situational gang members, as
expected, show a mixed and less criminally active pattern and eventually an earlier resolve to avoid such behavior. It was common for all
types of gang members to steal bikes, shoplift spray paint and junk
food, steal auto tape players, and even sell "hot stuff," but most of the
personal incidents were sporadic and inconsistent. An offense was
sometimes committed because of a dare from peers, and at other
moments it was a purely spontaneous event. The gang per se had
nothing to do with it. Most of the individuals eventually refrained
from continuing to break the law, whether in or out of the gang,
although, as the next section will show, being apprehended,
reprimanded, and detained operated as a factor for some persons in
changing the behavior. However, those individuals who start off as
multiple petty offenders tend eventually to become criminally
oriented.

There is a distinct difference between a person who commits one or
two infractions and someone who broadens his or her participation in
street life and later a life of crime (Haapanen and Jesness 1982;
Wolfgang et al. 1972). Much of the explanation for this interpersonal
difference stems from the type and degree of early life experiences,
overall social control breakdown (family and schools), and street
socialization. Lifelong street people are more likely to have had a

series of setbacks and troubling influences throughout life and turn to crime if only as a means of support. Beginning with petty crimes and not deterred by the punishment they receive, such individuals escalate into criminal careers. A male, 17, from Cucamonga, one of seven boys in a family of nine, provides an example:

> I was about 13 or 14 years old and I used to go out with my brothers to go out drinking or ripping off. The first time I got busted was for trying to rip off a tape player in a car. I shot the window with a gun and got in the car and was trying to get the tape player out when the owner of the car came out and caught me in the car. He got me and took me inside a factory and left me there with a security guard until the cops came. I was 15 then. I stayed in juvenile hall for three days. The very same day I got out, me and a couple of my friends got together and ripped off some pad. We needed some money, and we needed it to buy dope, uppers, and beer. It wasn't hard to get the money for it, but you had to know what you were doing. One way was with a friend who would take turns and go and knock on doors, and if someone answered the door, we would just ask for anyone's name, but if no one answered the door, we would just go inside and take what was there. Sometimes we would jump chúntaros and take their money. I was picked up the last time for armed robbery, assault with a deadly weapon, and grand theft. I did a year in a boys' home.

When interviewed, this youth, with the help of his girlfriend, was "trying to go straight." He was still hanging out with friends from the klika, however.

Sammie is a Corona male, 16, who came from a broken home. He lost his father when he was 5 years old, and his working mother was unable to adequately supervise her four children. He turned to the streets for direction and thereafter became involved in one setback after another. He was 8 years old when

> I used to take candy from the stores or steal small toys. I was caught by the store manager several times, but I was able to convince him that I wouldn't do it again. But the day came when I was caught trying to take out of the store a couple of small objects without having to pay for them. This time everything was different, my mother was told, and she really punished me. At that time, the only thing I could think of was running away from home. Later, in junior high, we used to use our money to smoke

grass. I didn't like school and I used to get arrested a few times
for truancy or for suspicion of making trouble. They would let
me off the hook only with a warning. I was put on six months'
probation one time for pushing and knocking down a teacher
who hassled me. They put me in a detention center, but I got in a
fight with two black guys and was put in solitary confinement
for three days. When I got out, I ran away from home and they
put me back in. Later, I started stealing cars because I thought it
wasn't cool to walk. They put me in the reformatory school, but
six days later I escaped. I was caught and sent to youth camp. I
later stole a lot of different cars and the police told my mother
that we should move away from the neighborhood. But we
couldn't afford to. We stayed and I got in a lot more trouble.
Gang fights, getting in and out of jail, and finally one time a
friend and I robbed a liquor store and the owner of the store got
hurt. This was deeper trouble and they put me away in county,
this time for a year . . . I'm the one who messed up. Maybe if they
had done something to me after the first time, I might of thought
about it before committing some other crime a second time.

Despite the apparent remorse in that personal assessment, he still is
drawn to the streets and no one has succeeded in providing any kind
of guidance or control.

A male, 21, from San Pedro, who had a similar background of street
socialization, family stress, drugs, and gang conflict, also began breaking laws early in life and later spent time in prison for second-degree
murder:

When I was age 5 or 6, the older guys used to write notes with
my mother's signature to have me get them cigarettes. At 9 years
old I would steal beer, wine, and I even stole a FM radio, from
the liquor store . . . At 12 years old, I broke into a house and took
some money and a knife. When I told the guys about it, they said
I would be a good homeboy . . . At 15 years old I got caught for
hot wiring a car and was on probation for a year. I kept on doing
it, though, and had to go to Y.T.S [Youth Training School] in
Chino for one year when I was 17 years old. Later on, at 19 years
old . . . that's when I got busted for second-degree murder because
of a gang fight at a party. My fingerprints were on a knife the
police found, but I did not do it. But I couldn't say anything.

In the three and one-half years in prison, he learned a baker's trade
and, when released, joined his wife and son and found work at a

bakery to support them. He presently hangs out with the homeboys, but he says he is more a family man now.

The lives of several other individuals showed this pattern of early, minor (but multiple) infractions burgeoning to serious offenses and eventual incarceration. A male, 19, from Santa Ana, as a regular gang member, fits in this category, but the last illegal act is the one most vividly remembered. As he recalled in a detailed interview:

I was at my parents' house and I decided to go to the park 'cause I hadn't seen my girl in three days. When I got there I saw some homeboys and got loaded. The next day me and a friend were going to get a job and start school [at a combined work-and-study community project], so we went home early. When I got home, Dad was leaving for work. My mom was in the hospital and my sister had taken all the kids somewhere [a family of nine children and two other relatives in the household]. Me and my brother were the only ones home, so we went back to the park. Nothing was happening there so we came home. Then a homeboy dropped in I hadn't seen for six or seven months. He gave me some reds. We didn't have no money, so we went to steal some beer from a Tic-toc store. Then we got drunk and loaded and went to pick up Paul [the guy he was going to get a job with]. At 1:00 A.M. me and my brother and Paul and Mike went to a 7-11 store to steal some more beer. I got a case from the back and set it on the counter as the clerk asks, "Cash or check?" All I could do was laugh, 'cause I knew I was going to run. When I went back for more beer my brother jumped the counter and hit the clerk over the head with my billy club. Then he handcuffed him and took him to the back of the store and opened and robbed the safe. [They hadn't initially intended to do this.] As this was happening I hear a cop and can't figure out what is happening. I look out and see a cop and get scared because of all the beer I had stacked up. I hid and when the cop walks in, I hit him over the head and closed the back door on him. I run for the front door and a lady is coming in and I grab her by the blouse and throw her to the side and take off. I turn down a street and see ten or fifteen cop cars [the other guys are already gone by now]. I hear gun shots and realize that the cop I hit is right behind me and the cop yells: "Shoot the son of a bitch."

A chase followed his exit from the scene, where he was shot in the hand and eventually subdued and taken to jail. The newspaper reported he had masterminded the whole affair and that he had also raped a lady. Charges brought against him were three armed robberies, three burglaries, two assaults with a deadly weapon, and an attempted rape. Presently he is doing time at Chino's Youth Training School for the offenses.

There are several other instances of serious crime in the life histories I collected. Generally speaking, this pattern emerged when the individuals were older and often included an arrest, conviction, and period of incarceration. Stealing (especially when younger) and robberies (usually when older) dominate the types of crimes committed. The rationale for criminal behavior among gang members appears to be based on the need for money or material goods. A male, 27, from South Fontana, for example, once decided to steal at work, and he served time for it. He said: "What I earned at work wasn't enough for my good times. I thought I could make some extra money by stealing carpets. It would be by the yard at first and then I began to get into rolls of carpet." In short, the level of participation in crime among gang members varies tremendously. Some start and end their crime careers with one or two offenses, while others, even after numerous serious crimes and much time in prison, remain rutted in this lifestyle. In most instances, it is individual motives and not gang or group ones that explain the occurrence of a crime (Moore and Vigil 1988). As noted, it usually is the need for money or material goods that undergirds the rationalization for criminal behavior.

The Criminal Justice System

Friction in barrio relations with law enforcement and the criminal justice system is a pervasive problem (U.S. Commission on Civil Rights 1970). Police and sheriffs, as street "social control" specialists next in importance to family and schools, are regularly brought into contact with barrio youth groups and gangs (Jackson and McBride 1985). As a result, law enforcement personnel have tended to be especially vigilant in their patrolling routines, and some barrio residents, especially youth, perceive this as unnecessarily intrusive. Although only a minority of the informants interviewed for this study commented specifically about police harassment, most indicated that there is an overall, implicit resentment in the barrio toward law enforcement.

More than half of my key informants have had some type of experience with arrest, detention, and/or incarceration. Regular gang members were more likely to have repeated police contacts and periods of detention and incarceration. Sometimes the contact that youth have with law enforcement is rather innocuous, such as shown in this interview account by a female, 21, from Ontario: "I was never really arrested before. I once came close to it. I tossed a bottle into a store. I don't know why. We ran but a truck stopped us and it was a policeman [off duty]. He made me clean it up and got mad when I was scared. He let me go after a while. I think that was the worst trouble I've been in."

In the view of gang members, police harassment ranges anywhere from how the police perceive and approach them to the actual verbal and physical exchanges that take place. One male, 16, from Cucamonga gave an account that combines several troublesome sore spots: "We weren't doing nothing, just riding around, like everybody else and the cops stopped us and started harassing us. We asked them how come they stopped us and he didn't want to give no answer. He just said, 'Shut-up, man!' And one of the cops hit one of the homeboys with a flashlight in the chest. I don't think cops should be doing that. If the cops wanted us to respect them, then they should respect us too." Being detained for no apparent reason, receiving disrespectful treatment, and getting hit without provocation, as occurred in this instance, are all part of an experiential pattern that gang members (and many non-gang members) recall with frequent consistency. Some informants also spoke of antipolice activities and expressions on their part, usually undertaken as individuals rather than groups. These ranged from the insults and other displays of disrespect emphasized by temporary gang members to several regular members' reports of throwing stones or bottles at the police. Mirandé (1981:69) has reported confrontations in rural barrios that are more clearly group affairs; and in a recent book (Mirandé 1987) has added further documentation.

To some degree, an antipolice bias stems from a broader antiauthority and anti-Anglo attitude. Authority figures from public institutions, like schools and law enforcement, have become something to avoid, dislike, and view suspiciously; they are, as Rodgers (1969) has noted, in a double-bind situation in areas where social control is losing out. A male, 22, from Ontario was quite honest about examining his attitude toward law enforcement and said in an interview: "I learned to hate police and white people at this stage. I believe that it might have been facilitated by the fact that the police were usually white. I say this because my feelings have changed about this now." Such sentiments contributed to his antiauthority feeling and general dislike of the police, an implicit view that others shared. A measure of fear of the police attends such an attitude. A regular gang member, male, 19, from Venice said that "the police will try to pin anything on you that they can. They have a *CRASH* unit [Community Resources against Street Hoodlums, a special Los Angeles Police unit targeted on eliminating street crimes] over there. They try to put you back in [prison] again." (In his case, although fear made the member guardedly respectful of the police, it was not sufficient to keep him out of prison.)

One young man, 17, vehemently stated that "the police start trouble when they come into the barrio." He reflects a commonly held belief among street youths that the police assume that "we are doing something wrong when we are just kicking back, maybe getting high or drinking beer, and just partying." Obviously "getting high and drinking beer" escaped this person's idea of what constitutes an illegal act, particularly if minors are around. Nevertheless, such sentiments indicate how normal policing incidents sometimes erupt into confrontations. Such events are triggered when one or both parties show disrespect or mistreatment toward the other. What often starts out as a relatively minor exchange can quickly escalate. A male, 16, from El Hoyo was particularly embarrassed by an incident that occurred in front of many people:

We seen an accident of a motorcycle cop and we started laughing. We don't like cops. After the accident he [another cop, who knows and dislikes them] turned around and got us in a corner, right against the wall, and got my brand new county shirt and tore it up. I told him, "You think you're bad 'cause you have that badge on, huh?" He takes off his badge, and says, "I don't have a badge on right now." I said, "I don't want to hit you 'cause you're a cop." I was high, and I don't like what they do. So they got me and beat me up right there. You know, they hit me with that stupid flashlight over the head—bam! I wanted to hit him, but I said, naw, I don't want to get *torcido* [arrested] for that, for hitting a cop, especially. He beat us up right there with all kinds of people going by and cars in the night. So then they split, and we went home bleeding and shit. They messed up my homeboy's eye, a big black eye. The next day we seen them, they look at us and stop and arrest us for nothing. They make up something, you know, "Oh, well, we got you for drunk" and this and that. They told my homeboy, "We got you for strong-armed robbery." We go to court and we try to fight the case, but the cops go and say this and that, and they believe the cops. And they take us in, and I just don't like it.

Wizard, the regular gang member discussed in Chapter 4, belonged to an earlier clique in the same barrio and also emphasized such harassment, which carried over to his experience in the county jail where he would fight with the guards. In a gentler vein, but still reflecting keenly felt irritation, is the experience of this male, 22, from South Fontana:

> We are all against the law. I feel that the cops are always picking on us and harassing us for no reason, no matter where we are or what we are doing. It is like you have a neon sign on your head that says, "Come on pigs." One time me and my girlfriend were walking down the street minding our own business, and a cop car stopped and they got out and started pushing me around, saying they saw me break into a house a couple of days ago. It was nothing but a bullshit story. Since I was with my girlfriend, I did not start any trouble, but I got real mad.

An unsettling conclusion dots the end of this account of Henry, the temporary gang member from Chino whose life history was summarized in Chapter 4:

> I still didn't believe what they said about the cops. But one time I got busted. They were following me, and I tried to lose them, and they said they got me for resisting arrest. See, they throw you in jail, call you names, and try to make you mad so you can hit them and they can hit you back. I was scared being arrested. And when they started saying stuff, I just got mad. The guy that said I was resisting arrest was a sheriff, and he started searching my brother. I know we have a right to know why we were picked up, but they didn't tell us. When I put my hands down, he said I striked him. Then he threw me down and I couldn't breathe. My brother tried to kick him, because he could see that I couldn't breathe. At the police station, I gave him a dirty look and started thinking about revenge. I really hated his guts. That scared me more.

Barrio-police riots are not frequent, but over the years there have been some major confrontations in East Los Angeles (Morales 1972). Most of these were charged by the sociopolitical actions and aspirations of the Chicano Movement and involved both Los Angeles police and county sheriff units at different times (Mandel 1982). There also have been smaller-scale hostilities that sprang from house parties or cruising events on the boulevard (cf. R. Rodríguez 1984). In addition, some rural enclaves (now surrounded by suburban and urban growth) have had major confrontations with law enforcement, in some instances rather serious affairs of several days' duration; Mirande (1981) offers detailed information and analysis of one such incident in the Riverside barrio of Casa Blanca. The 16-year-old from Cucamonga cited in the harassment incident above had this to say about one such near riot event:

> Like, one time, the cops came in and started harassing the homeboys, and the homeboys just got pissed off. One of them threw a rock, and it wasn't no big deal, it just hitted a police right here in the eye. They made a big thing out of it, though, they sent a lot of cops into the barrio. Streets were blocked off, nobody could come in or go out and all the cops had their guns, they were ready to shoot down just anybody. One of my homeboys was just kicking back doing nothing, then the cops just got him and broke his arm. But the cops will do that. Like when I got busted, they beat me up, too, pretty bad. That's the way they are, they'll beat you up, they will hit you in the back of your head or something. Then they will tell the courts that you fell and hit your head. If they were just like normal people, they would be scared to come in [the barrio]. The only way that they can hit you is when you're handcuffed or when they've got the badge or the gun.

The youth's version of these incidents plays down the seriousness of the injury suffered by the sheriff's deputy, who now must wear a steel plate (M. Miller 1984). A 16-year-old female member of the same barrio pointed out the repercussions in the aftermath of the same incident the male reported: "They were beating up on the guys and breaking the windows to their cars. Then the cops came to my house and started to kick the door . . . They said that they were gonna break the door open, so we opened it . . . When we opened it, they sprayed something into our eyes and it was burning our eyes. We had to come out with our hands up and then this lady cop searched us in front of everyone . . . After we were searched they made us sit on the dirt for about three hours." As noted in the previous chapter, police interactions with the Cucamonga barrio are characterized by unusual levels of bad feelings on both sides. Similarly, the series of events described here included extraordinary levels of violence. The majority of the youth-police contacts reported by my informants were of the milder forms of perceived harassment, with only a small number escalating into more serious affairs, such as beatings or riots. The mutual disrespect each party has toward the other doubtlessly provides the ingredients for such eruptions: minor, sometimes personal exchanges burgeon in tone (beatings, riots) and complexity (more police and youth).

The connection between the deviant activities of gang members—the gang conflicts, drugs, crimes, and police engagements—and the tendency to be arrested and incarcerated is clear (del Piñal 1973). However, "doing time" also is often a badge of honor and prestige among younger gang members. While police contacts often add an air of importance to a youth's image, heightening his reputation and respect among fellow gang members, going to jail earns much more respect. Henry, the temporary gang member described in Chapter 4, underscored this point when he said, "I almost made it."

Most of the Chicano youths I have interviewed who had been tried and incarcerated were regular gang members. Approximately even proportions of these regulars were detained in juvenile hall or camp institutions solely or had coupled this experience with time at a county or youth training facility. A smaller number were tecatos who had run the gamut from juvenile to adult penal institutions, with some ending up at a rehabilitation center. The peripheral/temporary gang members who had been incarcerated mostly spent time in institutions for young wards, like juvenile hall or camp. Such an experience sometimes hastens a youth's disaffiliation with the gang, as in the instance of Freddie, the peripheral member in Chapter 4. The range of variation in time spent incarcerated included one individual, a male, age 18 (a peripheral), who spent four days in juvenile hall, while another male, age 22 (a regular), had completed five and one-half years in various institutions, from juvenile hall to prison.

Some of the incarceration experiences recounted to me are instructive in aiding our understanding of gangs, especially of the "maturing-out" process, a matter dealt with in some detail by Joan Moore and her colleagues (1978), who described the continuity among drug life, prisons, and the barrio gang. Scaled from light to heavy involvement, the first type includes the peripheral and temporary members, who served only a short time in juvenile hall. For example, one male, 18, from Ontario was suspected (along with several others) of a drive-by shooting; he was detained four days in juvenile hall before being released. Soon after this experience, following the death of a close friend in another gang-related shooting, he abruptly withdrew from the gang. He is presently working fulltime and has focused his social interests on female companionship. Others in this group also had one-time-only or minimal involvement in law breaking and, obviously, served less time. One male, 18, from Corona spent six months in a youth camp (an unusually long period for a temporary gang member), but, while there, he gained some amount of recognition as a track star. Although he returned to the streets thereafter and continued to participate in some of the prosocial gang activities, his liaison with a supportive girlfriend appeared to be keeping him out of trouble at the time of my last contact with him.

A number of regular gang members with whom I have talked have also spent time in a juvenile hall or camp facility and (with the help of various external supports) appear to have reformed their lives on a more or less "straight" basis. For example, a female, 20, from East Los Angeles had become deeply involved with the gang during midadolescence, but the juvenile hall experience of one week helped her decide to seek more prosocial avenues. She is now working at a youth center, helping to counsel and direct other barrio youth. However, it must be noted that this group is younger (average age 16.6 years) than the regular gang members (24.5), who have done heavier time. Since most of them have remained in the barrio, where there are ample opportunities for conflict with the law, their declared intentions of going straight might be as much wish fulfillment as an actual final decision to avoid the antisocial features of gang life.

A larger group of regular gang members have served time in years, rather than months, some going through every type of institution possible—juvenile hall, camp, youth authority, and prison. For example, a 22-year-old male from El Hoyo has been in and out of one institution or another from the time he was 9 years old. He had a string of various offenses early, including burglary, curfew violation, glue sniffing, robbery, possession of dangerous drugs, loitering and disturbing the peace, intoxication at school, grand theft auto, joy riding, battery upon a police officer, and so on, and was consequently sent several times to juvenile halls and youth camps. Later, continuing in the pattern, he was remanded to the California Youth Authority and eventually ended up at the Youth Training School, where he is now. During the last seven years of his life, he has served five and one-half years' time with only seventeen months free in the community. His case is a strong example of a regular, hard-core committed gang member. Most of his crimes were individually motivated, but he was able to find willing crime partners in his and other barrios, especially with friends from other barrios he had met in prison. Much of his personal and family background reflects the varied conditions and situations that characterize gang members. As yet, he is the only one in a family of five other mother-raised siblings who has followed this path of crime and incarceration, although two of the others are also gang affiliated. A crucial reason for this difference is his strong and continuing identification with some of the more street-oriented gang members. As a result there is always someone around to support this behavior.

A male, 21, from San Pedro provides a less extreme example, more representative of most of the other regular gang members' criminal justice experiences. At age 14, he spent six months in camp for burglary; at 17 years, one year in Y.T.S. for a series of auto thefts; and at 19 years, three and one-half years in prison for second-degree murder, which he says he did not commit but, in the barrio code of not pulling *"rata"* [rat, snitching], took the rap for. Upon his release he is now working and raising a family.

A distinct group of regular gang members consists of the tecatos, who are mostly older, former gang members. However, they, too, had early contacts with the law. What separates them from the rest of the sample is that their drug addiction often virtually necessitated criminal acts to support the habit and that they served lengthy sentences for such infractions. Some of the younger cohort of gang members who already show an inclination toward heavy drug use can surely be expected to replicate these tecatos' experiences.

As we have seen, most gang youths learn early that incarceration is not to their liking, even though a certain amount of peer respect and personal prestige is gained because of it. They attempt and most often succeed at avoiding further such contacts by seeking other channels for fulfillment. Many, however, continue a cycle of crime and incarceration well into adulthood, continuing to find willing accomplices among their barrio peers (and sometimes juniors) or impelled by the demands of their drug abuse patterns.

Conclusion

Most gang individuals spend the bulk of their time in cruising, partying, socializing, and similar typical youth customs, but they create a public stir principally by their less frequent violence. Even the most involved gang members, like the regulars and peripherals, generally pursue more prosocial gang behavior. Gang violence accounts for only a small portion of their time, and even here the ventures are typically sprees rather than consistent, methodical undertakings. Gang membership certainly facilitates the tendencies toward violent behavior that some individuals might have, but it is the individuals themselves who initiate the actions. This is shown in the contrast in attitude and behavior among various types of committed gang members.

Alcohol and drug use is a social pastime, the abuse of which fits the same pattern, with regular members starting earlier and eventually becoming deeply involved. The same can be said for involvement with crime and the criminal justice system. Sometimes a harrowing brush with the law, a drug overdose, or detention works to make a person reevaluate his or her street gang involvement. Nevertheless, a considerable number of individuals remain in the gang and persist in the behavior, apparently unable to change a deep-rooted pattern, which stems from their stressful structural and sociocultural experiences.

7. Psychodynamics of Gangs

The acquisition and development of a self-identity is particularly noteworthy during adolescence, and early life experiences often determine the nature and trajectory of subsequent identity formation. For some Chicano youth in Southern California barrios the acquisition of a self-identity is beset with difficulties, and the street gang has become, in part, a type of coping strategy. The striving for self-identity, particularly during adolescence, is integrated and finds fulfillment through gang channels, and gang roles and functions are important to a certain segment of the barrio youth population. It is primarily those individuals who come from low-income, stress-ridden families and who are most alienated from public institutions, such as schools, who become gang members. The gang has surfaced as a competing force to these institutions, to become a source of emulation and identification. This attraction is made feasible because the gang combines different patterns, mixing the normal peer cohort friendship and emotional support activities with the more renowned street gang antisocial features.

To examine the formation and affirmation of a self-identity within the gang context, it is necessary to discuss how personal needs combine and intersect with group and role sociopsychological features, for each affects, and in turn is affected by, the other, especially during adolescence. As Erikson has said, "Psychosocial identity thus depends on a complementarity of an inner (ego) synthesis in the individual and of role integration in his group" (1968:61). While one's self-identity, for example, is affirmed and uplifted by a commitment to and identification with the gang—one learns what to think about oneself and how to act—it is the group itself and the roles that group members represent that provide the person with the ingredients for self-identification. Conversely, in the social and environmental realm, growing up in the barrio and becoming socialized and enculturated to street peer networks and beliefs make one group oriented early in life; and thus the gang role is more ascriptive. When adolescence is reached in these instances, there is already a sense of group associations with group lore and role patterns, which facilitates submergence to and self-identification with the group; indeed, the self ideal becomes the group in the name of the barrio gang. Further, group role patterns are very explicit, specific traits that provide a map for thought and behavior. In the process of enacting these role patterns one can, in turn, demonstrate allegiance to the group in an observable, public performance while also clarifying one's self-identity in a personal private way. Thus, the ego, group, and role psychologies of the gang combine into a sociopsychological network. Several authors have noted this in object relations theory where "the image of the self is dynamically linked to the image of the object or other" (Foulks and Schwartz 1982:256), and Caughey (1980) has rightly suggested that social identity and personal identity are interdependent. In other contexts, Spiro has affirmed that environmental and cultural features are accompanied by psychological developments (1978).

Although barrio Chicanos share structural and cultural experiences, it is those Chicanos with the most fragmented egos who during adolescence are especially attracted to the gang as a source of self-identity. To help curb or bring a "psychosocial moratorium" to this ego identity crisis period the gang provides roles for these adolescents, especially traits denoting age and sex qualities—how you act toward others, how you present yourself, and so on. In short, the gang as a social unit creates what Goffman (1959) has labeled "fronts" for thinking and acting, and, as a supportive network for emotional outlets, it functions to guide and direct members. Thus, the group operates to give many young males a role in society at the adolescent transition period, when the peer group dominates socialization and largely replaces the already attenuated family and authority influences. It also helps reconcile inner psychological conflicts over different types of "identities," including *ideal* (what I would like to be), *feared* (what I would not like to be), *claimed* (what I would like others to think I am), and *real* (what I am) (Caughey 1980:188; Avruch 1982:111). Some individuals have had preteen experiences with the gang, so they are generally familiar with the new patterns (their real and ideal identities are closer). Others, however, must make a somewhat marked adjustment and thus face an intensified peer pressure to measure up to gang standards (real and ideal are farther apart). Role modeling becomes their raison d'être, and, as Erikson (1963:261) has said of youths in similar situations, they are "primarily concerned with what they appear to be in the eyes of others." The interplay among ego, group, and role psychological features is clearly evident in this process, and it will be useful to keep in mind how these distinct separate features merge during adolescence.

The Barrio and Self-Identification Processes

Many of the gang's activities revolve around self-identity strivings, in effect, a continuous lifelong experience of synthesizing external objects into one's meaning of self. As noted earlier, gang members' pick-up games, partying, and casual socializing are nonviolent gang activities. These are fairly normal adolescent behaviors to impress one's peers. Such informal play also allows for male reality testing and learning of peer patterns, particularly of a sex/age nature (Rogoff 1981; Whiting 1980). In addition, other, socially unacceptable gang activities have most often gained the public's attention. The latter, in large part, evolved from previous generations' influence (i.e., gang lore and mythology, older models) and media sources (i.e., television and cinema violence), access to hand guns, and mind-altering drugs. Violence against others in the form of rampant gang fighting and slayings and against oneself through the careless use of drugs and other chemical substances represents the destructive, debilitative habits that separate the gangs from other adolescent peer networks. The influence of the streets is responsible for altering adolescent patterns of daring and excitement into requirements that, at least at times, one's daring and courage be proven by participation in this more celebrated "gang behavior." Yet, as Edgerton has reasoned in his report on deviance (1978), such personal and group activities must be perceived not as "freaks in a side show" but as "principal performers in the everyday dramas of life" (p. 444).

Peer group activity, of course, is important during this phase of life. Adolescence for Chicanos, as well as others, is generally a life stage passage from the familiar (childhood) to the new (adulthood), a transitional, marginal period where experimentation with new roles is expected and usually enacted. Biological and physical changes underway usher in the question of social maturity, for a bodily change must somehow be accompanied by a psychological and behavioral change. New objects of affection and emulation are sought to shape the self, as a person turns outward, away from the narrower childhood inward focus, to external influences. This life stage has been affected by the peculiar nature of cholo life, however, and combines sociocultural environment and psychological features (Edgerton 1973:25). A comparison of lives of the most committed gang members with those of the nongang barrio youths, and even some who are fringe gang members, shows a wide difference in their backgrounds. (Note the differences among the four individuals in the fourth chapter.) Core gang members more often grow up in very low-income, single-parent family situations with many siblings; their parents are more often dependent on unemployment and/or welfare payments. Stress from these sources has contributed to other facets of their lives, such as pressing street socialization and enculturation, guidance from street role models, breakdowns in social control, especially in schools, and, generally, problems with authority figures; schools in fact, have fared poorly in educating the Chicano community (Carter and Segura 1978). In short, these socialization paths—that is, "the process by which children learn to do, and want to do what is required . . . [and that results in] the desire for approval" (Edgerton 1978:446)—have operated to affect their sense of a favorable identity. Emotional problems, in their cases, have emerged early in life and, in part, account for their preteen deviance (e.g., runaways, petty infractions, and street fighting).

The shaping of a self-identity, as Erikson so succinctly pointed out, starts with early life experiences, when a person's racial background and parental influences, more than external forces, begin to make impressions (Erikson 1963:260). Historical patterns of racial and cultural discrimination and the effects of poverty and near poverty necessarily provide a backdrop to these developments, but they are not the sufficient condition to the assessment undertaken here. Self-identity usually begins under parental influences, and for gang members these are often very stressful. Although the family situation and source of stress varied among gang members—death of one or both parents, divorce, separation, or lack of harmony due to other problems—it was clear that one's meaning of self was affected by the experience and created the preconditions that made the gang a source of identification (Quicker 1983:40-44). These representative excerpts from life history interviews show this tendency:

> I felt bad because my mother had to be away most of the day and when she was home I had to share her with my brothers. I still felt lonely. [Pomona veterano]
> I got to be a hard kid to handle and started my life going from relative to relative. [female from Casa Blanca]
> I think my mother and father were at fault because all the time they were yelling at me, so I felt that I was not wanted, so I wanted to be with someone who cares. [male, 18, from Ontario]
> I didn't blame my mom at all. She tried her best to make it with the rest of us [eleven children], but lost the battle. [veterano

from South Fontana]

My mother tried to support us by working. It wasn't easy. We didn't get any supervision or anything. [male, 19, from East Los Angeles]

Other family members, peers, and older street models also contribute to identity formation at a young age, as for instance with family members:

I thought I would prove to him [uncle] that I was man enough. [male, 18, from South Fontana]
I liked to listen to my brother's stories . . . He said you get more respect. [male, 17, from Fontana]
My two brothers were into it, so it's nothing new for our family. [male, 16, from Corona]
I kept messing up in school, just like my brothers. [male, 17, from Van Nuys]
He [an older barrio resident] was strictly a gangster and he influenced a lot of the guys to be vato locos. [male, 18, from Ontario]
I was 9 years old and I used to hang around with pretty old people from there. [male, 17, from White Fence]
We learned more ways of the cholo life through this friend. [male, veterano, from Buena Park]

Socialization for such largely unsupervised and unprotected youths comes to depend considerably on the influence of street supervisors and protectors, including age peers and older models (Rogoff 1981:19). Self-identity formation, then, becomes street based for, as researchers have noted about gangs in general, "gang neighborhoods are female-based in the home and youth-dominated on the streets" (Cartwright et al. 1975:65). Enculturation of street values and habits proceeds along with their social activities. One street feature that demands almost immediate attention, and a ready, quick response, is fear. Fear under these circumstances is an omnipresent feeling in street life, especially if one is unprotected. It must be assuaged and managed. Thus, being and acting "tough" has evolved from this situation and is one of the central gang concerns (W. B. Miller 1958). Indeed, it has become a necessary "adjunct to their self-image" (Tangri and Schwartz 1967:188). As one male, 14, from downtown Los Angeles put it in an interview: "I was born into my barrio. It was either get your ass kicked every day or join a gang and get your ass kicked occasionally by rival gangs. Besides, it was fun and I belonged."

The effort to allay fear and be tough, like so many other adjustments, necessarily generates repercussions in other social, cultural, and psychological realms. For example, relying on one's peers to manage fear is generally helpful. But to receive such support requires reciprocity; thus, behavior is shaped in a mutually reinforcing way to benefit the self and others (Whiting 1980:109). Furthermore, for the members who have had particularly problematic lives, filled with anxieties, frustrations, aggressions, and fear-managing incidents, it is much easier for them to value and demonstrate physical toughness; as locos they feel like leaders, which uplifts the ego, allowing some success in at least one area and thus making them role models. Frightening people is as much a defensive as an offensive action, nonviolently beating someone to the punch with a hard look, body language, or word. The gang is sometimes a sanctuary for gang members who are lacking in size and strength. They must act even more loco to compensate for this drawback and to manage fearful situations. If they falter, they are assured of being backed by the gang. If this fails, they often resort to weapons.

There are many other background factors that clarify self-identity and gang relationships and the inner person's recurrent balancing and juxtaposing between ideal, feared, claimed, and real self-identities. Just living in the barrio provided ready sources of identification in the persons of relatives and other homeboys. Sometimes the gang is the only human unit a person can turn to if a pattern of uncertainty and hopelessness dominates his or her life. A 19-year-old man from Venice, who had older brothers in the gang and had himself been involved in various deviant and delinquent activities, serving time in youth camp and other penal institutions, gave this opinion of the sense of apathy in the barrio among older gang members who had turned tecatos; in some ways, he was also projecting thoughts about himself: "They never had anything going for them anyway. They gave up. They're using [heroin] the same. They're used to the same neighborhood. Right here. They may have wanted the chance to go out there and make something of themselves, but they never got into it. They had had maybe another problem or something. Maybe tomorrow, and tomorrow comes, then they say the next day. The next day comes and they say forget it." In these situations, their real identities were centered in the gang, and thus other sources of identification were difficult to envision or to attain.

Conflict in self-identity comes to a head during adolescence. Role diffusion and ambiguity in particular are important in this phase of ego development, especially in terms of age and sex identity. As noted, many of the gang members come from mother-centered households, where male influences are limited. Thus, "the danger of this stage is role confusion where this is based on a strong previous doubt as to one's sexual identity" (Erikson 1963:262). To punctuate this point, a male, 16 (Geronimo, one of the life histories in Chapter 4), recalled in an interview a rather significant event that had occurred a few years earlier: "I remember my Mom used to comb my hair. . . . she used to comb it to the sides. So one day I took the comb from her and started combing it back. That's when I started thinking I was all *chingón.*" This event coincided with his gang initiation.

Aggressive male behavior is a valuable aid to survival in the street life of the barrio. Male youngsters undergoing this role dilemma turn toward attitudes and behavior that overemphasize these "male" survival qualities. As part of self-identity strivings, each negotiates the feared self (insecure) with the ideal self (street role model) and strives to reshape the real self into the ideal. A father often encourages one to behave aggressively, as in the case of an interviewee from East Los Angeles: "When I got beat up one time as a kid, I came home crying. When I saw my father, he told me to go back out and not come back until I fought back and stopped acting like a sissy. I felt funny inside because I thought he would comfort me with words like—'What's the matter, hijo?' [son]." For many youths, however, the nonfamily male street models are the "ideal" source of those patterns. In an interview, a male, 22, from Pico Viejo explains it: "I started hanging around with the guys in the neighborhood and doing stuff, because there was nothing to do at the time. You may cut it loose [the barrio], but the guy across the street [another barrio] hasn't cut you loose. You're going to go back with your homeboys. You give up good for bad, too." As noted by Devereaux, self-identification is a process of intrapsychic and cultural linkages (1961).

The more fragile egos, of course, tend to have a greater concern to gain stability and direction in the gang, and in turn tend to benefit the gang by the strength of their commitment to it. This dynamic interaction is mutually beneficial to self and group. To this end, nonkin become carnales and homeboys as an especially charged emotional bond permeates the gang unit. This organizing custom appears to be related to the strong sense of familism among Chicanos, very typical of what Colman (1975:45) views as an inclination among certain ethnic groups to value communal and extended family ties. This is especially the case in deeply rooted, isolated barrios, as these words of a male, 16, from Cucamonga affirmed during an interview: "Most of the people in the barrio are related, that's what makes the barrio. . . . Even close friends become like a part of the familia."

However, there are also times when a person resolves a self-identity crisis by adhering superficially to group norms and goals, often motivated by feared and real identities, and thus they must work to achieve a role. This tendency is perhaps better highlighted by citing two individuals who were temporary gang members and represent typical examples of how gangs (as the ideal identity) affect the moderately problematic barrio adolescents. Both of them were from mother-centered homes, experiencing family stress, and had an uneven, mixed socialization to street and "square" (nongang) life. A 17-year-old female from Ontario began to associate and identify with cholas in junior high school because she wanted to belong to a group that was Chicano. Coming from an upwardly mobile family and as a good student, she was determined to prove to herself and childhood peers that she was not becoming a "Coconut"—"brown on the outside, white on the inside" (feared identity). She began to involve herself in chola activities and to champion their cause at school, a largely white institution. Some of the gang involvement included drinking alcoholic beverages and smoking pot at "ditch parties," but, within a year or two after starting high school, she quit the group. The other person is a 17-year-old Latino immigrant who became part of the gang in order to meld into the social environment (ideal identity). His cholo identification began in junior high school with a group of other Latino immigrants like himself who adopted cholo signs of identification and displayed stronger bonds of group solidarity when in this role. He used the cholo walk, talk, and dress (although he complained of the daily arduous task of starching and ironing his khaki pants) to gain stature and survive. "I liked being part of the gang, it made me get a chance to be bad. When I would dress and act like a cholo, I would feel together and tough. All I'd have to do was act cool and not stare at anybody. Whenever there was a chance for a fight, you would get out of it by just acting this way." Aided by a prodding mother and supportive brother, he left the group in high school, as the coping strategy of gang identification brought more problems than it solved.

A study of junior high school students in West Los Angeles further illustrates gang identity formation; it shows that many became involved in a "pseudo-gang" (more social group than street gang) because they sought acceptance by their peers (Cordero 1980). Several individuals, mostly recent Latino immigrants, had adopted the external trappings of the cholo in order to meld into the group; it was their way of assimilating the culture of the area, as a part of self-identification and role achievement. Most of them, however, remained with the group for only a short time, one for a week or two. Rather than being a "loner," or feeling rejected by others, youths often prefer to join the group. A 17-year-old female from Ontario explained her gang involvement when interviewed: "I didn't like feeling odd. There were so many of them, so I joined in right away."

The sociocultural environment features noted earlier are shared by many barrio youth. However, since only a small portion of that number become gang members on a regular basis, we must integrate subjective, psychological reasons into our framework of analysis. This is not to say that collective, sociocultural, and historical phenomena are unimportant in understanding the gang, as they certainly are; it is simply to underscore the subjective motivations that find expression in the small group—the gang. As Devereaux (1961:236) pointed out: "Social movements and processes are possible not because all individuals participating in them are identically (and sociologistically) motivated, but because a variety of authentically subjective motives may seek and find an ego syntonic outlet in the same type of collective activity." The wider society is required for this phase of self-development, and thus the peer group assumes the responsibility of assisting a person with identity formation. "To keep themselves together they temporarily overidentify, to the point of apparent complete loss of identity, with the heroes of cliques and crowds" (Erikson 1963:262).

The Nexus of Ego and Group

The ego identities of some barrio adolescents are embodied under the barrio name, which then becomes the groups's ego ideal. Thus, when one gang-affiliatd person asks, "¿De dónde eres?" (Where are you from?), a rival responds with his barrio name (El Hoyo, White Fence, Cuca, Chino, etc.) because the query is loaded with gang ascription connotations (cf. Geronimo, Chapter 4). There are several reasons why this occurs. In short, the barrio as a group becomes a replacement for the many other counselors who have failed. Bereft of guidance and supervision from family and schools and left to the harsh influences of the streets, some barrio youth have virtually no alternative but to seek membership in the gang. The latter becomes a functional substitute for these units and provides norms and mechanisms for personal security, social support and bonding, protection, and street survival. Given the realities of their lives and that of the streets, it is clear that a fragmented ego is benefited by identifying with a group ego ideal—better a group ego than an ego lacuna. Concrete personal needs—love, protection, supervision, aggression, and so on—are shaped and negotiated through the group. The latter becomes a coping unit for the street. Especially is this the case during the adolescent "psychosocial moratorium" where interest concerning a person's ego ideal (the real self) is suspended (with much individual variance in level of intensity and conviction) while the gang takes over and dominates self-identification. The group helps a person attain the ideal self (fearless). In a clear way, as will shortly be noted, a higher ego ideal is generated through group allegiance and solidarity.

Freud and Scheidlinger have offered several key suggestions on the nexus of ego and group psychologies. Freud (1923) said that the primary group facilitates self-identification, beginning with early environmental experiences and intensifying during adolescence. Upon joining a group, the ego learns group patterns and becomes submerged to the group ego ideal. Scheidlinger (1952) summarized such points in his work and suggested that the peer group provided ego outlets. He says that the group provides "positive personal ties; shared ideals and interests; protection, security, and affection; climate of equality and justice; common enemies outside of the group; and symbolic group ceremonials and activities" (pp. 141-142). In most ways, the gang carries out these functions. Even though there is a structural level (e.g., Suttles' [1968] complementary opposition to territorial outsiders) to group associations, there is also a sociopsychological counterpart that is reflected in the libidinal ties (emotional interest and backing, affection) that members have for one another. This is verified and reified in various ways, not least of which is the gang terminology showing strong emotional attachments. Members habitually say that they are carnales, *camaradas* (comrades), and homeboys to underscore the type of fictive kinship they share (Moore et al. 1983). As Freud (1923:48) said of group psychology in general, they (ego) identify with "one another in their ego."

The barrio name, thus, as a symbol for the group ideal, is central to group solidarity. Group identification reflects the similarity of barrio upbringing and natural development of friendly ties among individuals. Such networks encourage altruism at the expense of egoism. Egalitarianism is idealized (part of the ideal self within the group) but there nevertheless are times when personal, ego "trips" dominate. Although there is much talk of doing things for the homies and barrio, with little emphasis on who is doing it, there are occasional and situational leaders. Since the group ideal is paramount and, in fact, the symbolic leader, any show of egoism would undermine it.

For example, when opposing barrio gangs meet on the streets (on foot or in a car) or at other private (parties) and public (fairs) functions, it is quite common to hear the phrase "White Fence [or whatever barrio name] Rifa [controls]" yelled out, not "I [read: ego name] control." As a regular pattern, experiences acquired by previous cliques in the barrio, as a build-up of tradition and as a type of alter ego, serve as a source of mythology to stimulate the contemporary clique to measure up to past events, recognitions, and leaders (i.e., the barrio itself).

Most of a person's time is spent at the local hangouts (e.g., parks, parties) where opportunities to show group allegiance present themselves. In the context of normal, casual dialogue on personal or barrio events, there are ways for a new member to learn how to act and think. There is a need to adopt ways of talking, standing, even how to arrange your *máscara* (face; but, more elaborately, persona, as defined separately, *más* means "more," and *cara* means "face"—more faces). At one evening gathering I observed a newly inducted East Los Angeles gang member respond in a very nonchalant way to mention of the death of an important older member. An older gang member gave him a moderately stern look and replied: "He's from the barrio, *ese* [you]." The message was simple: anyone in the barrio is important, and you should feel what we feel about him. With casual reminders like this, an individual quickly incorporates the feelings of the group. Showing that one knows and understands is often communicated with eye and facial expressions. It is an affective, feeling way to convey group messages.

Separate individuals can fit into this group when symbols and identifiers that show conformity are adopted. Individuality is minimized in this way. Although it may happen earlier, group-directed nicknaming is a part of this process, much like a street baptism. Personal quirks, peculiarities, and aggressions are caricatured with a nickname, and in the eyes of the member thereby made normal. Gang members will affirm this distinction by branding their ego (or nickname) and barrio name on their bodies—tattoos—and on public structures and walls—placas.

These group characteristics include other behavioral habits in walk, talk, dress, and gestures and in ways of demonstrating gang loyalty, toughness, and *locura* (quasi-controlled insanity). The opportunity for showing one's identification with the group is enhanced by these behaviors, as proof that the self is as one with them. It is fairly certain that a person's commitment to the group can be, in large degree, measured by adherence to group traits. Are the body language, street slang, and style natural or affected? Does the person shower the body with tattoos and the barrio with placasos? How much is real or fake about the person? Such signs and symbols vary among individuals as they do among barrios. Group allegiances are shepherded by other practices and sanctions, such as maintaining your *palabra* (word) on various types of matters or laying a *leva* on a person who departs from group experience.

Group identification is strengthened in this climate of social and human reinforcement. One young man from Norco once said in an interview that there is no "in-between, for you're either with the group or against it." Several others stressed that it is the barrio (or the klika—peers—they belong to) that makes the decisions, not one individual. As one 19-year-old from Venice said: "To me, it's important to go back to your neighborhood and stay right there in your neighborhood. That way you won't have no problems or anything. You know what's there, what you've got, you can go and get what you want, anywhere, anyplace."

Several individuals mentioned in interviews that joining a gang made them "feel like somebody"; otherwise, they were a "nobody." An 18-year-old from Ontario helped start a klika in order for his "ego to go higher" when he was among his peers, although this group was principally involved with social activities like parties and cruising. For him, and others of his group, their street gang was adaptive because it protected them from neighboring barrio gangs and provided a source of identity. Another young man, a 17-year-old from El Monte Flores whose parents struggled to raise six other children, had a long and deep association with his peers dating from childhood. His ego had at an early age become as one with the barrio. "You see, well, where I live, I knew everybody in the street and everybody knew me. And just that little part where I live, everybody knows each other and just by that everybody backs each other." For him, it was natural to submerge himself in the barrio (group) and its activities, which he did time and again without question.

For many of the youngsters without adult supervision, the only guidance they receive is from peers. For the gang's approval, a member might behave in repugnant ways that initially have little intrinsic value to him. Showing that one can feel, act, and look hard or uncaring is a requirement for gang membership. The group will always stand behind you, even if you singly provoke or instigate an incident that requires group support. It does not matter, for the group is as one for those individuals who have crossed the line and committed themselves. Individual peculiarities and aggressions are tolerated in this climate of support. This habit is often reflected in the nicknames that show a personal quirk—Feo (homely or ugly), Puppet (face, hair, or body frame of a marionette), Gordo (fat or chubby), or Loco (crazy)—that perhaps affected the person's nonacceptance in other social groupings but that now is honestly recognized and nonetheless accepted by the group.

Thus, different subjective motives are able to fit into group patterns, particularly in the way that self-identity takes its form and shape in group life. Much of the show of commitment and attachment to the gang occurs in situations where established members witness one's efforts to conform to group ideals. However, in addition to the general importance of belonging to the group, there are other instances where individual egos benefit from the association. For example, some spoke of how the group gave them an opportunity to show their leadership abilities (gang disclaimers to the contrary), develop self-pride, and acquire prestige and self-esteem. This was evidenced in several of the cases cited earlier, in such common things as in dress: "I was all choloed-out"; walk: "I leaned laid back and moved slow"; and graffiti: "my placasos were all over the place." Sometimes gang members' accounts highlight personal, aggressive objectives of some individuals who want to show their gang loyalty, such as "If I were killed, I would go down with pride." Such assertions are usually phrased in group terms because it is the group's response toward the person that feeds the ego and makes him feel proud. A deeply involved 19-year-old male member from Chino, who learned the cholo and gang style at a young age, in an interview discussing why barrios fight, gave a rather interesting explanation of this phenomenon: "We can't talk because of our pride and their pride. No Chicano's going to lay his pride on the line so another can suck it up and make his pride bigger."

Group Roles

Starting at an earlier age, but accentuated during adolescence, a number of group role patterns and role symbols are incorporated into and onto the person to verify that ego and group have become as one. Thus, "symbols . . . are understood by the members of the social group who share language, beliefs, values, and rules of behavior . . . with all the nuances of style, gestures, postures, and facial expressions" (Whiting 1980:109). The most established gang members are the alter egos who, by example, represent the roles and convey the role symbols to other, younger novitiates. Their example, however, is what drives younger members to role achievement within the gang.

As part of the resolution of the adolescent self-identity crisis within the group, there are patterned group role expectations and symbols that need to be enacted and adopted. Some individuals, as noted, have backgrounds that fit them better for these gang roles, and as a result they become better enactors (real identity is closer to ideal identity). Other persons with less problematic backgrounds have a more difficult time of it; a few, as noted with the temporary and situational members, reflect a type of role dissonance and ambivalence (avoidance of feared identity). It is the proficient enactors who most influence the fringe gang members. The whole set of gestures and demeanors of these street models, like dress, talk, and walk, is an imagery for others to copy. For those individuals whose gang involvement is of short duration, these symbolic characteristics often become a role-set to be enacted, but, as Goffman has said of such behavior, "properly speaking this is not an image that is meant for his own eyes" (1956:489). For a variety of reasons, they are unable (or refuse) to wholeheartedly submerge their selves into the group. Thus, they play at the "part" only temporarily or when the occasion warrants it; as one young man said, "I would put on a regular shirt and pants and not walk or act like a cholo when I'd visit my girlfriend." Nevertheless, group roles and symbols of identification serve both regular and temporary gang members.

Group roles demonstrated by the group's heroes (real, legendary, and imagined) show ways for thinking and acting. In the process, they reduce the range of roles to select from and allay personal ambiguities over self-identity formation during this "psychosocial moratorium" period. Similar to the rituals that exist in other societies to ease this change, researchers have noted how role transition among urban gangs is aided by "rites of passage," which act to alleviate the adolescents' sense of confusion (Bloch and Niederhoffer 1958). The initiate is later held to the new role expectations by group witnesses acting as the public validation that the transition took place. A personal need to prove oneself is central to this ritual and most members do so informally by exhibiting courage, bravery, and daring in accepted street affairs, such as fighting (either friendly encounters among peers or more serious aggressions against rival barrio members). Criminal activities like robberies, shoplifting, burglaries, muggings, and so on, although less commonly a form of proof, are also a way of confirmation. Toward this end, with immersion into the group, with the self (real identity) now the barrio gang (ideal identity), thinking and acting are shaped by role, and a person is submerged into the group mentality; in short, "the individual is lost in union with others" (Colman 1975:43).

To consummate such an end, there are various informal and formal types of gang initiation rituals and ceremonies, which some gang members have mentioned in interviews, and barrios differ in how they handle it. Usually the process consists of a physical assault at the hands of three or four initiators, although occasionally a larger body will surround a person. Blows with hands and feet are permitted by all parties. Serious beatings are rare, but bruises and abrasions occur with some regularity. More often, the group merely observes how and if the person stands up forthrightly and defends himself. The ordeal permits the initiate to show that he can handle the new role, that is, prove his ability to fight and withstand punishment. Such a showing demonstrates one's abilities in at least one very important male, gang pattern: conflict.

Notwithstanding the nature or severity of the initiation, the ritual solidifies one's integration to the group and contributes to group lore, specifically showing that an initiate is tough. The latter quality is a highly respected male street trait. As noted, such an identity is forged by street "fear" coping and the movement away from a mother-centered household influence. Burton and Whiting (1961) have examined the cross-cultural association between adolescent initiation rites for males and situations that generate cross-sex identification ambiguities, saying that it is "clear that the gang is an institution with a function similar to that of initiation . . . in those societies with conflict in sex identity" (p. 94; also Whiting 1980). All gangs appear to emphasize exclusive relations and to admire daring behavior. Such patterns approximate elements of the rites that Burton and Whiting report, even though initiation is not common to all members. Veteranos of the group thus become teachers for the role the initiates seek and give feedback to ensure proper role behavior.

The expectations of the group are also important in learning the role. The role-set includes the role models and those who model that image. It is not mere conformity though, for the cholo style is a necessary facet of the role enactment, what Goffman would call the social ritual being played (1959:57). Thus, "whether his acquisition of the role was primarily motivated by a desire to perform the given task or by a desire to maintain the corresponding front, the actor will find that he must do both" (p. 27). The streets have helped forge a cholo identity that now affects an individual's personal identity. In sum, the self needs the group for self-identification, and the group presents self with various role expectations to ascertain group allegiance. When enacted, this reflects the merging of self into the group ideal of thinking and behaving.

Acting "bad" (a frequently used term) is representative of this role concern. It reflects a type of toughness and incorporates things that are desirable, particularly in the view of the gang. Temporary or situational individuals in the gang do things to acquire this feeling, which, of course, works to make them more accepted. It "looked like fun to get in fights and be rebels," one said. Another talked about being bad by "raiding other junior high schools." Others spoke of pride in appearing to be bad in the cholo walk or dress style. Group symbolic role traits, as noted, were mentioned quite often in this regard. In an interview a 20-year-old from Chino who spent only a short time on the fringes of the local group tried to act bad by "carrying a switchblade around and showing it to people," but the blade was broken and would be useless if he ever had to open it. For some, acting bad is a way of getting girls to look up to and be in awe of them; and for girls who act bad, it is a means of gaining recognition from the guys.

"Toughness" is a requirement for group membership that is proven in the ritual of gang initiation. Comments on acting and being tough show a strong concern about this type of behavior. A few cases illustrate this point. A 22-year-old male from South Fontana repeated his brother's habits and joined the barrio clique. He mentioned that "if anybody threatens a member we had to get together and beat the guys near to death. That's when you show how tough you are, because you have to be tough to make it in this world. We have to get them before they get us." A 17-year-old male from Varrio Nuevo who was only involved with the clique for social and athletic events summed it up in this way in an interview: "I was always the youngest and smallest of the crowd and always the last to be picked for any ball games. I always got my butt knocked down whenever we played ball. I learned that if you got up right away, no matter how much I might be hurting, they soon learned to accept me. I showed them I was tough and could take it, or either I was a dummy and didn't know any better." Another interviewee, a 16-year-old from East Los Angeles, said that "the veteranos get more respect because they have been through more, they're tougher." That statement underscores the role modeling that takes place within the barrio to learn what "tough" is. A 17-year-old male from White Fence even gives the movie role models credit for this behavior: "I wanted to do it because I wanted to be a tough guy. I used to watch a lot of gangster movies. Like James Cagney, Humphrey Bogart, and the regular gangster movies. I was always trying to impress people. I wanted to do my thing."

To "do his thing," as in the other cases, meant to do the "group" thing. It often is the case that joining a gang and wanting to act bad and tough stem from individuals' identifying with gang members, either friends or rivals, who have acted aggressively toward them. Indeed, to alleviate the fear that is instilled by such threats, a person is forced to feign that he is bad and tough. Destructive and violent gang actions often are nurtured in this climate of wanting to "prove" oneself; consider, for example, the youth described in Chapter 6, who went on a "drive-by" shooting to show his tough friend that he wasn't afraid.

Occasionally, individuals expressed a regard for leadership opportunities, as was the case with the young lady discussed above who took to representing cholo causes to avert a "coconut" label. These thoughts were uttered in private moments, for otherwise such opinions would tend to tarnish the group egalitarian standard. Those who were explicit about it made it clear that they enjoyed speaking up for the group. Generally, unofficial leadership status was given because they were responsible and backed up others; being a "big dude that no one would mess with" was also helpful. Respect for their fellow gang members characterized most of these leaders, as they could not afford to flaunt such powers when the gang code was explicit about no leaders. This explains simultaneous demonstrations of group loyalty and locura behavior as well.

Locura is a state of mind where various actions bordering on "craziness" take place. A loco exhibits this mind set by alternately acting tough, fearless, and daring and by exhibiting other spontaneous types of behavior, such as getting "loco" on drugs and alcohol. Some manage this role with authority, while others do so with trepidation and only when peer or situational pressures are overwhelming. This psychosocial role-set developed over a long period of time and has become a requisite for street survival; additionally, it is an acting and thinking pattern for identification and emulation. There are important advantages to having a loco in your circle. Such locos help the most when rival barrios are mounting "drive-by" campaigns against a barrio. He can often be a prized member of the gang in such affairs, sometimes acting as a deterrent to keep peace. However, almost as common is the loco who is a hindrance or detriment because he brings trouble to the community.

Among individuals within a barrio and between barrios there is a wide range of locura behavior. The worst case, hard-core loco individuals have generally undergone a traumatic early life, experiencing a type of "psychosocial death." They have developed feelings of self-hatred because of personal insecurity and family problems. Self-hatred is manifested by feelings of personal worthlessness and the worthlessness of others. Such a background makes them lash out at society without thought of retribution, for the aggressions and unhappy experiences of their early life are being acted out. One man, nicknamed "Psycho," as an example of this behavior, accidentally wounded a 5-year-old girl during a gang-related shooting. When he was asked about it, he replied: "I don't give a fuck. Why do you think they call me Psycho?" At the other side of the spectrum is the person who only is loco situationally, on a "drive-by" shooting. Role enactment characterizes the latter to ensure that the group accepts him. Numerous instances have been recounted to show this identification with loco role-playing, even with regular gang members. So, usually, the "craziest" individuals set the standard of behavior for the group, and, with some instigative prodding, they can encourage others to act according to the norm. The "psychosocial death" loco is important for this reason.

Tico, a 22-year-old, reflects this pattern. Early life experiences were dramatically problematic—raised in a broken family and foster homes, uneven and troublesome socialization to public institutions, ethnic identity confusions, and many traumatic childhood incidents. As an example, he recalled in an interview a street beating at the age of 9: "When I was little, they didn't care how smart you were or how young you were. They would beat the heck out of you. Man, I got beat up by just calling him a name and when I turned around, he jumped at me. I tried to run and slipped, and he kicked and beat the heck out of me. Yeah, I was real little and I tripped out on that." In junior high school he had become attracted to the cholo group life: "I started changing and these people [foster parents] kept on despising the way cholos were, and they wanted me inside before it was dark, and I just said fuck that shit. I'm going to do what I want. So I started going out and never coming back. I wouldn't come back all night. I would run away sometimes, and I would get busted for burglary." With the other cholo dress and demeanor habits, he launched a life of locura. He personally considered himself a "fuck-up" since he was a child, and by the age of 14 he emphatically emphasized: "I'm not scared of nobody."

Although this individual affected the cholo image, it is clear that his early life had dictated that he would play the part very well and get the most out of dangerous role enactments. Such a demonstration of locura as his, however, does not mean that he infrequently followed more usual cholo behavior—partying, friendship, cruising, and so on. It is just that the pressures of street life encourage a loco mind set that must be ready at all times. Daily life is spent, as he said himself, showing that "cholos have cora, too." It is important to remember that locura is but one type of role behavior among many available to a person who is seeking group confirmation. The complete cholo role-set is easier to perform for some persons, especially the early "psychosocial death" types. Nevertheless, it helps to act loco to gain headway into the group. The walk, talk, and dress role symbols are visual, public acts that indicate toughness to observers, but to do the loco role-set requires deeper changes.

A great deal of discomfort and anxiety accompany playing this loco role. The use of intoxicants and a striving to gain acceptance are what aid this behavior. It is these substances and motivations that soothe the apprehensions to allow for a suitable performance. While drug and alcohol consumption are problems in their own right, in combination with locura role expectations more serious consequences have developed. Even individuals who try to avoid trouble are more easily "locoized" with such substances.

Conclusion

Acquiring a self-identity in this group way fits in with other adolescent functions. The gang has taken on the responsibility of doing what the family, school, and other social agencies have failed to do—provide mechanisms for age and sex development, establish norms of behavior, and define and structure outlets for friendship, human support, and the like. Some of these group patterns have emerged as a result of barrio pressures, such as the need for surrogate kin, for many who come from broken, stressful family situations, and the need for protection in neighborhoods where physical violence is common, especially if their life is unsupervised. Other functions are more properly focal adolescent concerns, such as the need for role models and plenty of excitement and adventure to help expend youthful energies. Considered in combination, these group patterns help the shaping of a self-identity. The quid pro quo for making the group your ego ideal is to have the group protect you, calm your fears in a harsh environment, and give you a strong sense of emotional bonding through camaraderie, and, of course, for those particularly prone to such deviant activities, outlets for personal aggressions and hostilities.

Through various means, a positive self-identity has failed to materialize among certain Chicano youth. Because of this, some have sought what Erikson has labeled "a greater sense of identity in being withdrawn or in being delinquent" (1956:9). The multiple roots and origins of this identity ambivalence become especially troublesome during adolescence when the street gang takes over. To manage the crisis, the ego integrates itself to the barrio (group) ideal and the gang provides role expectations and functions to shepherd a person through this "psychosocial moratorium." There are uniform (and, in fact, uniformed) group ways to assuage the conflict and simplify an ego identification. To understand this process the nexus of ego, group, and role psychologies must be assessed. The moratorium can sometimes last throughout a young adult's life, some close to past 30 years old and beyond. Staying on the streets, they still find outlets in the gang. Most of the gang members, however, generally seek and find a way to grow out of this crisis period, sometimes after a great deal of experimentation and failures. In any event the urban gang has filled the vacuum usually occupied by other institutional units (e.g., family, school) that aid adolescent passage to adulthood. It must be understood that the unusual nature of underclass barrio life has revamped what is considered normal adolescent concerns. The group street life that has emerged is geared for such altered individual strivings and needs.

8. Conclusion

Most Mexican American barrios in urban areas of Southern California date from the massive immigration from Mexico in the early years of this century. Economic concerns (most of the new arrivals were unskilled or semiskilled workers who could only obtain low-paying jobs) and the entrenched anti-Mexican prejudice of the dominant society combined to dictate that these immigrants settle in marginal areas of the growing towns and cities or in rural enclaves—colonias—which would much later become urbanized. Subsequent waves of immigrants, also subject to racial discrimination and constrained by the need for inexpensive housing, tended to settle in similar locations. They preferred to live among others who would at least be familiar with their customs and language. Thus, virtually all of these immigrants and their offspring had to cope with the stresses generated by living in overcrowded housing in poorly developed neighborhoods, subsisting on poor wages, and dealing with public agencies and authorities who often disdained them. In time, through job seniority, improvement in pay and work conditions for unionized jobs, or entrepreneurial efforts, many of the immigrants and more of their children attained more prosperous positions. Some joined the American exodus to the suburbs; others improved their modest houses and yards but remained in the barrio. In short, most acquired coping skills in the course of adjusting to their marginal situations and fashioned for themselves what Arvizu (1974) has called a "constructive marginality," combining aspects of the Mexican and Anglo-American cultures. The development of bilingual and bicultural abilities aided this ultimately favorable adaptation (Buriel 1984; Vigil and Long 1981).

Yet, even within the earliest generation of immigrants, some (barrio residents most vulnerable to the strains of poverty, overcrowding, and discrimination) were less able to cope successfully. Their families were overwhelmed by what Dembo et al. (1984:20) calls "community factors that override individual characteristics in influencing family life." Increasingly they "fell behind" in their struggles, and the dimensions of the problems their children inherited were even more intractable. Over the generations this process has led to the emergence of an underclass; recent trends indicate that this population is increasingly children in single-parent households (Moynihan 1988). As has been observed in other ethnic groups, this process is accompanied by rising levels of juvenile delinquency (Glueck 1959). Normal youth cohorting became problematic and authorities began to recognize the youth gang phenomenon (Bogardus 1926). Barrio gangs gradually grew into established realities to which subsequent generations of youths have had to adjust.

Garbarino (1982) notes that traditional social control mechanisms in low-income, ethnic minority urban environments are transformed by the new working and living conditions. Children spend increasing amounts of time in the streets. Formal institutions, especially police and teachers, assume a much greater role in socializing youths to social norms and mores. Ironically, due to teacher-student "discontinuities" in language usage, contrasting cultural beliefs, and structural conditions, the most acute culture conflict often occurs in schools (Ogbu 1982). Encounters with the police are often similarly impaired. For youths from especially stressful home situations, such experiences commonly lead to the development of early learning problems, disrespect for authorities, and premature departure from school. Peers and older youths who have "dropped out" before them increasingly influence these youths, in effect functioning as "an interim kin group" (Garbarino 1982).

In Mexican American barrios, a cholo subculture emerged to reflect the street values, behavioral norms, and sociopsychological needs of such youths. This subculture combines Mexican traditions (which are continually renewed in the barrios by continuing immigration from Mexico) and American experiences, yet at the same time rejects aspects of both. Barrio adolescents encountering increased intergenerational strife are attracted to the core values and behavioral norms epitomized by the barrio street gangs. The members of these gangs are, in turn, drawn principally from among those youths whose lives most drastically reflect the multiple status "crises" brought about by marginal backgrounds. The subculture provides the gang member with a cholo front, which he presents in his social confrontations with peers as well as with the general public. The public usually sees only the front, and not the conditions that generated it. Yet the latter must be examined and understood if the destructive elements of barrio gang subcultures are to be effectively dealt with.

Multiple Marginality: Theory and Method

An interdisciplinary, multidimensional approach and assessment strategy is currently proving the most fruitful among researchers of youth issues and the gang phenomenon (C. D. Moore 1981; Garbarino 1982). The multiple marginality framework provides such an analytical basis for it is comprehensive and is guided by the anthropological notion of holism. Holism, as Keesing notes (1974), is more than just looking at everything: rather, it is a dynamic discussion and analysis at each level that enhances understanding of the complexity of barrio gangs. The ambiguities of modern life, in contrast to pre-industrial small-scale societies, generate complex problems that, in turn, require complex analytic approaches. A general orientation enables the interpretation of historical and ethnographic particulars. Geertz (1972, 1973) argues that it is "thick descriptions" which shed light on the different and separate interconnections in human thinking and acting. There is a need for such a construct in gang delinquency studies, even though we must proceed with caution in integrating gang theories that hold somewhat different assumptions.

Most of the elements of these gang theories are interwoven in the multiple marginality interpretation. The major difficulty with these theories of *emphases* is that they lack a historical developmental perspective and fail to utilize different ways of looking at the issue. For example, Cloward and Ohlin (1960) distinguish criminal, conflict, and retreatist subcultures within urban street populations. In the Chicano case and, I suspect, in similar minority groups, all three occur within a cohort, albeit at different times in the lives of the persons who make up that cohort. Aside from early home and street experiences that shape the intensity and duration of involvement, the conflict (e.g., gang-banging) phase is most common during early adolescence when fighting with rival barrios is intense. This is so because the youths must impress the veteranos and also act out their psychophysical identity changes. Later there is a shift in types and numbers of infractions and criminal activity (e.g., crime partners), and incarceration (e.g., pintos) becomes more prominent. Finally, for the regular, most heavily drug abuse retreatist members (e.g., tecatos), there is heroin. Without ascertaining the historic dimensions of a person's or cohort's life, one could easily label a gang and its members one or another subculture merely on the basis of single interviews or isolated periods of observation.

Similarly, while other gang theories may utilize particular variables to underscore their point, it is the collective synthesis of these variables that determines early involvement and subsequent regular gang membership. The advantage of a multiple marginality framework is that Bloch and Niederhoffer's (1958) point of "becoming a man" is incorporated as an analytical aspect in understanding the adolescent gang identity crises (e.g., the ego ideal becomes the barrio ideal). It is also important to include as an aspect of the framework, in turn, Cohen's (1955) model of subcultural developments among lower-class populations to acquire status (e.g., group autonomy, versatility); W. B. Miller's (1958) notion of lower-class culture (e.g., klikas, toughness); and Yablonsky's (1959) sociopathic argument (e.g., locura, gang conflict). Passing these theories through the prism of multiple marginality best reflects the complexity of modern urban society. Multiple marginality implies more than just many gang facets. It also entails the many situations and conditions that contribute to gangs.

Also common to the gang delinquency field are the theories of strain (e.g., Merton 1949), cultural deviance (e.g., Shaw and McKay 1942), and social control (e.g., Hirschi 1969). The interplay among all these factors is clearly exhibited in the lives of gang members. Geronimo's life history, for example, is best understood as an interplay of various influences dealing with aspects of his predicament: income disparities contribute to *strain*, stressful family situation weakens *social control*, and street associates influenced *deviance*. No single theory completely illuminates his gang involvement and behavior. There are many more children from his neighborhood who are also poor and from stressful families but who avoided Geronimo's level of gang involvement. Some were very adept at changing and shifting from a street to a conventional identity. In Geronimo's case, as in most others who were "high risk" candidates for regular gang membership, the cumulative, simultaneous dynamics of his situation led him to gravitate to the gang. This constellation of forces are intensely present in the lives of certain barrio youth who form gangs and join them.

The multiple marginality construct offers an integrative interpretation, a way to build theory rather than a theory itself. Although the multiple marginality argument initially emphasized the importance of historical-structural and cultural-ecological criteria, the sequence must be viewed as a whole. To reiterate, complex societies require complex frameworks of analysis. A multidimensional analysis identifies the crucial weaves within the broader fabric of the gang subculture. Indeed, it can show us how gang members experience multiple crises and confusions over living, working, associational, developmental, and identity situations and considerations.

Methodological approaches are closely associated with the

theoretical formulations. The life history and self-reflexive history method has provided novel details and insights in offering a the microcosms of gang life. Of course, much of the personal information must be contextualized ethnographically, that is, what places, times, and people. These methods differ markedly from other studies of gangs, especially Chicano variants, although other anthropological examinations of gangs exist (Keiser 1969; Snyder 1977). Moore (1978) and her associates, of which I am a member, have developed a "collaborative" team approach where academics and community researchers (former gang members) jointly set the research agenda. Horowitz's work (1983) on Chicano youth in Chicago relied on participant observation and key informants but encompassed a relatively short field experience. That community resembled the early generations of Mexicans in Los Angeles, whose youths were more a palomilla than a gang subculture. Klein's investigation (1971) utilized data from street gang worker case loads to compare black and Chicano gangs in Los Angeles. Each of these works has contributed to a greater understanding of Chicano gangs, but the combined methodologies of this study provide a broader basis for further insights. One of the major problems of urban research, especially gang-related studies, is that participant observation only goes so far. Because a field worker's presence makes observation obtrusive, one must consider and develop other means of gathering data. Interview and life history information buttressing field observances can round out the decisive events that occur in the world of gang reality. My own personal experience with gangs and gang members, as well as other types of "street" people, was particularly useful in placing the contemporary gang variant in historical context—for example, the changes from a gang to a gang subculture—and examining other private, deeper motivations—for example, locura and role "fronts."

Immigration, Adaptation, and the Future

After the sheriffs conducted a sweep of Barrio Cuca in 1978, arresting and jailing a number of very active gang members, the community remained fairly quiet for a couple of years. However, since the sheriffs only took one cohort away, it was only a matter of time before a new cohort surfaced. When it did, the barrio street life would be rekindled. The situations and conditions that created the street life and group were still there. The words of a Cucamonga city official notwithstanding ("we don't want to understand the problem, we just want to stop it"), the solution to gangs is not to be found in jailing each new cohort. We seem to forget that urban youth gangs have plagued

America since the turn of the century. The Boys Club of America was founded in the 1870s to help "pavement children." In the 1930s, motion pictures like *Dead End* provided audiences with a sympathetic portrayal of the problems of street youth. As long as certain environmental and economic patterns persist, the gang subculture will continue to recruit new members, especially given the reinforcement the subculture receives from those who return from prison life. There will always be cholos and among them individuals who are at risk of becoming gang members.

Future developments in the gang subculture in Southern California will clearly be affected by the demographic shifts underway today. As more and more neighborhoods become Latino, given the economic fluctuations and instabilities of our times, many other Latino immigrants are sure to join the ranks of the permanently unemployed and underemployed. Since there is already an established pattern, they and their children, even more swiftly than did earlier generations, may adopt habits and customs of the Mexican American underclass or create their own version (the gang subculture being one facet of the former). Many programs have attempted, with varying regularity and success, to combat this street phenomenon (through religion, e.g.; cf. Vigil 1982), but those that exist today are aimed more toward the symptoms than the cause.

Preparation for the expected increase in gangs and, obviously, gang members can be observed in official demands for more prisons (regular repositories for the more active gang members who advance to criminal careers) and the steady increase in specialized law enforcement units organized to combat street gangs. There is even a California Gang Investigators Association, which meets annually to discuss and share current information on the subject. Moreover, as Latinos continue to move into other urban areas around the country, early reports indicate that a local repetition of the Southern California experience may be in gestation (Moore and Pachón 1985; Hagedorn and Macon 1987). The cholo subculture and barrio gangs have also spread into new areas, including towns along the Mexican side of the border (Cuéllar 1987; Cummings 1987; Castro 1981) and even deeper within Mexico (Villela and Gastelum 1980). Moreover, as youths thoroughly anchored to gang and cholo patterns have grown up, they have even fashioned adult versions of choloismo.

Viewing the gang subculture in a broader, macro to micro way aids interpretation of how and why the subculture arose and outlines when and where youngsters gravitate to it as a solution to urban adaptation. It is a holistic interpretation precisely because social behavior is multilayered, and for many Chicanos it is the cumulative functionings of these marginal situations that account for their deep gang membership. Future researchers might more closely examine the linkages of family life, street peer socialization, and adolescent development or, put another way, how social control institutions are revamped by larger forces in urban settings. Many researchers have suggested or already charted this path (Dembo et al. 1984; C. D. Moore 1981; Mancini 1981; Garbarino 1982; Hirschi 1983; Goldstein 1981; Robins 1978), for it is clear that personal and environmental factors are intertwined and a comprehensive, multidimensional approach will yield the best insights in studies of this nature.

Glossary

BARRIO.   A neighborhood in a Chicano community, a district in a Mexican colony.

BRACERO.   Literally, field hand, one who works with his or her arms (*brazos*); contract Mexican field workers during and after World War II.

CALCOS.   Shoes.

CALÓ.   A pidgin or creole speech style of cholos, mixed Spanish and English; a jive, inventive language, originating with Gypsies in Spain and later diffused by bullfighters to Mexico.

CAMARADA.   Comrade, a buddy or friend.

CANCIÓN.   Song or tune.

CANTÓN.   Home, an abode.

CARNAL.   Literally, of the flesh; a brother, intimate friend.

CARNALISMO.   Placing value on brotherhood, from carnal; a strong social norm and cultural value.

CHINGAZOS.   Blows, or fighting.

CHINGÓN.   Someone who is in command and controls the social situation; the top guy; good fighter.

CHOLO.   A Chicano street style of youth who are marginal to both Mexican and Anglo culture; also used historically for cultural marginals and racial hybrids in Mexico and some parts of Latin America.

CHÚNTARO.   A Mexican national (a derogatory label).

CHURINGA.   An anthropological term taken from aboriginal Australians, referring to secret sacred objects in which ancestral souls were believed to repose.

COLONIA.   Colony, rural barrio.

CON SAFOS.   Phrase used in gang graffiti; meaning anything negative you say about this graffiti also applies to you.

CONTROLLA.   Controls barrio "turf"; alternate spelling (incorrect by Spanish standards) for *controla*.

CORA.   Cholo way of saying heart (*corazón*); one who has heart, compassion.

COSTROS KLIKA.   Clique in El Monte Flores, self-described as "gangsters"—probably from "Cosa Nostra."

CUENTA.   Tally sheet; used by barrio Mom-and-Pop storeowners to keep records of credit sales.

¿DE DÓNDE?   Where [are you] from? A phrase used by gang members to challenge or confront a stranger they see on the streets.

ENGABACHEADO.   Anglicized Mexican American; imputes disloyalty to Mexican lifeways.

ESE.   Guy; hey, guy.

ESTÁ ESCAMADO.   He's afraid, scared.

FIRME.   Firm, he's okay, he's firme; together, bonded.

GABACHO.   Anglo, or white.

GENTE.   People.

HIJO.   Son.

HUEVOS.   Balls, testicles; courage and daring.

JAÍNILLAS.   Girls, chicks.

KLIKA.   Clique; guys in a cohort within the gang.

LEVA.   Group sanction; social avoidance of gang member who has defied gang norms.

LIRA.   Guitar.

LISA.   Shirt.

LOCOS.   Crazies; usually, in gang context, short for vatos locos.

LOCOTE.   Act of getting crazy and/or high on drugs and alcohol.

LOCURA.   A mind-set complex that values crazy or unpredictable thinking and acting.

MÁSCARA.   Mask; used to refer to a person's face.

MOVIDA.   A move or manipulation of an object or person; something one did to show skill and ingenuity.

¡NUEVO-Y-QUÉ?   Utterance challenging another person or barrio, either through graffiti or spoken word, to respond to: "I'm from Nuevo [or any other barrio name] and so what? What are you going to do about it?

NO TE RAJAS.   You don't chicken out and run.

NUNCHAKU.   Karate sticks; used in martial arts (Japanese term).

ÓRALE.   Say; or, it's okay.

PACHUCO.   1930s-1940s label for mostly second-generation Mexican American youth; variant of zoot-suit style originating in El Paso, Texas, the latter town often referred to as "Chuco."

PALABRA.   Word; also, keeping your word.

PALOMILLA.   Literally, covey of doves; a Mexican term for an age/sex cohort.

PAYASA.   Female clown; gang nickname.

PEDO.   Literally, fart; real or potential trouble or friction that might involve fighting.

PINTO.   Ex-convict.

PISTO.   Alcohol; also, drunk.

PLACAS.   Graffiti signature; also used for police because of badges (*plaques*) of authority.

PLACASOS.   Personalized graffiti; signature; also referring to one's nickname.

PLAQUEANDO.   The act of creating a graffiti; going on a graffiti binge.

PLEBE.   Literally, plebian; common, humble folk, down to earth, working class who knows what's happening.

PLEITO.   Referring to potential trouble or fight.

POLVO.   Angel dust, or PCP.

QUINCEAÑERA.   A 15-year-old female's coming-out celebration.

RATA.   Rat; a snitch, one who tattles.

REMATE.   Swap meet in or near Mexican American neighborhood.

RIFAMOS.   We're the best, we're better than your barrio; used in graffiti, *rifa*, to mean our barrio is the best.

TECATO.   Heroin addict; habitual drug user.

TIENE HUEVOS.   He has balls, i.e., courage.

TONTO.   Dumb, stupid.

TORCIDO.   Literally, twisted; arrested.

TOTAL.   Everything, complete domination; used in graffiti to signify dominance.

TRAGO.   A drink; draught of liquid, usually alcohol.

TRUCHA.   Beware, be alert.

VAISA.   Hand; hand grip, like a vise.

VATO LOCO.   Literally, crazy guy; refers to wild and violent behavior.

VETERANO.   Vetaran; older gang member who has been through it all and is now a role model for younger members.

YESCA.   Marijuana.

References

Achor, Shirley
  1978   *Mexican Americans in a Dallas Barrio*. Tucson: University of Arizona Press.

Acuña, Rudy
  1981   *Occupied America: A History of Chicanos*. 2d. ed. New York: Harper and Row.

Alvarez, Robert
  1988   "National Politics and Social Responses: The Nation's First Successful School Desegregation Court Case." In *School and Society: Learning Content through Culture*, ed. H. T. Trueba and C. Delgado-Gaitan. New York: Praeger Publishers. [In press]

Alvírez, David, Frank D. Bean, and Dorie Williams
  1981   "The Mexican American Family." In *Ethnic Families in America: Patterns and Variations*, ed. Charles H. Mindel and Robert W. Hobenstein, pp. 269-292. New York: Elsevier.

Anonymous
  1966   "School Bias toward Mexican Americans." *School and Society* 94(4): 378-380.

Arroyo, L., and V. Nelson-Cisneros, eds.
  1975   Special Issue on Labor History and the Chicano. *Aztlan—International Journal of Chicano Studies Research* 6. [University of California, Los Angeles, Chicano Studies Center]

Arvizu, S. F.
  1974   "Education for Constructive Marginality." In *The Cultural Drama*, ed. W. Dillon. Washington, D.C.: Smithsonian Institution Press.

Auletta, Ken
  1982   *The Underclass*. New York: Random House.

Avruch, Kevin
  1982   "On the 'Traditionalization' of Social Identity: American Immigrants to Israel." *Ethos* 10(2):95-116.

Baker, Bob
  1979   "Gang Murders, Spreading across County, Reach Record Rate." *Los Angeles Times*, November 14.

Banfield, Edward
1970   *The Unheavenly City*. Boston: Little, Brown.

Barker, G. C.
1950   *Pachuco, an American-Spanish Argot and Its Social Function in Tucson, Arizona*. Tucson: University of Arizona Press.

1972   *Social Functions of Language in a Mexican-American Community*. Tucson: University of Arizona Press.

Barrera, Mario
1979   *Race and Class in the Southwest: A Theory of Racial Inequality*. Notre Dame: University of Notre Dame Press.

Bearak, Barry, and Richard E. Meyer
1985   "No Tactic Yet Found to Win Poverty War." *Los Angeles Times*, August 1. [Five-part series, America and Its Poor]

Bernard, H. Russell, and Pertti J. Pelto, eds.
1972   *Technology and Social Change*. New York: Macmillan Co.

Bion, Wilfred R.
1975   "Experiences in Groups." In *Group Relations Reader*, ed. Arthur D. Coleman and W. Harold Bexton. Sausalito, Calif.: GREX.

Bloch, H. A., and A. Niederhoffer
1958   *The Gang: A Study in Adolescent Behavior*. New York: Philosophical Library.

Bogardus, Emory S.
1926   *The City Boy and His Problems*. Los Angeles: House of Ralston, Rotary Club of Los Angeles.

1929   "Second Generation Mexicans." *Sociology and Social Research* 13:276-283.

1934   *The Mexican in the United States*. USC Social Science Series, no. 8. Los Angeles: University of Southern California Press.

1943   "Gangs of Mexican American Youth." *Sociology and Social Research* 28:55-56.

Brandt, M. Richard
1972   *Studying Behavior in Natural Settings*. New York: Holt, Rinehart and Winston.

Burgess, E. W.
1925   "The Growth of the City: An Introduction to a Research Project." In *The City*, ed. R. E. Park, E. W. Burgess, and R. O. McKenzie, pp. 47-62. Chicago: University of Chicago Press.

Buriel, Raymond
1984   "Integration with Traditional Mexican American Culture and Sociocultural Adjustment." In *Chicano Psychology*, ed. Joe L. Martínez, Jr., and Richard Mendoza, pp. 95-130. 2d ed. New York: Academic Press.

Buriel, Raymond, Silverio Calzada, and Richard Vasquez
1982   "The Relationship of Traditional Mexican American Culture to Adjustment

and Delinquency among Three Generations of Mexican American Male Adolescents." *Hispanic Journal of Behavioral Sciences* 4(1):41-55.

Burton, R. V., and J. W. M. Whiting
1961   "The Absent Father and Cross-Sex Identity." *Merrill-Palmer Quarterly* 7:85-95.

Camarillo, Albert
1979   *Chicanos in a Changing Society: From Mexican Pueblo to American Barrios in Santa Barbara and Southern California, 1848-1930.* Cambridge: Harvard University Press.

Carter, Thomas P., and Robert D. Segura
1978   *Mexican Americans in School: A Decade of Change.* New York: College Board.

Cartwright, Desmond S., B. Tomson, and H. Schwartz
1975   *Gang Delinquency.* Monterey, Calif: Brooks/Cole.

Castañeda, Alfredo, Manuel Ramírez III, Carlos E. Cortes, and Mario Barrera, eds.
1974   *Mexican Americans and Educational Change.* New York: Arno Press.

Castro, Gustavo López
1981   *El cholo: Origen y desarollo.* Mexicali, B.C.: Universidad Autónoma de Baja California.

Caughey, John L.
1980   "Personal Identity and Social Organization." *Ethos* 8(3):173-203.

Chicano Pinto Research Project
1979   *A Model for Chicano Drug Use and for Effective Utilization of Employment and Training Resources by Barrio Addicts and Ex-Offenders.* Los Angeles: Final report for the Department of Labor and National Institute of Drug Abuse.

1981   *Barrio Impact of High Incarceration Rates.* By Joan W. Moore and John Long. Los Angeles: Final report for National Institute of Mental Health.

Chicano Survey Reports
1979   Ann Arbor: Chicano Projects, University of Michigan.

Clinard, Marshal B.
1960   "Cross-Cultural Replication of the Relation of Urbanism to Criminal Behavior." *American Sociological Review* 25:253-257.

1968   *Sociology of Deviant Behavior.* New York: Holt, Rinehart and Winston.

Cloward, R. A., and L. B. Ohlin
1960   *Delinquency and Opportunity: A Theory of Delinquent Gangs.* New York: Free Press.

Cohen, Albert K.
1955   *Delinquent Boys: The Culture of the Gang.* Glencoe, Ill.: Free Press.

Colman, Arthur D.
1975   "Group Consciousness as a Development Phase." In *Group Relations Reader,* ed. Arthur D. Colman and Harold Bexton, pp. 38-46. Sausalito, Calif.: GREX.

Cornelius, Wayne A., Leo R. Chávez, and Jorge G. Castro
   1982   *Mexican Immigrants and Southern California: A Summary of Current Knowledge.* University of California, San Diego, Center for U.S.-Mexican Studies, Research Report Series, no. 36.

Cuéllar, José B.
   1987   "Cholismo: On the Development and Distribution of an International Mexican Barrio Subculture." Paper presented at the 47th Annual Meeting of the Society for Applied Anthropology, April 9.

Culp, Alice Bessie
   1921   "A Case Study of the Living Conditions of Thirty-five Mexican Families of Los Angeles with Special Reference to Mexican Children." M.A. thesis, University of Southern California, Department of Sociology.

Cummings, Laura
   1987   "Factores en la reproducción del cholismo en dos ciudades fronterizas del norte de México." Paper presented at the 47th Annual Meeting of the Society for Applied Anthropology, April 9.

Decker, Cathleen
   1983   "Gang-Related Murders Fall by 38% in Los Angeles." *Los Angeles Times*, January 7.

de la Garza, R. O., Z. A. Kruszewski, and T. Arciniega, eds.
   1973   *Chicanos and Native Americans: The Territorial Minorities.* Englewood Cliffs, N.J.: Prentice-Hall.

del Piñal, Jorge H.
   1973   "The Penal Population of California." In *Voices*, ed. Octavio I. Romano. Berkeley, Calif.: A Quinto Sol Book.

Dembo, Richard, Nola Allen, and Harold J. Vetter
   1984   *A Framework for Understanding Nondelinquent and Delinquent Life Styles in the Inner City.* [N.p.]

Derbyshire, R. L.
   1968   "Adolescent Identity Crisis in Urban Mexican Americans in East Los Angeles." In *Minority Group Adolescents in the United States*, ed. E. B. Brody. Baltimore: William and Wilken Co.

Devereaux, George
   1961   "Two Types of Modal Personality Models." In *Studying Personality Cross-Culturally*, ed. Bert Kaplan, pp. 227-241. Evanston, Ill.: Row, Peterson and Co.

Dickie-Clark, H. F.
   1966   *The Marginal Situation.* London: Routledge, Keagan Paul.

Douglas, Mrs. Helen W.
   1928   "The Conflict of Cultures in First Generation Mexicans in Santa Ana, Calif." M.A. thesis, University of Southern California, Department of Sociology.

Edgerton, Robert B.
   1973   *Deviant Behavior and Cultural Theory.* Addison-Wesley Module in Anthropology, no. 37. Reading, Mass.: Addison-Wesley Publishing Co.

1978 "The Study of Deviance—Marginal Man or Everyman?" In *The Making of Psychological Anthropology*, ed. George D. Spindler, pp. 442-476. Los Angeles: University of California Press.

Emprey, La Mar T.
1978 *American Delinquency: Its Meaning and Construction*. Homewood, Ill.: Dorsey Press.

Epstein, A. L.
1967 "Urbanization and Social Change." *Current Anthropology* 8(4):275-296.

Erikson, Erik H.
1956 "Ego Identity and the Psychosocial Moratorium." In *New Perspectives for Research on Juvenile Delinquency*, ed. Helen L. Witmer and Ruth Kotinsky, pp. 1-23. Washington, D.C.: U.S. Children's Bureau Publication, no. 356.

1963 *Childhood and Society*. New York: W. W. Norton and Co.

1968 "Psychosocial Identity." In *International Encyclopedia of the Social Sciences*, ed. D. Sills, 7:61-65. New York: Macmillan and the Free Press.

Feldstein, S., and L. Costello, eds.
1974 *The Ordeal of Assimilation: A Documentary History of the White Working Class*. New York: Anchor Press/Doubleday.

Fogelson, Robert
1967 *The Fragmented Metropolis: Los Angeles, 1850-1930*. Cambridge, Mass.: Harvard University Press.

Foulks, Edward F., and Frances Schwartz
1982 "Self and Object, Psychoanalytic Perspectives in Cross-Cultural Fieldwork and Interpretation: A Review Essay." *Ethos* 10(3):254-278.

Fox, Richard G.
1977 *Urban Anthropology: Cities in Their Cultural Settings*. Englewood Cliffs, N.J.: Prentice-Hall.

Frazier, E. Franklin
1957 *Race and Culture Contacts in the Modern World*. New York: Alfred A. Knopf.

Freud, Sigmund
1923 *Group Psychology and the Analysis of the Ego*. New York: W. W. Norton and Co.

Frias, Gus
1982 *Barrio Warriors: Homeboys of Peace*. Los Angeles: Diaz Publishing.

Fuentes, Dagoberto, and José A. López
1974 *Barrio Language Dictionary*. La Puente, Calif.: Sunburst Enterprises.

Fuller, E.
1974 "The Mexican Housing Problem in Los Angeles (1920)." In *Perspectives on Mexican American Life*, ed. C. E. Cortez. New York: Arno Press.

Galarza, Ernesto
1964 *Merchants of Labor*. Santa Barbara: McNally and Loftin, Publishers.

1971   *Barrio Boy.* Notre Dame: University of Notre Dame Press.

Gamio, Manuel
1969a   *Mexican Immigration to the United States.* New York: Arno Press.

1969b   *The Mexican Immigrant.* New York: Arno Press.

Garbarino, J.
1982   *Children and Families in the Social Environment.* New York: Aldine.

Geertz, Clifford
1972   "Deep Play: Notes on the Balinese Cockfight." *Daedalus* 101:1-37.

1973   *The Interpretation of Culture.* New York: Basic Books.

Gettin, Jack, and David Reyes
1983   "The Newest Slums—Out in the Suburbs." *Los Angeles Times,* October 2.

Ginn, M. D.
1947   "Social Implications of the Living Conditions of a Selected Number of Families Participating in the Cleland House Program." M.A. thesis, University of Southern California, Department of Sociology.

Glueck, S.
1959   *The Problem of Delinquency.* Boston: Houghton Mifflin Co.

Goffman, Irving
1956   "The Nature of Deference and Demeanor." *American Anthropologist* 58:473-502.

1959   *The Presentation of Self in Everyday Life.* New York: Doubleday and Co.

Goldstein, M.
1981   "The Family." In *Adolescence and Stress,* ed. C. D. Moore. Rockville, Md.: National Institute of Mental Health.

Gómez-Quiñones, Juan
1982   *Development of the Mexican Working Class North of the Rio Bravo: Work and Culture among Laborers and Artisans, 1600-1900.* University of California, Los Angeles, Chicano Studies Research Publications, Popular Series, no. 2.

Gonzales, Alfredo
1981   "Mexicano/Chicano Gangs in Los Angeles: A Socio Historical Case Study." D.S.W. dissertation, University of California, Berkeley, School of Social Welfare.

Gordon, Milton
1964   *Assimilation in American Life.* New York: Oxford University Press.

Graves, Theodore D.
1967   "Acculturation, Access, and Alcohol in a Tri-ethnic Community." *American Anthropologist* 69(3-4):306-321.

Griffith, Beatrice
1948   *American Me.* Boston: Houghton Mifflin Co.

Griswold del Castillo, Richard
1980   *The Los Angeles Barrio, 1850-1890.* Los Angeles: University of California Press.

Gustafson, C. V.
1940   "An Ecological Analysis of the Hollenbeck Area of Los Angeles." M.A. thesis, University of Southern California, Department of Sociology.

Haapanen, Rudy A., and Carl F. Jesness
1982   *Early Identification of the Chronic Offender.* Sacramento, Calif.: Department of the Youth Authority.

Hagedorn, John, and Perry Macon (Joan Moore, Principal Investigator)
1987   *Milwaukee Gang Research Project (Final Report).* Milwaukee: Center for the Promotion of Policy Relevant Urban Research, University of Wisconsin—Milwaukee.

Hall, Calvin S., and Gardner Lindzey
1968   "The Relevance of Freudian Psychology and Related Viewpoints for the Social Sciences." In *The Handbook of Social Psychology,* ed. Gardner Lindzey and Elliot Aronson, 1:245-319. Reading, Mass.: Addison-Wesley Publishing Co.

Hallowell, A. I.
1955   *Culture and Experience.* Philadelphia: University of Pennsylvania Press.

Handlin, Oscar
1951   *The Uprooted.* New York: Grosset and Dunlap.

Haro, Carlos Manuel
1976   "An Ethnographic Study of Truant and Low Achieving Chicano Barrio Youth in the High School Setting." Ph.D. dissertation, University of California, Los Angeles, Department of Education.

Hauser, Philip
1968   "The Social, Economic, and Technological Problems of Rapid Urbanization." In *Industrialization and Society,* ed. Bert Hoselitz and Wilbert E. Moore. The Hague: Mouton Publishers, UNESCO.

Haviland, William A.
1980   *Cultural Anthropology.* New York: Holt, Rinehart, and Winston.

Heller, Celia S.
1966   *Mexican American Youth: Forgotten Youth at the Crossroads.* New York: Random House.

Hill, Merton
1928   "An Americanization Program for the Ontario Schools." In *California Controversies,* ed. Leonard Pitt. Rpt. Glenview, Ill.: Scott, Foresman, and Co., 1968.

Hinojos, F. G.
1975   "Notes on the Pachuco: Stereotypes, History, and Dialect." *Atisbos: Journal of Chicano Research,* Summer. [Stanford: Chicano Studies Center]

Hirschi, Travis
  1969   *Causes of Delinquency.* Berkeley: University of California Press.

  1983   "Crime and the Family." In *Crime and Public Policy*, ed. J. Q. Wilson. San Francisco: ICS Press.

Hoffman, Abraham
  1974   *Unwanted Mexican Americans in the Great Depression: Repatriation Pressures, 1929-1939.* Tucson: University of Arizona Press.

Homans, G. C.
  1950   *The Human Group.* New York: Harcourt, Brace and World.

Horowitz, Ruth
  1983   *Honor and the American Dream: Culture and Identity in a Chicano Community.* New Brunswick, N.J.: Rutgers University Press.

Humphrey, Norman D.
  1944   "The Changing Structure of the Detroit Mexican Family: An Index of Acculturation." *American Sociological Review* 9:622-626.

Hymes, Dell, ed.
  1971   *Pidginization and Creolization of Languages.* London: Cambridge University Press.

Jackson, Robert K., and Wesley McBride
  1985   *Understanding Street Gangs.* Costa Mesa, Calif.: Custom Publishing Co.

Jessor, R., T. D. Graves, R. C. Hanson, and S. L. Jessor
  1968   *Society, Personality, and Deviant Behavior: A Study of a Tri-Ethnic Community.* New York: Holt, Rinehart and Winston.

Johnston, Tracey J.
  1979   "The Vida Loca." *New West*, January 29.

Kapferer, Bruce
  1978   "Structural Marginality and the Urban Social Order." *Urban Anthropology* 7(3):287-320.

Keesing, Roger
  1974   "Theories of Culture." *Annual Review of Anthropology.* Stanford, Calif.: Stanford University Press.

Keiser, R. Lincoln
  1969   *The Vice Lords: Warriors of the Street.* New York: Holt, Rinehart and Winston.

Kienle, John Emmanuel
  1912   "Housing Conditions among the Mexican Population of Los Angeles." M.A. thesis, University of Southern California, Department of Sociology.

Klein, Malcolm W.
  1968   "Impressions of Juvenile Gang Members." *Adolescence* 3(9):53-78.

  1971   *Street Gangs and Street Workers.* Englewood Cliffs, N.J.: Prentice-Hall.

Langness, L. L., and Gelya Frank
  1981   *Lives: An Anthropological Approach to Biography.* Novato, Calif.: Chandler and Sharp Publishers.

Leeds, Anthony
   1974   "Housing Settlement Types, Arrangements for Living, Proletarianization, and the Social Structure of the City." In *Latin American Urban Research: Anthropological Perspectives on Latin American Urbanization*, vol. 4, ed. Wayne A. Cornelius and Felicity M. Trueblood. Beverly Hills: Sage Publishing.

Lomnitz, Larissa A.
   1977   *Networks and Marginality: Life in a Mexican Shantytown.* New York: Academic Press.

   1978   "Mechanisms of Articulation between Shantytown Settlers and the Urban System." *Urban Anthropology* 7(2):185-205.

McWilliams, C.
   1968   *North from Mexico—the Spanish-Speaking People of the United States.* New York: Greenwood Press.

Mancini, J.
   1981   *Strategic Styles: Coping in the Inner City.* Hanover, N.H.: University Press of New England.

Mandel, Jerry
   1982   *Police Use of Deadly Force in Hispanic Communities (Final Report).* Washington, D.C.: National Council of La Raza.

Matza, David
   1964   *Delinquency and Drift.* New York: John Wiley and Sons.

   1966   "The Disreputable Poor." In *Class, Status, and Power*, ed. Reinhard Bendix and S. M. Lipset, pp. 289-302. New York: Free Press.

Mazón, Mauricio
   1985   *The Zoot-Suit Riots: The Psychology of Symbolic Annihilation.* Austin: University of Texas Press.

Merton, Robert K.
   1949   *Social Theory and Social Structure.* Glencoe, Ill.: Free Press.

Miller, Denise
   1983   "The Cucamonga Kings: Street Gang or Media Monsters?" Manuscript, James Diego Vigil collection.

Miller, Marjorie
   1984   "Cholos Return to Their Roots, and Find They Bloom." *Los Angeles Times*, September 9.

Miller, Walter B.
   1958   "Lower Class Culture as a Generating Milieu of Gang Delinquency." *Journal of Social Issues* 14(3):519.

   1975   *Violence by Youth Gangs and Youth Groups as a Crime Problem in Major American Cities.* Washington, D.C.: U.S. Department of Justice.

Miller, William P.
   1977   "The Rumble This Time." *Psychology Today* 10 (May).

Mirandé, Alfredo
  1981   "The Chicano and the Law." *Pacific Sociological Review* 24(1):65-86.

  1987   *Gringo Justice*. Notre Dame: University of Notre Press.

Molohon, Kathryn T., Richard Paton, and Michael Lambert
  1979   "An Extension of Barth's Concept on Ethnic Boundaries to Include Both
          Other Groups and Developmental Stages of Ethnic Groups." *Human Rela-
          tions* 32(1):1-17.

Monthly Labor Review
  1974   "Conditions of Mexicans in California." In *Readings on La Raza: The Twen-
          tieth Century*, ed. M. S. Meir and F. Rivera. New York: Hill and Wang.

Moore, C. D., ed.
  1981   *Adolescence and Stress: Report of an N.I.M.H. Conference*. Rockville, Md.:
          National Institute of Mental Health.

Moore, Joan
  1968   "Social Class, Assimilation, and Acculturation." In *Spanish-Speaking People
          in the United States: Proceedings of the 1968 Annual Spring Meeting of the
          American Ethnological Society*. Seattle: University of Washington Press.

  1978   *Homeboys: Gangs, Drugs, and Prison in the Barrios of Los Angeles*.
          Philadelphia: Temple University Press.

  1985   "Isolation and Stigmatization in the Development of an Underclass: The
          Case of Chicano Gangs in East Los Angeles." *Social Problems* 33(1):1-12.

  1986   "Chicano Gangs and the Development of an Underclass." Paper prepared for
          the conference Turks in Berlin: Mexicans in Los Angeles: What Can We
          Learn From Each Other? Berlin, September.

Moore, Joan, and Alberto Mata
  1981   *Women and Heroin in Chicano Communities*. Los Angeles: Chicano Pinto
          Research Project.

Moore, Joan W., and Harry Pachón
  1976   *Mexican Americans*. 2d ed. Englewood Cliffs, N.J.: Prentice-Hall.

  1985   *Hispanics in the United States*. Englewood Cliffs, N.J.: Prentice-Hall.

Moore, Joan W., and James Diego Vigil
  1988   "Chicano Gangs: Group Norms and Individual Factors Related to Adult
          Criminality." [Forthcoming in *Aztlán*]

Moore, Joan W., James Diego Vigil, and Robert Garcia
  1983   "Residence and Territoriality in Gangs." *Journal of Social Problems*
          31(2):182-194.

Morales, Armando
  1972   *Ando sangrando (I Am Bleeding)*. La Puente, Calif.: Perspectiva Publisher.

  1982   "The Mexican American Gang Member: Evaluation and Treatment." In *Men-
          tal Health and Hispanic Americans*, ed. Rosina M. Becerra, Marvin Karno,
          and Javier I. Escobar. New York: Grune and Stratton.

Morrison, Patt
 1983 "Gang Girls Get a Hint at What They Could Be." *Los Angeles Times*, March
      29.

Moynihan, Daniel P.
 1988 "The War on Poverty Must Continue." *Los Angeles Times*, March 7.

Muller, Thomas
 1984 *The Fourth Wave: California's Newest Immigrants.* Washington, D.C.: Ur-
      ban Institute Press.

Murphy, Suzanne
 1978 "A Year with the Gangs of East Los Angeles." *Ms.*, July, pp. 55-64.

National Association of Latino Elected and Appointed Officials (NALEO)
 1985 *Poverty's Invisible Victims: Hispanic Children; Number of Latino Poor
      Children Doubles in California in Past Decade.* Washington, D.C.: NALEO
      News Release.

National Commission for Employment Policy
 1982 *Hispanics and Jobs: Barriers to Progress.* Washington, D.C.

Ogbu, John
 1982 "Cultural Discontinuities and Schooling." *Anthropology and Education
      Quarterly* 13(4):290-307.

Olmedo, Esteban L., and Amado Padilla
 1978 "Empirical and Construct Validation of a Measure of Acculturation for Mex-
      ican Americans." *Journal of Social Psychology* 105:179-187.

Park, Robert E.
 1928 "Human Migration and Marginal Man." *American Journal of Sociology*
      33(6):881-893.

Peattie, Lisa R.
 1974 "The Concept of 'Marginality' as Applied to Squatter Settlements." In *Latin
      American Urban Research: Anthropological Perspectives on Latin American
      Urbanization,* vol. 4, ed. Wayne A. Cornelius and Felicity M. Trueblood.
      Beverly Hills: Sage Publishing.

Peñalosa, Fernando
 1980 *Chicano Sociolinguistics.* Rowley, Mass.: Newbury House Publishers.

Perlman, Janet
 1976 *The Myth of Marginality.* Berkeley: University of California Press.

Poggie, J. J.
 1973 *Between Two Cultures: The Life of an American Mexican.* Tucson: Universi-
      ty of Arizona Press.

Poirier, Mike
 1982 *Street Gangs of Los Angeles County.* Los Angeles: Self-Published. P.O. Box
      60481, Los Angeles, CA 90060.

Quicker, John C.
 1983 *Homegirls: Characterizing Chicana Gangs.* San Pedro, Calif.: International
      Universities Press.

Ramos, George
1983   "American Dream Lives in the Barrio." *Los Angeles Times*, July 27.

Ranker, Jess Elwood, Jr.
1958   "A Study of Juvenile Gangs in the Hollenbeck Area of East Los Angeles." M.A. thesis, University of Southern California, Department of Sociology.

Redfield, M. P. , ed.
1962   *Human Nature and the Study of Society: The Papers of Robert Redfield.* Chicago: University of Chicago Press.

Reisler, M.
1976   *By the Sweat of Their Brow.* Westport, Conn.: Greenwood Press.

Reisner, Robert G.
1968   *Graffiti.* New York: Canyon Books.

Robins, L. N.
1978   "Etiological Implications in Studies of Childhood Histories Relating to Antisocial Personality." In *Psychopathic Behavior,* ed. R. D. Hare and D. Scholling. New York: Wiley.

Rodgers, B. W.
1969   "Developmental Exposure and Changing Vocational Preferences in the Out-Island Bahamas." *Human Organization* 28:270-278.

Rodríguez, Patricio E.
1980   "Barrio Psychology and the Education of the Chicano Learner." Manuscript in Chicano Studies course, California State University, Los Angeles.

Rodríguez, Roberto
1984   *Assault with a Deadly Weapon: About an Incident in E.L.A. and the Closing of Whittier Blvd.* Los Angeles: Rainbow Press.

Rogoff, Barbara
1981   "Adults and Peers as Agents of Socialization: A Highland Guatemalan Profile." *Ethos* 9(1):18-36.

Romo, Ricardo
1983   *East Los Angeles: History of a Barrio, 1900-1930.* Austin: University of Texas Press.

Rosenquist, C. M., and E. I. Megargee
1969   *Delinquency in Three Cultures.* Austin: University of Texas Press.

Rubel, A. J.
1965   "The Mexican American Palomilla." *Anthropological Linguistics* 4:92-97.

1966   *Across the Tracks: Mexican Americans in a Texas City.* Austin: University of Texas Press.

Samora, J.
1971   *Los Mojados: The Wetback Story.* Notre Dame: University of Notre Dame Press.

Sample, Herbert A.
1984   "Youth Gangs Take a Shine to Custom Cars." *Los Angeles Times*, February 5.

Sánchez, G. I.
1967   *Forgotten People: A Study of New Mexicans.* Albuquerque: Calvin Horn Publishers. [Originally published in 1940]

Sánchez, Rosaura
1983   *Chicano Discourse: Socio-historic Perspectives.* Rowley, Mass.: Newbury House Publishers.

Santana, Ray, and Mario Esparza
1974   "East Los Angeles Blow-Outs." In *Parameters of Institutional Change: Chicano Experiences in Education*, pp. 1-9. Hayward, Calif.: Southwest Network.

Scheidlinger, Saul
1952   *Psychoanalysis and Group Behavior.* New York: W. W. Norton and Co.

Schermerhorn, R. A.
1970   *Comparative Ethnic Relations: A Framework for Theory and Research.* New York: Random House.

Sellin, Thorsten
1938   *Culture Conflict and Crime.* New York: Social Science Research Council.

Serrano, Rudolfo A.
1979   *Dictionary of Pachuco Terms.* Bakersfield: California State University, Bakersfield.

Shaw, C., and R. McKay
1942   *Juvenile Delinquency and Urban Areas.* Chicago: University of Chicago Press.

Shoham, S., N. Shoham, and A. Razek
1966   "Immigration, Ethnicity, and Ecology as Related to Juvenile Delinquency in Israel." *British Journal of Criminology* 7:391-409.

Short, James F., Jr., and Fred L. Strodtbeck
1965   *Group Process and Gang Delinquency.* Chicago: University of Chicago Press.

Siegel, Barry
1982   "Immigrants: Sizing Up the New Wave." *Los Angeles Times*, December 12, 13, 14. [Three-part series]

Simross, Lynn
1984   "Digging Up Roots of an Early Mexican Barrio: Former Residents of Jimtown Gather for First Reunion." *Los Angeles Times*, October 29.

Snyder, P. Z.
1977   "An Anthropological Description of Street Gangs in the Los Angeles Area." [A working note, prepared for the Department of Justice, by Rand Corporation, Santa Monica, Calif.]

Spiro, Melford E.
1978   "Culture and Human Nature." In *The Making of Psychological Anthropology*, ed. George D. Spindler, pp. 330-360. Los Angeles: University of California Press.

Steward, Julian H.
1955   *Theory of Culture Change.* Urbana: University of Illinois Press.

Stonequist, Everett V.
   1937   *The Marginal Man.* New York: Russell and Russell.

Suttles, Gerald D.
   1968   *The Social Order of the Slums: Ethnicity and Territory in the Inner City.*
   Chicago: University of Chicago Press.

Tangri, S. S., and M. Schwartz
   1967   "Delinquency Research and the Self Concept Variable." *Journal of Criminal Law, Criminology, and Police Science* 58:182-190.

Thrasher, Frederic M.
   1963   *The Gang.* Chicago: University of Chicago Press. [Originally published in 1927]

Tittle, Charles R., Wayne J. Villemez, and Douglas A. Smith
   1978   "The Myth of Social Class and Criminality: An Empirical Assessment of the Empirical Evidence." *American Sociological Review* 43:643-656.

Torres, D. M.
   1979   "Chicano Gangs in the East Los Angeles Barrio." *California Youth Authority Quarterly* 32(3):5-13.

Tuck, R.
   1956   *Not with the Fist: Mexican-Americans in a Southwest City.* New York: Harcourt, Brace.

Twillen, Calvin, and Edward Koren
   1978   "Our Far-Flung Correspondents: Low and Slow, Mean and Clean." *The New Yorker,* July 10.

United States Commission on Civil Rights
   1970   *Mexican Americans and the Administration of Justice in the Southwest.*
   Washington, D.C.: U.S. Government Printing Office.

   1971   *Report I: Ethnic Isolation of Mexican Americans in the Public Schools of the Southwest.* Washington, D.C.: U.S. Government Printing Office.

United States Department of Commerce
   1983   *1980 Census of Population and Housing—Los Angeles and Long Beach, California.* PHC80-2-226. Washington, D.C.: U.S. Government Printing Office.

   1983   *1980 Census of Population and Housing—Los Angeles and Long Beach, California.* PHC80-2-226. Washington, D.C.: U.S. Government Printing Office.

   1983   *1980 Census of Population—General Social and Economic Characteristics.*
   PC80-1-C6. Washington, D.C.: U.S. Government Printing Office.

Vigil, James Diego
   1976   "Adolescent Chicano Acculturation and School Performance: The Role of Social Economic Conditions and Urban-Suburban Environmental Differences." Ph.D. dissertation, University of California, Los Angeles.

   1979   "Adaptation Strategies and Cultural Life Styles of Mexican American Adolescents." *Hispanic Journal of Behavioral Sciences* 1(4):375-392. [UCLA Spanish-Speaking Mental Health Research Center]

1982a "Chicano High Schoolers: Educational Performance and Acculturation." *Educational Forum* 48:59-73.

1982b "Human Revitalization: The Six Tasks of Victory Outreach." *Drew Gateway* 52(3):49-59.

1983 "Chicano Gangs: One Response to Mexican Urban Adaptation in the Los Angeles Area." *Urban Anthropology* 12(1):45-75.

1984 *From Indians to Chicanos: The Dynamics of Mexican American Culture.* Prospect Heights, Ill.: Waveland Press. [Originally published as *From Indians to Chicanos: A Sociocultural History.* St. Louis: C. V. Mosby Co., 1980]

1987 *An Ethnographic Enumeration of a Barrio in Greater East Los Angeles.* Washington, D.C.: U.S. Bureau of the Census.

Vigil, James Diego, and John M. Long
1981 "Unidirectional or Nativist Acculturation?—Chicano Paths to School Achievement." *Human Organization* 40(3):272-277

Vigil, James Diego, and Denise Miller
1981 "Cucamonga: A Community Study with a Focus." Paper delivered at conference, Chicano History and Culture Week, November 16-21, Department of Chicano Studies, California State University, Los Angeles.

Villela, Samuel, and Silvia Gastelum
1980 *Los cholos: Los "Cholos" de Culiacán: Transculturación chicana en bandas juveniles de Sinaloa.* Culiacán: Universidad Autónoma de Sinaloa.

West, Ted
1976 "Scenes from a 'Revolution: Low and Slow.'" *Car and Driver*, August.

Whiting, Beatrice B.
1980 "Culture and Social Behavior: A Model for the Development of Social Behavior." *Ethos* 8(2):95-116.

Whyte, Williams F.
1973 *Street Corner Society.* Chicago: University of Chicago Press. [Originally published in 1943]

Willis, Paul E.
1977 *Learning to Labour.* Farnborough, England: Saxon House.

Wolck, Wolfgang
1973 "Attitudes toward Spanish and Quechua in Bilingual Peru." In *Language and Attitudes*, ed. Roger Shuy and Ralph W. Fosold. Georgetown: Georgetown University Press.

Wolfgang, Marvin, Robert M. Figlio, and Thorsten Sellin
1972 *Delinquency in a Birth Cohort.* Chicago: University of Chicago Press.

Yablonsky, L.
1959 "The Delinquent Gang as a Near-Group." *Social Problems* 7:108-117.

Yinger, J. M.
1960 "Contraculture and Subculture." *American Sociological Review* 25:625-635.

Youth Gang Task Force
1981 *Report on Youth Gang Violence in California.* State of California Department of Justice. Sacramento.

Ziegler, Peggy
　　1978　"Arrests Follow Probe of Gangs in North Town." *Daily Report* (Ontario, Calif.), November 15.

Zucker, Martin
　　1978　"Walls of Barrio Are Brought to Life by Street Gang Art." *Smithsonian*, October.

Index